Empire by Mandate

CAMPBELL L. UPTHEGROVE

Empire by Mandate

A History of the Relations of Great Britain with the
Permanent Mandates Commission of the League of Nations

BOOKMAN ASSOCIATES

New York

1. Mandates
2. League of nations
3. Permanent Mandates Commission
I Title

325.31
U71e

MANUFACTURED IN THE UNITED STATES OF AMERICA
PRINTED BY RECORD PRESS, NEW YORK

Preface

Sir D. Maclean said in the British House of Commons in July, 1919, that the mandates system would impose no new conditions on Great Britain, inasmuch as the British colonial policy was analogous to the principles of the mandates.[1] This statement was confirmed shortly when Great Britain received the largest number of mandated territories. This factor, together with their long experience as a colonizing nation, offers a challenge for a study of Great Britain's administration in the mandated territories.

The mandates system set up under Article 22 of the Covenant of the League of Nations was admittedly temporary in nature and the system itself envisaged an eventual termination of the mandates and the recognition of their independent status. An important feature of the system was the acknowledgment that such a development should be consummated only when the peoples concerned evidenced their ability to stand by themselves under the strenuous conditions of the modern world. This has also been Great Britain's policy in dealing with her dependencies. Therefore it is clear why the mandate principle was said to have been borrowed from British colonial practice. Roughly speaking, British colonial practice was to be internationalized. The Permanent Mandates Commission was the important international institution created for international colonial practice by the League of Nations. It has been described as an international Areopagus, to which a state which is a trustee for the League renders an annual account of its trust.

The success of the mandates system depends greatly upon the relations between Great Britain and the Permanent Mandates Commission since Britain has the largest number of mandates, and more experience with colonial problems. It may again be said that this fact offers a challenge for a study of Great Britain as a mandatory, for mutual cooperation between Great Britain and the Permanent Mandates Commission is necessary if successful principles and practices for the mandates are to be developed.

The materials used for this study were secured from the von KleinSmid Library of World Affairs of The Los Angeles University of International Relations, the E. L. Doheny, Jr. Memorial Library of The University of Southern California, the Los Angeles Public Library, and the Library of the University of California at Los Angeles.

In the execution of this study the writer is indebted to Dr. G. G. Benjamin, Dr. O. C. Coy, Dr. E. M. Eriksson, and Dr. T. W. Wallbank of the History Department, and Dr. J. Eugene Harley and Dr. C. C. Rodee of the Political Science Department of The University of Southern California for their valuable criticism.

CAMPBELL L. UPTHEGROVE.

Los Angeles, California
June, 1941

Contents

Empire by Mandate

CHAPTER ONE

The Mandates System

The origin. The disposal of the former German colonies in Africa and the Pacific and of the non-Turkish provinces of the Ottoman Empire confronted the allied and associated powers at the end of World War I. During the war, it was realized that an advance in the direction of internationalizing colonial policy must be made if the peace of the world were to be preserved in the future. The fear that political control would inevitably lead to commercial monopoly by the nationals of the controlling state had dominated the relations of the powers with each other in questions involving unexploited territories inhabited by backward peoples.[1]

Leading writers favored a policy that would demand any nation acquiring a colony to follow the principle of the "open door." They thought that if such a principle was definitely established, commercial operations, following the genuinely cooperative tendency of modern finance, would be organized on an international basis. In this way one of the most fertile causes of modern belligerent support of private companies by foreign offices would be removed.[2] The conclusion is hardly more than an expansion of the suggestions of H. N. Brailsford made in 1915.[3]

The idea of the colonies being held in trust for civilization seems to have come as the only means of escaping from prewar economic imperialism and, at the same time, safeguarding the interests of the weaker populations inhabiting them.

The League of Nations—"A Practical Suggestion" published by General Smuts, December 16, 1918, was the first concrete plan for such trusteeship.[4] The proposal consisted of twenty-one articles, and the first nine dealt with mandates. The setting up of a League of Nations was envisaged as the primary and basic task of the Peace Conference, and the League was to be considered as the reversionary in the most general sense of the peoples and territories formerly belonging to Russia, Austria-Hungary, and Turkey, and as clothed with the right of ultimate disposal in accordance with certain fundamental principles. Revision to the League of Nations should be substituted for any policy of national annexation.[5] General Smuts was influenced by the publications of certain students of imperial and foreign affairs in England who were writing about the coming peace.[6] R. S. Baker claims Smuts took his plans from other thinkers more radical than himself, including the Inter-Allied Labor and Socialist programs of February, 1918.[7] W. G. Ormsby-Gore, formerly a member of the Mandates Commission, names Philip Kerr as General Smuts' coadjutor in this matter.[8]

However, before Smuts' proposal, the British Foreign Office in November, 1918, presented the Foreign Office Memorandum.[9] It proposed a standing international conference to hold regular meetings; a permanent secretariat should be established; the new body would include the whole world and not Europe alone; and finally, the member states were to become part of a great world organization. There was to be organized not only a society of states but also a society of peoples.[10]

Elsewhere, as in Great Britain, politicians as well as writers took up these ideas and began to narrow their sphere from general colonial policy to the disposition of the former German colonies and of parts of the Turkish Empire. President Wilson, in his Fourteen Points, enunciated in January, 1918, demanded a free, open-minded and absolutely impartial adjustment of all colonial claims and that the interests of the populations concerned must have equal weight with the equitable claims of the government whose title is to be decided.[11]

At first, Wilson regarded the colonial settlement like the boundary settlement in Europe, as a matter to be dealt with prior to and apart from any League of Nations, as a settlement of concrete political matters on the foundation of which and for protection of which the League was to be created.[12] However, Baker tells that before seeing the Smuts' plan, President Wilson thought the German colonies should be declared the common property of the League of Nations and administered by small nations.[13] George L. Beer, Chief of the Colonial Division of the American Delegation, was much disturbed about an apparent vagueness in the President's reference to the League of Nations, especially on the question of mandates. On the latter point, the idea had been thrown out that the mandatory state should be chosen from among those which had no previous interest in the colony assigned. Beer regarded this as very dangerous and an academic type of thinking, for he thought the President, in his anxiety to secure an unbiased and unselfish attitude on the part of the mandatory, had overlooked the point which was fundamental, that colonial government requires experience both in the governing state and in the colony on the part of its administration.[14]

What is believed by many to be the best prototype of the mandates system as later adopted was the famous Roosevelt proposals during the Algeciras Conference in 1906, as revealed in the correspondence between the German and American governments of that period.[15] W. R. Batsell contends the use of the term "mandate" by Roosevelt in 1906 was by no means the first use of the word "mandate" in its present connotation, that it was used by practically every writer to describe the status of Bosnia-Herzegovina between 1878-1908.[16]

Luther H. Evans reviews what he considers the various direct antecedents of the mandate system. The United States had the moral mandate of the world to intervene in Panama and built the Canal.[17] France acted on a moral mandate from the rest of the world when she intervened in Syria in 1860.[18]

Thus Baty has said:

We come now to the consideration of the novel institutions of Mandates. Their germ cannot be found as is sometimes imagined in the Treaty of Berlin (Article 25), which conferred upon Austria the right and probably imposed on her the duty, to occupy and administer Bosnia and Herzegovina. So far as can be seen, the institution of mandate now assumes for the first time a place in international affairs.[19]

Smuts' proposal for a mandates system applied to the peoples and territories of the former empires of Europe, including the Turkish Empire.[20] Since he regarded the barbarian inhabitants of the German colonies as too unfit for political self-determination, in the European sense, he advocated annexation for them.[21] The mandatory state should administer its trust on behalf of the League, as far as possible, with the consent of the population concerned. He rejected the idea that the mandatory state should derive any benefit from its administration, and declared that the policy of the open door should be upheld and that only such native troops should be raised as were necessary for internal police.

President Wilson at once realized its value, and felt that this application to the German colonies would be more in accordance with his general principles than the equitable distribution he had been advocating.[22] He embodied the essentials of the idea in his second draft, January 10, 1919, of a proposed covenant, adding the notion that the League should be the residuary trustee of the peoples and territories.[23] David Hunter Miller, legal adviser to Wilson during the Peace Conference, claimed most of Smuts' proposals with regard to the colonies were already ripe in Wilson's mind and Wilson took from Smuts nothing but his phraseology.[24] Baker, who more than anybody else has access to all of Wilson's papers, is of the contrary opinion, and gives all credit for the mandatory principle to Smuts.[25] But, while Wilson practically transferred Smuts' ideas and even style into his own plan, he also added a new provision that not only was not found in Smuts' script but was even against its spirit. Smuts was concerned solely with territories formerly belonging to Russia, Austria-Hungary, and Turkey. With regard to the German colonies in the Pacific Ocean and Africa, he expressed himself as follows: That they are inhabited by barbarians, who not only cannot govern themselves, but to whom it would be impracticable to apply any idea of self-determination in the European sense.[26] Wilson took the same principles of mandatories and applied them to the German colonies.

Wilson prepared a third draft with the aid of the legal adviser of the American Delegation, Mr. David Hunter Miller. The third draft resembled the second, but prohibited member states from interfering with the free exercise of religion, and also bound the signatory powers to exercise no discrimination in their fiscal and economic relations.[27]

At the same time, the British had perfected a plan of their own, which, in many points, disagreed with that of Wilson. It was, therefore, decided to straighten out these difficulties before a plan should be put before the commission on the League of Nations. This was done by the respective legal advisers to the American and British delegations, David Hunter Miller and Cecil J. B. Hurst. This draft was known as the Hurst-Miller draft and became the basis for discussion by the commission.[28]

14

Curiously enough, the mandate plan did not come up for discussion in the commission on the League of Nations directly nor did the commission draft the main parts of Article 22 of the Covenant which embodies that plan.[29] The disposal of the German and Turkish territories was a matter of such political and economic importance that it arose in discussion in the Supreme Council at a very early date.[30] It was here that President Wilson so vigorously supported the mandate plan and its application to the German colonies against the opposition of the prime ministers of New Zealand, Australia, South Africa, and Canada.[31]

The plan, known as the Mandates System, was adopted on January 30, 1919, by the Supreme Council, and transmitted to the Peace Conference Commission on the League of Nations, and with very slight changes was incorporated as Article 22 of the Covenant which consists of the first twenty-six articles of the Versailles and other treaties.[32] The language of Article 22 is practically the same as the Smuts' resolution of January 30, 1919, and adopted by the council as the principles by which the German possessions and Turkish near-eastern provinces were supposed to be governed. The British delegation finally agreed upon the text of the resolution only after a heated and violent debate.[33] This resolution of the council was finally adopted as a compromise between the imperialistic desires of certain of the dominions of the British Empire and Wilson's insistence on the mandatory principle. President Wilson had thus prevented annexation, got the principle of mandates accepted for all the territories and postponed final allocation of mandates until the League of Nations was in operation, though he had been obliged to recognize the prior claims of the occupying powers to receive mandates, the special claims of the dominions in respect to the open door, and of France in respect to recruiting natives.[34] Twenty-one years later W. E. Rappard wrote:

The solution finally adopted was clearly a compromise between national acquisitiveness and international justice. But although the former may be said to have prevailed, thus planting a dangerous germ of future dissension, something very significant had been gained also for the latter and perhaps another important milestone laid on the road of progressive colonial evolution.[35]

Article 22. Article 22, which deals with the mandates, was not written by the commission on the League of Nations. The text actually adopted was introduced in the League of Nations Commission on February 8 by General Smuts, as a substitute for the Hurst-Miller article. Thus both the original proposal and the final form of Article 22 was largely the work of General Smuts. There are, however, notable differences with respect to the territories covered, the roles of the League, and the principles applied which developed out of the proposal mentioned between December 16, 1918, and January 30, 1919.[36] Whereas General Smuts originally thought of applying the mandatory system to the broken empires of Austria-Hungary, Russia, and Turkey, from which he expressly distinguished in principle the German Colonial Empire, the Wilson draft omitted Russia and added the former German colonies.

For the period between the armistice and the final adoption of the Covenant, President Wilson and General Smuts, and particularly the latter, may be regarded as the authors of the mandate system.[37] But the credit for the inclusion in the Covenant of the League of the mandatory principle and of making the Covenant an integral part of the Treaty of Versailles is due almost solely to President Wilson, who fought for it bravely, stubbornly, and single-handed.[38]

Article 22 contains two conceptions of mandate which are bound together by the common idea of a trust. The territories detached from Turkey emphasized the notion of the guardianship of minor nations. The notion of the conduct of government in a paternal way for the benefit of the native population and in the interest of civilization is emphasized with respect to the territories in Africa and Oceania. The mandatory is under definite obligations both to the population and to the League, and does not acquire sovereignty in the way that a state has sovereignty over its colonies. There are at least ten theories regarding the location of sovereignty in mandated communities, which may be arranged in four main groups according as sovereignty is attributed to the principal allied and associated powers, the mandatories, the mandated communities, or the League of Nations.[39] At the same time, powers of internal and external administration are exercised by the single mandatory state which acts on behalf of the Society of Nations and is accountable to that society. International responsibility is manifested in various ways. The mandate is defined in a document finally approved by the mandatory and in the form that the council enacts it, and can be changed only with the consent of the League; and, in theory, it would appear that it may be revoked by it if the council should find that the mandatory was not fulfilling its obligations.[40] The League has the right of ultimate disposal, and the Assembly of the League exercises a certain general and moral influence over the execution of the mandate.

Two new conceptions in political science and international law have been introduced by the mandate system: (1) A system of national responsibility for the government of a country under the control of an international body. (2) A system of guardianship of peoples, similar to the guardianship by individuals of minor persons.[41]

Seven principles are revealed in analyzing the provisions of Article 22 of the Covenant. They are: (1) Colonial territories taken from the enemy are not to be annexed by the victorious powers; (2) these colonial territories are to be put under the joint sovereignty of the allied and associated powers; (3) they are entrusted to the tutelage of certain individual advanced nations; (4) this tutelage is to be exercised by the mandatories under the supervision of the League; (5) the open door is to be maintained in colonial territories so far as the mandatory has any power over them as such; (6) natives shall be used in a military capacity only for local defense and police; (7) the people of the mandated territories are to have a voice in the choice of the mandatories.[42]

In order to carry out these principles, the mandates were divided into three categories, A, B, and C, in accordance with their location, economic status, and cultural development. Class A mandates are lands which have reached such a high stage of development that they may be recognized as independent nations, but need administrative advice until they can exist unaided. Palestine, Trans-Jordan, and Iraq, which Great Britain later received, are in this category. Smuts' original plan was concerned with this territory.[43]

Class B mandates are those less advanced, and cared for by the mandatory power with a greater amount of supervision and with definite guarantees to the League for the welfare of the inhabitants. They were formerly owned by Germany. Some of the territory in this class consisted of British Togoland, British Cameroons, and Tanganyika. Smuts did not intend to have the German colonies governed under the mandatory principles.

Class C mandates include southwest Africa and the Pacific Islands, both of which belonged to Germany. Because of their sparseness of population, their small size, and their remoteness from centers of civilization, they have been assigned to neighboring mandatory powers and are governed as integral portions of their own empires, subject to certain safeguards from the natives. Nauru, later awarded to the British Empire, belonged to this group. General Smuts thought it would be impracticable to apply any idea of political self-determination in the European sense and he would not have interfered with the interest of Great Britain and her dominions in annexing these colonies.[44]

Two sorts of obligations are obtained in Article 22 of the Covenant: (1) The general obligation to secure the well-being and development of the inhabitants of the mandated territories, and (2) the specific obligations relating to the B and C territories.[45] According to the provision, the conditions set forth in these two paragraphs, with the possible exception of that relating to commercial equality, are safeguards in the interest of the indigenous population. Moreover, most of them are equally beneficial to the states members of the League. It is Great Britain's obligation to secure in the mandated territories conditions which will guarantee the prohibition of abuses, such as the slave trade and liquor traffic. In a different manner, regulation of the arms traffic is laid down primarily in the interests of the natives. Freedom of conscience or religion is evidently required as much for the sake of keeping the peace among the various European sects as for the sake of allowing freedom to the native in deciding what he would like to believe. The prevention of military training of the natives for other than police purposes and defense of territory is an immense protection for the natives under the rule of a mandatory having compulsory military services in its colonies; nevertheless, it is also a protection to the states who feared that the mandated territories might be used as reservoirs for the raising of great black armies to strengthen the military power of the mandatory state.[46] The obligation to prevent the establishment of fortifications or military and naval bases in the mandated territories was undoubtedly laid down primarily in the interests of the members of the League.

The specific obligation which has aroused the most contention regarding its purpose is the obligation in the paragraph relating to the B territories requiring the mandatories to establish conditions which will secure equal opportunities for the trade and commerce of other members of the League. Paragraph 6, relating to C mandates instead of enumerating again the duties of the mandatory powers, says simply that the territories can best be administered under the laws of the mandatory as integral portions of its territory, subject to the safeguards in the interests of the indigenous population. Article 22 of the Covenant of the League of Nations may rank as the Magna Charta of the colored races. The well-being and development of people not yet able to stand alone by themselves forms a sacred trust for civilization.[47]

The assignment and drafting of the mandates. The Allied Supreme War Council on May 7, 1919, conferred the Nauru mandate upon the British Empire and selected Great Britain as mandatory for one third of Togoland and one sixth of Cameroons and Tanganyika.[48] The Turkish territory, a part of which consisted of Palestine and Mesopotamia (Iraq) was assigned to Great Britain by the principal allied powers at San Remo, May 5, 1920.[49] The next step was to confer legal rights of authority and administration upon Great Britain and to define in charters the terms of the separate mandates. Article 22 of the Covenant of the League of Nations defines the governing principles. The charters for the various mandated territories are, in a way, executive conventions for the application of these principles.[50]

On June 28, 1919, the Supreme Council entrusted the drafting of the mandates to a commission from the principal allied and associated powers under Lord Milner.[51] Three types of mandates were prepared and designated as A, B, and C corresponding to the three classes of territories described in Article 22 of the Covenant. This commission met in July in London, but some of the interested governments made several important reservations, and an agreement was not immediately reached.[52]

The procedure eventually followed was that the principal allied powers submitted draft mandates to the council, which, after satisfying itself that they were in accordance with the provisions of the covenant, finally adopted them with slight amendments.[53]

After the mandatory principle had been accepted, the final distribution and definition was delayed for a long period of time. In August, 1920, the Council of the League met at St. Sebastian, Spain, and at this meeting a report was presented and adopted dealing with the responsibilities imposed upon the League by Article 22. The report was presented by M. Paul Hymans, the Belgian member on the council.[54]

According to the report, the following action should be taken: (1) That the mandatory powers be carefully chosen;[55] (2) that the frontiers of the territories be delimited;[56] (3) that the mandatory powers chosen be invested with the authority and the necessary powers by means of instruments which would bind them legally; (4) that these instruments should involve the application of the principle laid down in Paragraphs 4, 5, and 6 of Article 22, and should vary according to the nature of the people that were to come under them; (5) that the body provided for by Article 22 to help ensure the observance of the mandate be created.[57]

In practice, the distribution of the mandates was as follows: The Supreme Council, composed solely of representatives of the principal allied and associated powers, allocated the mandates and notified the Council of the League to that effect. The Council of the League took official cognizance of this allocation and informed the respective powers appointed by the Supreme Council that, in the eyes of the council, they were designated as mandatories, and, at the same time, notified them of the terms of the mandates. This action, in addition to the drawing of boundaries and rules for governing mandated territories by the powers before the Council of the League was formed, made the residuary trustee idea seem like a farce.[58]

It has also been charged that if the Covenant permits the British dominions and India to be at the same time members of the League of Nations as independent states with full voting powers and the powers to be mandatories of the League, and at the same time allows them to be parts of the British Empire in subordination to Great Britain, the distribution was not impartial; for by it the British Empire received nearly all that was to be distributed.[59]

The actual framing of the mandate charters, Hymans proposed to leave to the respective mandatory powers.[60] However, they had to be written in the spirit of Article 22. If found by the council to be so written, that body would then approve them. Only in case the mandatory power failed to indicate the terms of its mandate would the council take the matter in its own hands and itself write the mandates.

With the adoption of the Hymans' Report by the council, October 28, 1920, there ended an important phase in the establishment of the mandate system.[61] The coming into force of many of the mandates was, however, delayed by a number of considerations, not dependent upon either the mandatory power or the council. The C mandates came into legal force December, 1920, when they were confirmd by the council.[62] Nauru, a member of this group, had been allotted the British Empire by the Supreme War Council.

The delay in the definition of the A and B mandates was principally due to the intervention of the United States. During the council session in February, 1921, when it had been expected that the B mandates would finally be approved, an important note was received from the American government requesting that the draft mandates should be communicated to it for its consideration before submission to the council. Reference was further made to a note of November 20, 1920, from the American to the British government, expressing the view that the approval of the United States was essential to the validity of any determinations which might be reached respecting the mandates.[63] The vigorous American objection to the Franco-British San Remo oil convention of April, 1920, on the ground of economic discrimination incompatible with the mandate principle, was one of the main reasons for delay in legalizing the French and British positions in the Near East.[64]

The council, before the receipt of the American note, had already decided to postpone the consideration of the A mandates. In view of the desire expressed by the United States, the consideration of the B mandates was also deferred.[65]

On July 17, 1922, when preliminary agreements between the United States and the mandatory powers had been reached, the B mandates were confirmed by the council and entered into force at once.[66] Great Britain by this action was now the mandatory for the British Cameroons, British Togoland, and Tanganyika.

The mandate for Palestine was approved on the same occasion, but with the understanding that it should not come into force until the president of the council had been notified by the governments of France and Italy, that the negotiations then pending between them in regard to certain questions relating to the mandate for Syria had resulted in final agreement.[67] On September 29, 1923, the council was duly informed by the representatives of France and Italy that these negotiations had been successfully concluded, and took note of the fact that the mandates for Syria and Palestine would thereby automatically and simultaneously come into force. The mandate for Mesopotamia (Iraq) came into force September 24, 1924.[68] The cause of the delay will be discussed in the chapter on Iraq.

Great Britain now controlled, as mandates, territory totaling about one third the size of Australia in area and containing a population a little larger than that of Canada. In other words, mandate territories are roughly one fourteenth of the entire British Empire, and their peoples are one forty-fifth of the population of the British Empire.[69] There was nothing unusual about the fact that Great Britain received the largest number of mandates, as there was no escaping the fact that the British have been more successful in dealing with backward peoples and in helping young nations than any other of the so-called great powers.[70]

The establishment of the Permanent Mandates Commission.

A permanent Commission shall be constituted to receive and ex- amine the annual reports of the Mandatories, and to advise the Coun- cil on all matters relating to the observance of the Mandates.[71]

While mentioned by the Covenant of the League of Nations, this commission was not organized by it, and one of the first tasks of the Council of the League of Nations was to organize this commission. N. Bentwich says:

The Permanent Mandates Commission is a novel institution of international law and international politics. It may be described as an international Areopagus, to which a State which is a trustee for the League renders an annual account of its trust.[72]

In view of this statement, it is not surprising that considerable dif- ferences of opinion were disclosed in the council as to the organization of the commission. M. Hymans of Belgium thought that the manda- tories, if represented on the commission, ought not to vote in cases where they were interested in order to convince the public that man- dates are not a convenient fiction of a temporary character, but that the League is a reality.[73] M. Mitsui of Japan and A. J. Balfour of England demurred and M. Tittoni of Italy suggested that the non-mandatories should have a majority.[74] M. Hymans proposed two months later that the Assembly should appoint the nonmandatory members but this was quickly vetoed. Tittoni then made the extraordinary proposal that the mandatories should pay the expenses of the commission, but should not vote on it, and Ishii of Japan suggested that there was no need of setting up the commission at all until the mandates were confirmed. Hymans, however, pointed out the deplorable consequences if the public were given the impression that the League was unwilling to accept the duty of supervision entrusted to it by the Covenant. A plan was drawn up for a commission of fifteen, seven to be elected by the mandatories and eight by the council, on nomination of nonmandatory powers.[75]

At the eleventh session Mr. H. A. L. Fisher of Great Britain proposed a commission of only five, all nonmandatories, to save expense, but the Secretary-General pointed out that the mandatories would have to send representatives in that case, which would be as expensive. It did not seem advisable that the commission should have no function but criticism; the intention had been that the commission should be able to cooperate positively in all matters concerning the progress and well-being of the populations, placed under mandates. Bourgeois of France added that mandatories were needed in the commission to insure uniformity in the jurisprudence which would be created by the decisions of the commission. Its moral authority would be endangered if it were out of touch with the mandatories. He suggested a commission of seven, three appointed by the mandatories.[76]

On November 26, 1920, Hymans reported a suggestion prepared by the Secretary-General for a commission of nine, a majority nonmandatory, all to be appointed by the council on expert qualifications. Thus, only four of the seven mandatories would have a member. In practice, the three British dominion mandatories, Australia, New Zealand, and South Africa, have had no national on the commission while Great Britain, France, Japan, and Belgium have each had one. Inasmuch as the commission members from the mandatory powers were not to be representatives of those powers, it was proposed that these powers should be entitled to send a representative before the commission when their mandates were being considered. These accredited representatives would take part in the discussions, and at Balfour's suggestions, it was added that they should be permitted to append comments to the commission's report before it was submitted to the council.[77] At the same time, the Director of the Labor Office, referring to Articles 22 and 23(a) of the Covenant, as well as Articles 421 and 427 of the Treaty of Versailles, asked that a member of the Labor Office be appointed on the commission. The council agreed that the Labor Office might appoint an expert to be present in an advisory capacity at all meetings where labor questions were discussed.[78] The first assembly suggested that members of the Commission should not be dismissed without consent of a majority of the assembly and that one member should be a woman.[79] On November 29, M. Hymans also read the new draft constitution of the Permanent Mandates Commission, prepared by the Secretary-General of the League, and the council adopted the draft with the addition of a certain number of amendments.[80]

The commission was established in 1921 by the council.[81]

Duties and scope of work. The work of the Permanent Mandates Commission is to receive and examine the annual reports of the mandatory powers and to advise the council on all matters relating to the observance of mandates.[82] The commission is a purely advisory body: it has no power to render any decisions or to make direct recommendation to the mandatories, but it is evident that its observations and recommendations have, to a great extent, formed the basis of the decisions of the council.

Any one of the mandatory powers on the Council of the League of Nations by a single veto may overrule a recommendation from the Mandates Commission. In this case, an impasse seems to have been reached which only the exercise of considerable tact can prevent from developing into a regrettable break between the council and the commission. It raises the question of whether the Mandates System could operate at all were mutual confidence for some reason or other to be destroyed.[83]

The commission met at least once a year, and later twice a year, at Geneva, examined and discussed each individual annual report in the presence of the duly accredited representative of the mandatory power who offered any supplementary information required.

24

After the representative had withdrawn the commission decided on the observations to be submitted to the council. These observations were communicated to the mandatory power, which was entitled to add any comments of its own and such comments have been published simultaneously with the reports of the mandatory powers and the observations of the commission.[84] The Mandates Commission maintained a permanent Secretariat with an office at Geneva, which dealt with all the material received from the mandatories and prepared the work for the commission. The mandatory was required in each case to send to the commission copies of all laws and regulations and other legislative enactments passed during the year. These were examined to ascertain that they were in conformity with the principles of the mandate.

The powers of the commission have not been fully defined by either the Covenant or the commission's constitution, and differences of opinion have arisen in regard to four questions. They are: (1) Is the commission an independent body or merely an instrument of the council? (2) Is the commission limited to advice on the observance of the mandates or can it recommend improvements in the texts? (3) Is the commission limited to the investigation of representatives of the mandates, or can it hear petitions orally and conduct investigations in the mandated areas? (4) Is the commission limited to consideration of the activities of the mandatory on matters mentioned in the mandates or can it advise on the entire administration of the areas? [85]

In its first report to the council, the commission made its position clear on the first question by declaring:

> The Covenant provides that "the Permanent Mandates Commission shall be constituted to receive and examine the annual report" which the mandatory powers are pledged to send to the Council concerning the territories under their charge, and "to advise the Council on all matters relating to the observance of the mandates." Such investigations and such advice can only be of value if inspired by absolute independence and impartiality of judgment concerning the data furnished to us. We know that the Council intended us to act in that spirit, since it insisted that the Commission should be composed of experts answerable only to the League of Nations as a body, and, further, insisted that the majority of these members should be nationals of nonmandatory states.

Allow me, Mr. President and Gentlemen, to assure you that this is the manner in which we as a commission unanimously interpret the mission entrusted to us, a mission of which we hope to prove ourselves worthy.[86]

The commission and council have been clear that the commission's duties are limited to advice on the observance of mandates, but the Mandates Commission has tendered suggestions for the modification of the mandates, which the council has often transmitted to the mandatory powers.[87]

The third question has aroused much discussion and it will be treated in the discussion of petitions.[88] The fourth question is very difficult to answer. In Hyman's report accepted by the council in August, 1920, the importance of the commission examining the entire administration of the mandated territories was emphasized.[89] The constitution of the commission adopted at this time by the council seems to contemplate the same wide scope, and thus the commission had considered itself competent to consider all phases of administration in the mandated territories.[90] Opposition to this theory has occurred in the boundary negotiations of French and British mandated territories in West Africa, on the subject of oral hearings of petitioners and a recommendation for a more extensive questionnaire. This will be discussed when those subjects are covered.[91]

Personnel. At first, the Permanent Mandates Commission consisted of nine members, the majority of whom could not be nationals of nonmandatory powers. The members were appointed individually by the council for an indefinite period and were not government representatives for the states of which they were nationals. They were selected on the grounds of their personal merits and competence and it was expressly stipulated that they could not hold any office of direct dependence on their governments while members of the commission. The International Labour Office was given the right to appoint an expert who could attend in an advisory capacity all meetings of the Permanent Mandates Commission at which matters relating to labor were to be discussed. The commission itself may, moreover, summon technical experts to act as advisors in special questions.

The members first selected were: M. Beau of France, former Governor-General of French Indo-China; Mr. W. G. Ormsby-Gore, Great Britain, member of the House of Commons; M. Pierre Orts, Belgium, former Secretary-General of the Department of Foreign Affairs; M. Kunio Yanagida, Japan, former Secretary-General of the House of Peers; of the nationals of the nonmandatory powers, Mme. Bugges-Wicksell, Sweden, Doctor of Law and Delegate of Sweden at the First Assembly; M. Freire d' Andrade, Portugal, former Governor-General of Mozambique and former Minister for Foreign Affairs; the Marquis Theodoli, Italy, former Under-Secretary of State of the Ministry for the Colonies; M. van Rees, Netherlands, former Vice-President of the Council of the Dutch East Indies, Secretary-General of the Dutch Colonial Institute; and Mr. W. Cameron Forbes, United States, former Governor-General of the Philippines.[92] Forbes was unable to accept the position and his place was taken by M. Ramon Pina, Spain, former Under-Secretary of State of the Ministry for Foreign Affairs.

Changes in the commission's personnel have occurred owing to various causes: Mr. Ormsby-Gore and M. Pina were appointed to government positions and had to resign; their successors were Sir Frederick Lugard, Great Britain, former Governor of Hong Kong and former Governor-General of Nigeria, and Count de Ballobar, Spain, former Consul at Jerusalem.[93]

In 1924, the places of Count de Ballobar and M. Yanagida, who resigned, were taken by M. Palacios, Spain, Professor of the University of Madrid, and M. Chiyuki Yamanaka, Japan, former Counsellor of the Embassy.[94] M. Merlin of France replaced M. Beau of France, who died in 1926. Merlin was former Governor-General of Indo-China and former Governor-General of French West Africa.[95]

The council created a new seat on the commission in September, 1927, in order to appoint a member of German nationality: Dr. Ludwig Kastl, formerly a senior official in the German Colonial Administration, former chief of the reparations sections, of the Finance Ministry, Director of the Reichsverband der Deutschen Industrie.[96] With this appointment it was no longer possible for even the most cynically minded to dispose of the institution as a mere "screen" or "fig leaf." [97] In 1925, M. Rappard resigned his post in the Secretariat of the League of Nations. John H. Harris in *Contemporary Review* said:

It [The Mandatory System] closes the five-year period with the resignation of the Director M. William Rappard, under whose universally approved guidance the machinery of the mandatory system was erected.

The Permanent Mandates Commission represents, without doubt, one of the most generous pieces of disinterested public services performed by the League; civilization owes to every member of the Permanent Mandates Commission a debt it cannot easily repay.[98] The commission, while not wishing to increase its size, regretted so much the prospective loss of M. Rappard's cooperation that it decided to ask the council to appoint him as a supplementary member, with all the rights of an ordinary member save that in the event of his retiring his place would not necessarily be filled again. At its meeting in Rome in December, 1924, the council adopted this suggestion, and since the sixth session M. Rappard has been sitting as supplementary member of the commission.[99] M. V. Catastini succeeded Rappard as Chief of the Mandates Section.[100]

Harold A. Grimshaw, an Englishman, was the representative from the International Labor at Geneva. He died in 1929 and C. H. Weaver succeeded him and attended the Sixteenth Session in November, 1929.[101] In 1928, M. Nobumichi Sakenobe, former Plenipotentiary, was selected to fill the vacancy caused by the resignation of M. Yamanaka of Japan.[102] The council appointed, on June 9, 1928, Mlle. Valentine Dannevig to the vacant post on the commission caused by the death of Mme. Anna Bugge-Wicksell. She was a Norwegian, head mistress of the Vestheim Girl's High School, and had a great reputation as a teacher, had travelled widely, and as a member of the City Council of Oslo had gained a thorough practical knowledge of public affairs.[103]

Due to ill health, General Freire d' Andrade resigned, and was replaced by Count de Penha Garcia.[104] His reputation in international colonial questions dated back many years. M. Kastl of Germany felt obliged, owing to his numerous other duties, to hand in his resignation.[105] The council filled the vacancy by appointing Dr. Ruppel. He had been an official in the Cameroons Administration from 1910-1913, and from 1913-1919 was chief in the German Colonial Ministry, and in 1919, was attached to the German delegation at Versailles as an expert on colonial questions.[106] Merlin died May 8, 1935, and Manceron was appointed May 22, 1935. He had a brilliant administrative, diplomatic, and colonial career in France and in Africa.[107]

M. Catastini relinquished his post as Director of the Mandates Section at the twenty-eighth session in 1935.[108] M. E. De Haller became the Acting Director of the Mandates Section at the twenty-ninth session. The Secretary-General secured Catastini's services as an expert and Catastini was to attend the session not as a member or as a Secretariat official, but in a position *sui generis,* so that the commission should continue to benefit from his knowledge and experience.[109] M. E. De Haller was appointed Director of the Mandates Section in 1938.[110]

Baron Frederick Mari van Asbeck was appointed a member of the commission on January 19, 1935, in place of M. van Rees. He brought wide experience and recognized competence in colonial matters and international law. A native of the Netherlands, he was a former professor of law in the Batavia school of higher studies.[111] Lord Lugard tendered his resignation from membership on the commission after thirteen years on July 24, 1936. Lord Hailey was his successor. Hailey had been Director of the African Survey,[112] formerly Governor of the Punjab and of the United Provinces of Agra and Oudh.[113] M. Manceron died April, 1937, and Governor Giraud was appointed to take his place.

Giraud began his career in the Madagascar Civil Service and, from 1907-1917, he acted as Chef de Cabinet to the Lieutenant-Governor of the Middle Congo. From 1917-1919, he occupied a similar post in the Cameroons. He was Director-General of the Economic Services of the Governor-Generalship of French West Africa, 1919-1927, and was responsible for the study and solution of economic and social questions. In 1928, Giraud was appointed Colonial Governor. Since 1927, he has been Director of the *Agence economique de l' Afrique-Occidentale française* at Paris.[114]

Lord Hankey succeeded Lord Hailey, who resigned in 1939. Lord Hankey was Secretary of the Committee of Imperial Defence, 1912-1938; Secretary of the War Cabinet, 1916, and of the Imperial War Cabinet, 1917; Secretary of the Cabinet, 1919-1938; Clerk of the Privy Council, 1923-1938; Secretary-General of the Imperial Conferences held in 1921, 1923, 1926, 1930, and 1937; Secretary of the British Delegation to the Peace Conference, 1919, the Washington Conference, 1921, the Genoa Conference, 1922, the London International Conference on Reparations, 1929; Secretary-General of the Hague

Conference, 1929-1930, the Lausanne Conference, 1932. On his retirement in 1938, Sir Maurice Hankey was raised to the peerage. He is one of the Directors of the Suez Canal Company.[115]

The withdrawal of Japan, Germany, and Italy from the League ultimately caused the withdrawal of the members of the commission from those countries. Dr. Ruppel was not listed as a member after 1934, while Mr. Sakenobe attended till 1938, and Marquis Theodoli, the Italian member, resigned in 1938.[116]

There have been thirty-seven sessions of the commission; the first meeting was in October, 1921, and the final meeting was in December, 1939.

The Permanent Mandates Commission, a vigilant, independent, powerful, competent body, composed of men of experience, accustomed to administration, having life tenure, a majority of whom must be from states not having mandates, made it its business to know and to judge. In reporting to the council, the mandatory does not report solely to itself: it reports to this commission and thereby to the opinion of mankind. The effect is real; the whole course of events is different in mandated regions because of the consistent courageous analyzing of public judgment by this commission.[117] The Permanent Mandates Commission is regarded in all mandatory countries with genuine respect and confidence; it enjoys a degree of authority and wields an influence which the authors of Article 22 could hardly have foreseen.[118]

Conclusion. Article 22 of the Covenant lays down three main principles for the government of the backward peoples: (1) The well-being of the native inhabitants must be regarded as a sacred trust of the Administration. (2) There must be equal opportunity for the trade and enterprise of the subjects of all states of the League of Nations, and no preference or discrimination in favor of subjects of the mandatory power. (3) There is to be no establishment of military or naval bases, and no military training of natives for other than police purpose and the defense of the territory.[119]

The value of the mandates system will be due to its ability to focus public attention on the sacred trust of good colonial administration and advance the idea of trusteeship of backward people in place of the prewar concept of outright imperialistic exploitation.[120] The Mandates Commission expected to depend on public opinion. Though public opinion works slowly and sometimes is ineffective, in the long run the advantage of the issue of the reports by the commission, if it can be continued, will be found to be substantial.[121]

The mandate principle was said to have been borrowed from British colonial practice, and it is a principle on which the occupation and administration of areas formerly controlled by the native inhabitants has been justified.[122] Since Great Britain has more mandates and colonies than any other power, it follows that mutual cooperation between Great Britain and the Permanent Mandates Commission is necessary if successful principles and practices for the mandates are to be developed.

CHAPTER TWO

General Problems Affecting the Mandated Territories of Great Britain

I. The National Status of the Inhabitants of Territories under B and C Mandates

The Treaty of Lausanne provided definitely for the nationality of the inhabitants of the A mandates.[1] The guiding principle adopted was that Ottoman subjects habitually resident in the detached territory became *ipso facto* nationals of the state to which such territory is transferred.[2] The nationality of inhabitants of the territories placed under other mandates was a matter left in the air by the covenant and the peace treaties. Nothing was said about it in the mandate instruments. The inhabitants had lost their German nationality without gaining the nationality of the mandatory under whose administration they were placed. Their condition originally appeared then to be that of stateless persons; and not possessing any nationality, the moment they left their country for a foreign one they could not claim the benefit of any commercial treaty made between the mandatory and the other foreign state.

A great difference of opinion existed among the members of the Permanent Mandates Commission at its first session in October, 1921, concerning the right of the mandatory to impose its nationality upon inhabitants of the mandated territory and those who held that the mandatory's nationality could only be acquired by voluntary naturalization. Therefore, it was decided to draw the council's attention to this matter.[3]

The council, in accordance with suggestions, appointed a subcommittee of the Permanent Mandates Commission to examine this question.[4] The report of this subcommittee was submitted to the council May 12, 1922, by Marquis Alberto Theodoli, chairman of the Permanent Mandates Commission. According to the council's resolution, B and C mandates were alone under consideration. The British Government submitted to the subcommittee the three following considerations which were submitted to the Council of the League of Nations.

The British Government considered:

(a) That the mandate in itself did not affect the nationality of the inhabitants of a mandated territory:

(b) That where special clauses were provided for the administration of mandated territories as an integral part of the territory of the Mandatory Power, they should not affect the nationality of the now native inhabitants of the mandated territory:

(c) That neither should these special clauses affect the nationality of the native inhabitants of the territories.[5]

According to Article 127 of the Treaty of Versailles, the terms of which "the native inhabitants of the former German oversea possessions shall be entitled to the diplomatic protection of the governments exercising authority over those territories," have already been applied in conformity with the consular instructions of the British Foreign Office, these native inhabitants are treated as persons enjoying British protection without having received British nationality. Moreover, the British Government considered that it would be preferable not to authorize the naturalization of Europeans inhabiting the territories under British mandates of Class B, in view of the impossibility of conferring upon such inhabitants imperial naturalization, and the serious drawbacks from an administrative point of view of local naturalization within the British Empire.[6]

The council considered the report and requested the Permanent Mandates Commission to submit definite proposals on the basis of its examination.[7] This was considered by the Permanent Mandates Commission at its second session, August 1-11, 1922, and it drafted a resolution proposing that native inhabitants be given a distinct status, that the mandatory define this status, and that the mandatory be entitled to provide by law for "the individual and purely voluntary naturalization of any inhabitants of the mandated area." [8] This was in agreement with the views of the other mandatory powers, namely Australia, Belgium, France, Japan, New Zealand, and South Africa. All these powers were agreed that it would not be proper to assimilate these inhabitants to their own nationals, or to the inhabitants of their own colonies, but that in general it would be better to give them a special status conformable to the requirements of the new principle of the mandates.[9] Nationality is often spoken of as the reciprocal relations of allegiance and protection on the part of the person and the state.[10] The commission's resolutions were accepted with slight modifications by the council in its meeting of April 23, 1923.[11]

Mandated territories had been mentioned twice in the report of the proceedings of the British Imperial Conference held in 1923, and the question of the acquisition of the nationality of the mandatory power by the inhabitants of territories under B and C mandates had been discussed by the conference. The commission recommended that the council request the British government to communicate to it information on this point.[12] However, when this came before the council on December 10, 1924, Austen Chamberlain, the British member of the council, said it would be necessary to communicate with the government of the United States and with the governments of the Dominions before it was possible to give any undertaking in regard to it.[13]

In 1928, the Permanent Mandates Commission desired to learn what action the mandatory powers had taken regarding the council's resolution of April 23, 1923, and the council's decision dated March 5, 1928, requested this of the mandatory powers.[14] The council was especially interested in the steps taken to give effect to Paragraph 4 of the resolution, which provided that native inhabitants who receive the protection of the mandatory power should in each case be designated by some form of descriptive title, which will specify their status under the mandate.[15] In response to the commission's request, Great Britain replied that the question of legislation to enable the inhabitants of such territories to obtain Imperial naturalization was discussed at the Imperial Conferences of 1923 and 1926 and the terms of the bill to give effect to the conclusions reached was still under consideration by the various governments concerned.[16] As regards the fourth paragraph of the resolution, Great Britain believed that the question of the descriptive title to be accorded to the native inhabitants of the British Cameroons, British Togoland, and Tanganyika is of practical importance only in so far as it concerns the description to be entered on passports granted such persons. They decided to use "British protected person, native of the mandated territory of British Cameroons,

British Togoland, and Tanganyika." [17] The status of the native inhabitants of a mandated territory is distinct from that of the nationals
of the mandatory powers and cannot be identified therewith by any
process having general application. [18]

As to the status of inhabitants of A-mandated territories it may
be said that there are no special council decisions. [19] The Palestine
mandate expressly provides for Palestinian citizenship, and in the
Re Ezra Goralshvi case, the Supreme Court of Palestine held that
Palestinians were not subjects of the mandatory. [20] A British subject,
however, does not lose that status on acquiring Palestinian nationality. [21]

Thus, with Great Britain and the other mandatories acting with
the council, they determine the status of either inhabitants or territory of the mandated areas. [22] This action supports Wright's suggestion that there will be a close approach to truth in ascribing sovereignty of the mandated territories to the mandatory acting with the
consent of the Council of the League. [23]

II. *Loans, Advances, and Investment of Private Capital*

During its third session in July, 1923, the Permanent Mandates
Commission examined the conditions under which the financial assistance necessary to supplement the revenues of a mandated territory or
to create public works could be obtained, and how private capital
could be encouraged to assist in the development of these territories.
The commission expressed the view that mandated territories were
exposed to an economic disadvantage in consequence of the popular
doubts as to the stability of the mandates, and asked for a pronouncement by the council in order to remove this lack of confidence. [24]

M. Branting, the Rapporteur of the Council, in his report of September 22, 1923, suggested that special attention of the mandatory
powers should be invited to this grave and important question. [25] At
the fourth session of the Mandate Commission, 1924, the British accredited representative told of the Palestine loan which the British
government had decided to float and it was made clear that this would
require a special act of Parliament. The question arose whether such
an act provided the precedent for all British territories.

Sir Frederick Lugard, the British member of the Permanent Mandates Commission claimed, if the British government guaranteed the

principal and interest of a loan, the security for the subscribers was the British taxpayer. The problem of the Mandates Commission was how the mandated territory might itself be able to afford sufficient security for the raising of a loan in the public market. Security could only be obtained by removing the uncertainty which undoubtedly existed in regard to the possible revocation or transfer of the mandates, or any other element of doubt which might exist.[26]

Marquis Theodoli, the Chairman, presented two more questions. The first one was whether it was proposed to take in Palestine any security for this loan and whether the taxpayers in Palestine would be in any way responsible. The second question: could a government take guarantees in a mandated territory without the intervention of the Council of the League?

This question was of a more delicate nature in regard to A mandates than to the B and C mandates. In the case of the A mandates, it was recognized that the mandated territory was under a system of trusteeship only until it was ready and able to stand alone.[27]

According to Sir Frederick Lugard, the British government had informed him that it was waiting to send a direct reply to the council in regard to the question raised by the commission in 1923, concerning loans to mandated territories. Ormsby-Gore did not think this information represented the final views of the British government.[28]

The Permanent Mandates Commission had made recommendations to the council, and the council had asked the mandatory powers for their views.[29] Great Britain's reply was that in case of a direct loan or advance, one which is not subscribed to by the public, the new mandatory would be responsible for repayment, but in the unlikely event of a transfer it would be content to submit the matter to the League. It may be observed that even in the case of a loan publicly subscribed, the shareholders would probably be almost exclusively nationals of the mandatory whose interests the mandatory would be urged to defend.[30]

The Permanent Mandates Commission considered this reply outside its competence and did not review it.[31] Sir Frederick Lugard was requested at the fourth session, June-July, 1924, by the commission to draw up a memorandum to be communicated to the members of the commission before its fifth session.[32] While it was outside the competence of the Mandates Commission to review Great Britain's reply, moreover, it was too late for the Permanent Mandates Commission to submit any clearer or more precise presentment of the question. However, Lugard realized his recommendations, if accepted by his colleagues, would be of some use to the council in its examination of Great Britain's reply. He suggested that the concurrence of the council and assembly in the following propositions would go far to remove the reasons given for the reluctance of capital to enter the territories:

(1) Revocation of a mandate may, for practical purposes, be regarded as inconceivable. It could only take place in the event of gross violation of the mandate and at the instance of the international court, which may be relied upon to safeguard all private interests.

(2) Loans and advances, whether made by the mandatory power or raised by public subscription, should be secured as a first charge on the revenues of the mandated territory and not by the hypothecation of any specific work or undertaking. Resignation or transfer of a mandate, however improbable (except on the acquisition of self-government by a territory under A mandate), would require the sanction of the League of Nations, and this would only be accorded if the new government or mandatory guaranteed the service of the loans on the security of the revenues.

(3) Important works essential to public services should be undertaken by the mandatory power alone, in order that their ownership and control may not remain in private hands, and in case of transfer or resignation of the mandate, they may pass to the new government. In such an event, the new government or mandatory would, as a condition of the League's approval of the change, be required to confer all titles to land and other contracts made by the retiring mandatory to private companies or individuals.[33]

The council adopted a resolution on March 11, 1925, requesting the Permanent Mandates Commission to prepare a draft decision in accordance with Paragraph (b) of the decision of the council of December 12, 1923.[34] M. Rappard prepared the draft decision for the sixth session of the Mandates Commission. According to Rappard the League of Nations had been examining two distinct questions concerning advances of capital to mandated territories, although these questions were linked together when they first came up for consideration.[35]

The first was how far it was possible to overcome the hesitation of financiers who were willing to invest in the mandated territories under a regime which did not appear to offer sufficient guarantees of security. The second question was purely academic. The commission had been rendered rather anxious concerning the possibility of a mandatory power acquiring financial rights over essential public works greater than those which should be allowed under the mandatory system.[36] Great Britain's reply refers to only one of the two aspects of the problem. It examined the question of the right of a mandatory power to secure its advances to a mandated territory by mortgages on public works and the responsibility which would be assumed by a new mandatory in the very improbable event of a mandate being transferred.[37] Concerning the first question, Rappard argued that the mandated territories were much more fully guaranteed under the administration of the mandatory powers than were their own colonies. With the second question, there had as yet been no example of a mandatory power making advances and taking security for these advances by a mortgage on public works. The case was purely hypothetical.[38]

The commission at its sixth session proposed to submit for the consideration of the council a draft resolution that

(1) Declared that obligations assumed by a mandatory Power in a mandated territory, and rights of every kind regularly acquired under its administration, shall have under all circumstances the same validity as if the mandatory Power were sovereign;
(2) Decides that: (a) In the event of the cessation of a mandate or of its transfer—however improbable this may be—to a fresh mandatory Power, the Council without whose approval no change can take place, will not give such approval unless it has been assured in advance that the new Government undertaking the administration of the territory will accept responsibility for the fulfillment of the financial obligations regularly assumed by the former mandatory Power and will engage that all rights regularly acquired under the administration of the latter shall be respected: (b) Moreover the Council, when this change has been effected, will continue to use all its influence to ensure the fulfillment of these obligations, as has already been expressly provided in the mandates for Syria and Lebanon and for Palestine.[39]

Following the recommendations of the Mandates Commission, the council, in its resolution, declared, first:

That the validity of financial obligations assumed by a mandatory Power on behalf of a mandated territory in conformity with the provisions of the mandate and all rights regularly acquired under the mandatory regime are in no way impaired by the fact that the territory is under mandate. Secondly, the cessation or transfer of a mandate will not take place unless the Council had been assured in advance that the financial obligations regularly assumed by the former Mandatory will be carried out.[40]

Loans and the investment of private capital into the less highly developed territories have often led to annexation. Therefore, loans to a mandated territory are watched with interest by the Mandates Commission as it considers annexation irreconcilable with the mandate principle.[41] Lugard's statement that "revocation of a mandate may for practical purposes be regarded as inconceivable," and Rappard's declaration "that mandated territories were much more fully guaranteed under the administration of the mandatory powers than were their own colonies" gave greater stability to the mandates. The case of the Mavrommatis Palestine Concession also helped, for the fact that a case involving the interpretation of a mandate had been brought before the Permanent Court of International Justice was an important precedent in that it showed that the status of a mandate territory was safeguarded by international law, as well as by the supervision of the political institutions of the League of Nations.[42]

Great Britain's reply to the commission's question on loans was that in the case of a direct loan or advance to a mandate by the mandatory, the new mandatory would be responsible in case of transfer. Important as the statement was at this time, it became of greater importance later, as it became one of the criteria for Iraq to meet before assuming statehood.[43]

Annexation is not the only problem to be considered with the problems of loans. Another important one is that all purchases made by the mandated territory out of the proceeds of the loans or guarantees must be made in the lending country.

III. *The Purchase of Supplies by the Administration of Mandated Territories*

A debate in the House of Commons on December 9, 1926, concerning the Palestine and East African loans resulted in the Permanent Mandates Commission making an inquiry as to the method of purchasing supplies and materials by the authorities in a mandated territory for public works. An amendment was proposed to the Palestine and East African Loans (Guarantee) Bill to the effect that all purchases of plant, machinery, or equipment made out of the proceeds of such loans should be made in the British Empire. This amendment, however, provided that this obligation should not apply to purchases of any such plant, machinery, or equipment required for mandated territories.[44]

At the eleventh session of the Mandates Commission (June 25-July 6, 1927), M. Orts referred to this debate.[45] Amery, the Secretary of State for the Colonies, opposed the amendments, mainly because all purchases would be made through the crown agents for the colonies, who had instructions not to place any order outside the British Empire without special reference to the Secretary of State.[46] The Secretary of State thought the stipulation that all purchases must be made in the United Kingdom or the British Empire was not a violation of the terms of the mandate as Article 7 of the mandate reads as follows:

> The Mandatory shall ensure to all nationals of States Members of the League of Nations, on the same footing as to his own nationals, freedom of transit and navigation, and complete economic, commercial, and industrial equality, provided that the Mandatory shall be free to organize essential public works and services on such terms and conditions as he thinks just.[47]

During the Eleventh Session, M. Rappard asked Sir Donald Cameron, Governor of Tanganyika, if it were necessary to purchase agricultural machinery which could not be obtained from the United Kingdom or the British Empire, would the Governor feel precluded from using the loan money in order to do so. Cameron told of a recent purchase of machinery from the United States out of the revenue. Therefore, when equipment could not be purchased within the Empire there was no hesitation in recommending outside purchases.[48] The Tanganyika Report for 1926 reported complete equality existed.[49] It was difficult for the commission to make a decision regarding this as it was clear that, since the money provided by this loan was to be used on public works, a stipulation that all orders regarding those works should be placed in the United Kingdom or in the British Empire was quite in order and was not against the terms of the mandate. Therefore, the Permanent Mandates Commission did not make any criticism as it could not be justified.[50]

In October, 1927, at the Twelfth Session of the Mandates Commission, the subject became much more important than it had at first appeared. A question of principle was involved which directly interested not only all the mandatory powers but all the state members of the League.[51] M. Orts was appointed to report upon the subject, and he was of the opinion that the whole question bore for the moment on the declaration of Amery. That declaration was very clear. It was, therefore, easy for him to make a report on that subject and to decide whether the declaration of Amery was or was not well founded. The mandatory power had resorted in a particular case to to a particular practice. Had it been right or wrong in doing so? That was the question at issue. Mr. Orts feared that if the commission expected a statement of the principles which should in the future define the right of the mandatory power, it would be disappointed: he feared that it would be disappointed; it seemed difficult to formulate a general principle in view of the number of hypotheses which might present themselves.[52]

The Chairman asked M. Orts to examine in his report the case of orders for goods on account of the government of Iraq which were reserved by the crown agents solely for British firms, and at the same time to study the theses put forward by Amery on the subject of Tanganyika.[53] The commission came to no final conclusion on the subject at this session, and during the thirteenth session it became apparent that the question assumed quite a different aspect in the case of Palestine, since no exception of this kind applied to the A mandates.[54] A loan had been issued for a considerable sum, the proceeds of which were partly intended for public works in Palestine. As the commission feared there was a tendency to reserve these purchases for British industry, it recommended to the council to request the mandatories of A and B mandates to inform them of what system they used for the purchase of supplies by the public authorities of the mandated territories.[55] The council at its fifty-first session, 1928, adopted the recommendation.[56]

The B mandates reserve to the mandatory powers freedom of action only in regard to "essential" public works and services. What is understood by "essential works"? Some have rightly held that this adjective does not connote the importance of the works, but the fact that they are of public utility. According to this view, all public works undertaken by the administration in the public interest, and all public services are of an essential character.[57]

Orts concluded that in A as well as in B mandated territories the mandatory power responsible for the administration is entitled to organize all public works and services as it thinks fit and is not bound to call for public tenders for the execution of such work or the provision of the supplies required for the operation of such services. The commission is entitled to examine the whole administration of the territory and must be able to decide in each case whether the mandatory power, in allocating the contracts for public works or the supply of material by private contract, has deliberately and for good reasons of its own resorted to a practice which is not as a rule to be recommended from the standpoint of sound administration.[58]

The British Government sent a document containing the regulations governing the purchase of material and supplies by the public authorities in Palestine and Trans-Jordan, Tanganyika, Togoland, and the Cameroons under British mandate.[59] According to these regulations, purchases made locally or in adjacent countries are decided after submission to public tenders. Articles which the country does not produce or which cannot be obtained locally on advantageous terms are purchased through the Crown Agent.[60] According to a more recent letter from the British Government, these rules are not applicable in the case of the Government of Iraq,

. . . who, while as a matter of convenience placing the majority of their orders through the Crown Agents for the Colonies, not infrequently purchase stores through other channels.

This reply was not considered satisfactory by the commission in November, 1929, at its sixteenth session. The commission asked the council to request the British Government to state:

(1) Whether, as regards the purchase of material and supplies for the administration of territories under A and B mandates, the Crown Agents are authorized to place orders indifferently with firms of every nationality, or if, in conformity with what would appear to be the rule in the case of orders placed by the colonies and protectorates, orders may not be placed outside the British Empire without special reference to the Secretary of State.

(2) Whether in practice, nationals of States Members of the League of Nations are allowed to submit tenders for supplies required by the administration of territories under A and B mandates.

(3) Whether in practice the Government of Iraq, when dealing with supplying firms and not through the Crown Agents, advertises its intending purchases, and whether nationals of all States Members of the League are allowed to submit tenders.[61]

Great Britain replied that there was no discrimination with firms because of their nationality; however, in the case of Togoland and the Cameroons, which are administered as integral parts of the Gold Coast and Nigeria and have no separate administrations, supplies would naturally be ordered with supplies for the respective British colonial administrations.[62] Concerning the rules about public works in territories under British mandate, it is the general practice of the mandatory governments to carry out such works through the agency of their public works departments. In those cases in which contracts are invited, no discrimination is made between the contractors on the ground of nationality.[63] As to Iraq, when the crown agents for the colonies act for the government of Iraq, nationals of all states members of the League of Nations are allowed to submit tenders for supplies required for the administration of the territory in question.[64] On the other hand, if the department concerned decides not to place the order through the crown agents in London, they do not deal directly with supplying firms abroad, but only through their agents in Iraq, who should be government contractors. Any government contractor may tender. Government contractors may be of any nationality and may tender on behalf of manufacturers of any nationality.[65]

Orts did not think he could alter his conclusions reached during the thirteenth mandate commission session. Mainly since the administration was responsible for the organization of public services and works, it was clear that it should be entitled to use its own judgment in selecting the staff.[66]

M. Kastl of Germany could not support the conclusions of M. Orts' report. He thought it was essential to draw a distinction between the organization of public works and services, on the one hand, and the purchase of supplies for such works and services on the other. It might be true to say that the responsibility incurred by the mandatory power conferred upon it full freedom to organize public works as it thought fit, but it could not be admitted, in virtue of the same principle, that the mandatory power was free to organize the purchase of supplies, which, according to the principle of equality, should be effected by public tenders open to all.[67]

Lord Lugard accepted the general conclusions of M. Orts' report.[68]

The Chairman of the Mandates Commission, at its twenty-second session in November, 1932, expressed the view that a conclusion be reached on this question.[69]

The Mandates Commission thought it necessary to define the scope of the provision of the mandate in which, so far as concerns essential public works and services, exception is made to the principle of equality. In the commission, it was clear that two different opinions were held.[70]

The principle that equal opportunities for trade and commerce applied only to private enterprise was the view expressed by Mr. Orts. As a corollary of its administrative responsibility, the mandatory power enjoyed, in principle, complete freedom in that sphere—that was to say, in matters of public works and services it had the right to place orders or conclude contracts with whomsoever it thought fit.[71] Opposed to this point of view is the group to which the word "essential" in the text of the mandate clearly demonstrates the desire of the authors to lay down a clear distinction between public works and services which by reason of their special character, are excepted from the system of economic equality, and other works and services. Supporters of this view are of the opinion that, if an exception is not authorized under the terms of the mandate, the mandatory powers should, in the case of the purchase of material and undertakings relating to public works, invite public tenders which would be open to nationals of all the state members of the League of Nations, that procedure being the best means of safeguarding the interests protected by the principle of economic equality.[72]

Dr. Ruppel, the German member on the Mandates Commission, thought Great Britain's claim to an absolutely free hand for Togoland and the Cameroons was not consistent with the economic equality clause contained in the mandates for those territories. Secondly, as regards public works, it was said that it was the general practice to carry out such work through the agency of the Public Works Department. In his opinion, that practice, transferred from British colonies to the mandated territories, did not take sufficiently into account the special obligations imposed by the mandates.[73]

Lord Lugard desired to know what meaning should be attached to the word "essential." Did M. Orts hold this view that in practice all public works and services were essential? Lastly, did he consider that the administration was not bound to call for public tender when incurring expenditure in public utility works which was met out of current revenue?

In M. Orts' view, the term "essential" applied to all works and all services of public utility, irrespective of their importance.

M. Orts asked the commission to ask the council to approve the first part of the report, and the commission was aware that there could be no idea of securing unanimity on a doctrinal interpretation of the mandates.[74] Orts also replied that, when he had first embarked upon the study of this question, he, too, had felt that it was a matter of principle, the solution of which would have important consequences in practice. The discussion in commission had shown that this was not the case. The question in effect was whether all public works and public services were essential or only some of them. Everyone agreed that the mandatory power was entitled to make arrangements for essential works and services at its own discretion. The only point still in doubt was whether works of minor importance or supplies for subsidiary services should be put up for public tender or no. It must certainly be agreed that, reduced to these dimensions, the matter was, in practice, of only very relative interest. That was indeed an additional reason why the commission should not lose further time in academic discussion.[75]

While the commission was divided on the doctrinal interpretation of this provision of the mandates, it was unanimous in recognizing that administrative practice adopted in this matter remains subject to the supervision which the commission exercises over the general administration of countries under mandate. It was, therefore, for the commission to decide in each case that arises whether the mandatory power, in concluding a private agreement for the carrying out of public works or the supply of material, has conscientiously and for good reasons adopted a practice which, from the point of view of good administration, may be open to objection.[76]

The replies led the Mandates Commission to conclude that the rules enunciated by the mandatory powers in connection with the carrying out of public works and services did not call for any criticism. And the commission made a reservation regarding the rule followed in Togoland and the Cameroons under British mandate. It notes that the administrative union between those two territories and the adjacent British possession places certain difficulties in the way of the adoption of rules differing from those adopted in those possessions. The commission did not think it necessary to submit any proposals to the council for a doctrinal interpretation of the relevant article of the mandate. It agreed once more to confine its activities to the supervision of the application given in the various mandated territories to the rules drawn up by the mandatory powers themselves.[77] The council approved its conclusions at its seventieth session in February, 1933.[78]

It has been impossible to avoid discrimination by the mandate powers in favor of their own nationals in the resources and commerce of the mandated territories.[79] Nevertheless, Great Britain has declared there was no discrimination with firms because of their nationality. The Mandates Commission was responsible for the failure to answer the question concerning the position taken by Amery, the British Colonial Secretary, in stipulating that, in return for the guarantee of a loan, all purchases be made in the territory of the mandatory power consistent with the terms of the mandate. During the commission's attempt to answer it, a discussion arose as to the exact meaning and scope of the clause "essential public works and services" in which there was no conclusive agreement as to what public works and services could be called essential or unessential. No discrimination was made between contractors on the ground of nationality in the cases in which contracts were invited.

The Mandates Commission has elaborated a specific doctrine of mandatory law under which such territories may not become the prey of unrestrained exploitation; it has made annexation difficult, and the investment policies and practices have been more clearly exposed to the public view.[80]

47

IV. *Treatment Extended in Countries Members of the League of Nations to Persons Belonging to Territories Under A and B Mandates and to Produce and Goods Coming Therefrom*

The council at its fifty-first session in September, 1928, requested the Permanent Mandates Commission to make a general study of the question of the treatment of persons belonging to territories under the mandate of states members of the League of Nations and the treatment of products and goods from these territories.[81]

According to the resolution of the council, September 1, 1928, the enquiry which the council expects the commission to make must cover two entirely distinct questions. First, the treatment of persons belonging to mandated territories who leave their country of origin to settle permanently or temporarily in the territory of states members of the League. This question concerns the personal interest of such persons. The second question deals with the treatment of produce coming from the mandated territories and imported into the territory of states members of the League. In contradistinction to the first, this question concerns the interests of the exporting territories and their inhabitants.[82]

M. Rappard submitted a report on this subject at the fifteenth session of the Mandates Commission.[83] After studying the question the Mandates Commission recommended to the council to ask the mandatory powers in charge of A and B mandates whether they consider it necessary to contemplate the conclusion of an international convention intended to secure to the territories under A and B mandates the benefit of reciprocity in respect to economic equality which these territories are obliged to grant to states members of the League of Nations, at least in respect to commercial exchanges, or whether, in their opinion, it would be preferable and sufficient for them to pursue the end in view by means of direct and bilateral negotiations.[84]

The British Government replied March 6, 1930, that the system of direct bilateral negotiations had worked well in the case of the mandated territory administered by them. It, however, was not free from difficulty and a conclusion of an international convention would be welcomed, though it was not regarded as necessary. Great Britain presumed that any such convention would be drafted so as to entitle mandated territories only to most-favored nation treatment and not so as to require a power accepting the convention to extend to the mandated territories of another power the treatment which it accords its own possessions.[85]

During its eighteenth session, 1930, the commission, following M. Rappard's advice after having taken note of the replies from Great Britain, Belgium, and France, decided to draw the attention of the council to the desirability of inviting all states members of the League of Nations to give favorable consideration to any request which may be made to them by the mandatory powers, with a view to obtaining for the nationals or, at any rate, for the goods of the territories under A and B mandate, advantages corresponding to those enjoyed by their own nationals and their own goods in the aforesaid territories.[86]

Rappard thought it unwise to lay a proposal before the council for the summoning of an international conference on this subject. The asking of all the states members of the League of Nations to give a favorable response to any request received from the mandatory powers would obviate the delays, the expense, and the hazards of an international convention, and yet would tend to secure to the territories under A and B mandate and to persons belonging to those territories, advantages corresponding to their interests and their desires, and at the same time conforming to the dictates of justice and to the spirit of the mandate system.[87] This procedure was in accordance with the precedents established by the council on two occasions and sanctioned by the assembly.[88] The council adopted the resolution September 9, 1930.[89]

Again Great Britain was willing to cooperate and welcomed an international convention to deal with the treatment of produce coming from the mandated territories and imported into the territory of states members of the League. The Mandates Commission opposed the calling of an international conference. The question of the treatment of persons belonging to mandated territories who emigrate was not very important as the emigration is very low.

V. Application of International Conventions to Mandated Territories

Great Britain is required to apply any general international convention to the mandate that is applicable to contiguous territories.

A general international convention is one to which several states are party. Some general international conventions are those concerning slavery, traffic in arms and munitions, liquor traffic, drug traffic, or those dealing with commercial equality, freedom of transit and navigation, aerial navigation, railway post, telegraph and wireless, literary, artistic, and industrial property. The Convention of St. Germain, as well as the Berlin and Brussels Acts, were general treaties.[90] Special treaties are those concluded between two states or bilateral conventions for mutual benefit.

The B mandate contains no references to special treaties, and the Permanent Mandates Commission considered that special international conventions entered into by a state do not apply *de jure* to territories in regard to which the state in question has been entrusted with a mandate. As a result, a situation prejudicial to the inhabitants of the mandated territories and to the economic development of these territories arose. The inhabitants could not claim the benefits of any treaties which have laid down the legal status of nationals of the mandatory state within the territory of other states. Also they could not claim the benefits of the most favored nation clauses.[91]

Sir Frederick Lugard maintained that the point at issue was to secure for the mandated territories the option of the most favored nation clauses, and he thought this question was a matter for the council or the Assembly, which might definitely decide whether the status of a mandatory should be considered as equivalent to that of a colony or protectorate.[92]

Since the interest of the inhabitant of a mandated area is affected, the commission questioned whether further measures might not be adopted to give the fullest practical effect to the principle enunciated in Article 127, Section I, Part IV, of the Treaty of Versailles, which states:

. . . that the native inhabitants of the former German oversea possessions shall be entitled to the diplomatic protection of the Government exercising authority over those territories.[93]

The Permanent Mandates Commission, at its third session in 1923, adopted a recommendation to the effect that the members of the League of Nations should consider the possibility of extending to the territories under B mandate the advantages which are conferred upon the contiguous colonies and protectorates of the mandatory state by special treaties and conventions entered into by that state with any other member of the League of Nations, on the understanding that reciprocity will only be recognized if it does not in any way effect the principles of economic equality.[94] The council forwarded the suggestions of the commission to the mandatory powers and requested them to inform the council of their views as to the advisability and possibility of the proposed measure.[95]

A letter of April 29, 1924, from the British Government to the Secretary-General of the League of Nations as regarding the extension of special international treaties to territories under mandate observed that, so far as territories administered by Great Britain under B mandates were effected, (a) in commercial treaties with foreign powers negotiated by them, provision had been made for the accession of mandated territories, and it proposed to make similar provision in subsequent treaties, while steps were also being taken to insert in extradition treaties, when negotiated, a provision under which they may be made applicable to mandated territories; (b) in the case of earlier treaties, which did not apply to mandated territories and contained no provision for extension to such territories, Great Britain announced she was willing to take up the question when any foreign power considered it desirable.[96] Early in 1926, the British Government made it clear again that the statement of April 29, 1924, concerned only the B mandates. Because of Iraq's special status it was necessary to consult the Iraq Government in all cases except those to which it was bound by the treaty with Great Britain to adhere.[97]

At its sixth session the Mandates Commission, realizing that bilateral or multilateral conventions could not be applied automatically, recommended that all states, whether members or not of the League, which concluded special treaties or conventions with the mandatory powers should agree to extend the benefits of such treaties or conventions to mandated territories if circumstances render such extension possible and expedient and if the provisions of these international agreements are consistent with the stipulations of the covenant and the mandate.[98] The council approved this at its thirty-fifth session in September, 1925.[99]

The President of the United States, on July 12, 1926, proclaimed two treaties signed with Great Britain relating to rights in British

Togoland and the Cameroons.[100] From the standpoint of international law the most interesting feature of these treaties is the assumption that American consent is necessary for British administration of the mandate, and that Great Britain can grant permanent rights with respect to the terriories.[101]

The Mandates Commission, at its twelfth session, took note of two lists drawn up at its request by the Secretariat. One indicates the general and special conventions applied in each mandated territory, and the other shows the mandated territories in which each general international convention is applied. Sir Frederick Lugard proposed that these lists should be sent to all the mandatory powers for verification; also he proposed that this document should be periodically brought up to date and printed.[102]

Also at this session, M. Bourdillon, counsellor to the High Commissioner for Iraq, announced that Iraq had decided to adhere to four international conventions. He wished to draw attention to one constitutional point; certain international conventions contained a provision that Great Britain might adhere to them on behalf of Iraq.[103] A resolution adopted at the forty-ninth session of the council decided that the accession of Iraq to international conventions should in the future be effected by the Iraq Government as a separate contracting state. Such action was not incompatible with the arrangements made for the government of Iraq under Article 22 of the covenant.[104] Steps were taken to secure for Iraq the benefits of future commercial treaties between Great Britain and other states by the conclusion of a special protocol that was appended to the principal treaty, providing for the separate accession of Iraq.[105]

The commission again considered the problem at its thirteenth session, and it was suggested that the council should first request the commission to proceed, within the limits of its competence, to examine the problem very minutely, and to communicate the results.[106]

In the annual report on the British Cameroons, the commission noted that the accession of the British Cameroons to the Treaty of Commerce and Navigation concluded in 1926 had been considered but not recommended. The accredited representative for the Cameroons was reminded that under the terms of the resolutions adopted by the council, the mandatory powers had been asked to explain why they had not acceded on behalf of their mandated territory to a treaty.

The accredited representative replied that the probable reason was that there was no trade between the British Cameroons and Greece, and that in future reports this practice would be followed.[107]

In the 1928 Tanganyika report for the fifteenth session of the Mandates Commission, thirty-six international conventions and treaties were listed as having been adhered to on behalf of the territory.[108] Lord Lugard thought there were several omissions in the list. No mention had been made, for instance, of the Convention on the Traffic in Women and Children and the Convention on the Preservation of Game. However, these omissions were probably accidental.[109]

On March 5, 1928, the council, in conformity with the recommendations of the Mandates Commission, asked the mandatory powers to revise the list of conventions and treaties.[110]

At its twentieth session, June, 1931, the Mandates Commission proposed to the council that the table of general international conventions applied in the territories under mandate should, without further delay, be distributed to the members of the council and to the members of the League of Nations and published, and that this document should be constantly kept up to date with the help of the particulars which it is incumbent on the mandatory powers to supply.[111] Later it also proposed that the table relating to the bilateral conventions applied to the mandated territories should, until further notice, preserve the character of an internal document for the exclusive use of the Mandates Commission.[112]

M. Orts of the Mandates Commission had contended that a distinction should be made between general conventions and bilateral or special conventions. The application in the territories under mandate of general international conventions, or accession, on behalf of the territories under mandate, to the general conventions to which they are parties constitutes for the mandatory powers the execution of an engagement which they are not at liberty to evade. On the other hand, the council and assembly resolutions, relating to the application to the territories under mandate of certain special conventions are not of the same imperative character, but are of the nature of recommendations, the text of which allows considerable latitude to the mandatory powers as regards their application. He concluded that the publication of the general conventions made applicable to the territories under the mandate would give rise to objection. This might not be the case with regard to the publication of the list of special conventions which have voluntarily been made applicable by the mandatory powers. Such publication might give rise to comparison between the various degrees of good will shown by the various mandatory powers in deferring to the wishes of the council and assembly, and might lead to conclusions which would not be justified, especially as no time limit was laid down within which these recommendations were to be put into effect. A publication of this form without the consent of the powers might look like indirect pressure in a matter where the execution of the recommendations in question should depend exclusively on the inclinations of the powers.[113]

Nevertheless, the mandatory powers unanimously replied that they saw no objection to the publication of the revised versions of the tables of bilateral conventions applied in mandated territories, but the commission thought there could be no serious objection to suspending its publication, which would entail considerable expense. By doing this, the tables of conventions would provisionally retain the character of documents reserved for the Mandates Commission's internal use.[114]

As to the extension of special treaties to mandated territories, Great Britain informed the commission that it had already made this provision in its new commercial treaties, and intended to continue to do so. In the case of earlier treaties which did not apply to mandated areas, England announced she was willing to take up the question when any foreign nations considered it desirable.

Great Britain and the remaining mandatories unanimously agreed to the publication of the revised version of tables of bilateral conventions applied in the mandates. The Mandates Commission objected and suspended publication of the treaties because it feared public publication would appear like indirect pressure on the various mandate-holding nations.

VI. *Military Recruiting in Mandated Areas*

Article 3 of the mandate for the British Cameroons reads:

The Mandatory shall not establish in the territory any military or naval bases, nor erect any fortifications, nor organize any native military force except for local police purposes and for the defense of the territory.[115]

This question was of great importance to Smuts, Clemenceau, and Lloyd George during the World War and the Peace Conference. The prolonged resistance of the German East Africa colony and a large number of troops raised in Africa for local purposes had made necessary a reconsideration of the Middle African situation in light of these facts.[116] General Smuts expressed his sentiment regarding it May 22, 1917, in a speech in London:

I hope that one of the results of this war will be some arrangement or convention among nations interested in Central Africa by which the military training of natives in that area will be prevented as we have prevented it in South Africa.[117]

During the Peace Conference, M. Clemenceau demanded an unlimited right of levying black troops to assist in the defense of French territory in Europe if France were attacked in the future by Germany.[118] Lloyd George replied that he had exactly the same power as previously. What the document did prevent was the kind of thing the Germans were likely to do, namely, organize great black armies in Africa which they could use for the purpose of clearing everybody else out of that country. That was their proclaimed policy and if that was encouraged among the other nations, even though they might not have wars in Europe, they would have the sort of thing that happened in the seventeenth and eighteenth centuries in India when France and Great Britain were at war in India, while they were ostensibly at peace in Europe.[119]

During the examination of the report on the sphere of the Cameroons under Britain at the third session of the Mandates Commission, Mr. W. G. Ormsby-Gore, the accredited representative, asked the commission whether a mandatory was precluded from accepting, from the population of the territory under mandate, recruits who volunteer for service in an armed force belonging to a neighboring colony, a detachment of which may be temporarily quartered in the territory.[120] No special force had been maintained for the defense of the mandated territory. A company of the Third Battalion of the Nigeria Regiment, West African Frontier Force, was stationed in the mandated territory for the maintenance of order.[121] A number of Cameroons' natives presented themselves voluntarily for enlistment. Of these, 189 men were enlisted and posted to the various companies of the battalion. It was thought possible that this point might be raised by the Mandates Commission, as a native regularly enlisted in any unit of the West African Frontier Force was liable to serve in any part of West Africa. If so, the point to be cleared up was whether Article 3 of the Mandate should be construed as preventing the mandatory power from accepting natives of the mandated areas for voluntary enlistment in a force organized before the mandate was granted.

M. Rappard thought it was the intention of Article 3 of the Mandate to prevent the mandatory power from using its position as mandatory to increase its military strength elsewhere than in the mandated territory.[122]

M. Orts held the question of principle remained the same whether the question was one of voluntary enrollment or of obligatory service, whether three hundred or three million men were concerned. What should be cleared up was the question whether it was in conformity with the spirit of the system that the exercise of the mandate should confer upon the mandatory the means to develop its military power.

The text of Article 3 of the British Mandate gave no specific answer to the question. What Article 3 forbade was the organization in the territory itself of a military force other than that necessary for police and local defense. Could advantage be taken of these terms to consider as legitimate a practice which consisted in enrolling men in the territory in view of the fact that these men would be put into units organized on the other side of the frontier in the neighboring colony?

Sir Frederick Lugard, Great Britain's representative on the Commission, said that it would be equally a violation of the principle if the men were sent from the Cameroons to Nigeria to be recruited there. He was inclined to agree with M. Orts on the question of principles.[123]

The commission was unanimously of the opinion that the spirit, if not the letter, of the mandate would be violated if Great Britain enlisted the natives of the mandated territory (wherever they presented themselves for engagement) for service in any military corps or body of constabulary which was not permanently quartered in the territory and used solely for its defense or the preservation of order within it.[124]

At the twenty-seventh session of the Council of the League of Nations in December, 1923, the following resolution was submitted:

The Council decides to refer the consideration of military recruiting in mandated territories raised by the British Government to the Mandates Commission and to the British Government in the hope that the Council would have received the following year that an agreement had been arrived at on this matter.[125]

Lord Robert Cecil of the Council defined the point of view of the British Government. The recommendation as originally drafted might be taken to imply a limitation of the rights and powers of the British Government beyond the limits of mandated territories, and the British Government would feel that such an interpretation would be open to obligation. The emendation of the *Rapporteur*, as well as the resolution, was adopted.[126]

On June 4, 1924, the British Government announced that it was willing to pay due regard to the views of the Mandates Commission, and decided not to maintain their right to recruit natives of a mandated territory for enlistment in His Majesty's forces outside the boundaries of the mandated territory.[127] At the same time, the British Government expressed the wish that it should be understood that they receded in no way from the attitude taken up by their predecessors as to British sovereign rights in British territory or British protected territory.[128]

Sir Frederick Lugard said there was no reservation. The letter from the British Foreign Office merely laid down a general principle that the sovereignty of British colonies and protectorates could not be infringed and that the decision of the British Government should not form a precedent. No reservation was made in regard to the actual point which had been raised.[129]

Ormsby-Gore declared that the British Government merely stated that it was beyond the competence of the Mandates Commission to say what the British Government should or should not do in a British colony. The British Government had the right to facilitate or prohibit the enlistment in British colonies of natives from mandated territories, but it had agreed not to practice such enlistment and had, therefore, fallen in with the wishes of the commission.

After noting the declaration of Ormsby-Gore the commission decided to record that it had never been its intention to infringe in any way the sovereign rights of the British Government.[130]

The logical conclusion is that the British Government would, for instance, be perfectly free to enlist, for military service in the protectorate of Nigeria, any number of natives originally coming from the British Cameroons who had settled in Nigeria or were there only temporarily. The acceptance of the mandate has not deprived the mandatory power of any of its rights in its own colonies. This acceptance has, nevertheless, laid on it a moral obligation to observe not only the letter of the provisions of the mandate but also their spirit.[131]

VII. *Liquor Traffic*

A general prohibition of liquor traffic is contained in the Convention of St. Germain, 1919, which applies to the whole of Africa, including colonies and protectorates.[132] But the mandates direct control and not prohibition, and the council early had certain inconsistencies in the texts of the covenant, the mandates, and certain international conventions drawn to its attention by private societies.[133] Opinions differed whether all alcoholic beverages must be prohibited in the territory, whether they must be prohibited only to natives, or whether only dangerously intoxicating spirits need be prohibited. The council, in July, 1922, passed a resolution asking the Permanent Mandates Commission to investigate the matter.[134]

During the third mandates session, Sir Frederick Lugard made a report in which he held prohibition of alcoholic beverages was not intended for the mandated areas.[135] Also, at the third session of the Mandates Commission in 1923, with a view to restricting the import of spirits into the backward countries, it was recommended that the governments of France and Great Britain be invited to agree that the duties of all spirituous liquors imported into the territories placed under their respective mandates in Africa should not be less than the duties in the adjoining territories on similar spirits of equal strength.[136] The commission also recommended that the two powers should consult with each other from time to time in order to maintain this uniformity of duty. In a letter dated March 13, 1924, the British Government informed the Secretariat that it was engaged in conversations with the French authorities in regard to this question.[137]

Hanotaux, the French member of the Council, thought the Mandates Commission had a tendency to go beyond the powers with which it was entrusted. Its duty was to advise the council on questions relating to the execution of the mandates. The Mandates Commission could not on its own initiative make proposals in regard to the general administration of the mandated territory as a whole.[138] The English member of the council, Lord Robert Cecil, thought that the task of the commission would be very difficult if it were not able to make suggestions for the better execution of the mandates. He, however, made it clear that the commission could not communicate directly with the governments. Such a procedure would be strongly resented. The commission should report to the council, and it was for the council to decide whether its recommendations should be forwarded to the governments or not.[139]

The Mandates Commission at its fourth session, 1924, suggested authoritative definition be given to such phrases as the "liquor traffic" and "trade spirits." [140] In a reply to questions in Parliament on May 7, 1924, the British Colonial Secretary defined the term "liquor traffic" as the importation of cheap distilled liquors for sale or barter as an article of trade with African natives. Such distilled liquors were generally known as "trade spirits." [141] In answering the Mandates Commission's suggestion, Great Britain saw no reason to differ from the definition of the terms given by Mr. Thomas, the Colonial Secretary in the House of Commons on May 7, 1924.[142] In a resolution adopted on June 9, 1926, the council resubmitted the matter to the commission, which at its tenth session interpreted the phrase, "shall exercise a strict control over the sale of spirituous liquors in B mandates to apply to all distilled beverages with over 20 per cent alcohol." [143] The council referred this to the mandatory powers on December 6, 1927, requesting them to inform it whether they would soon be able to indicate their acceptance of the recommendations of the Mandates Commission.[144] Prior to this on May 14, 1927, the British Government had stated that it considered the recommendations of the commission on this question satisfactory.[145] After an acceptance by all the mandatory powers and another endorsement by the Assembly and the commission, the council approved on March 4, 1929.[146]

In 1928, in accordance with the resolutions of the Assembly, the council in September and December, 1927, began a study of the causes of the increased importation of alcoholic liquors into territories under B mandates, where such an increase had been noted, and of the measures to be taken to remedy this situation. The commission at its thirteenth session expressed the wish that the mandatory powers should make known to which parts of the mandated territories on the continent of Africa Article 4, Paragraph 2, of the St. Germain Convention concerning the liquor traffic in Africa has been applied.[147] This article prohibits the importation, distribution, sale, and possession of spirituous liquors in those regions of the Central African zone where their uses had not been developed. The increase of the imports of spirits was attributed chiefly to the growing wealth and purchasing power of the natives and to the opening up of the country by railways and motor transport.[148]

A considerable obstacle to the control of liquor traffic was the difference between the customs systems and monetary units in adjacent British and French mandated areas.[149] The duties were increased in both French and British mandated territories, but the commission thought a much greater increase was necessary in order to be effective.[150] The commission believed the French and British Governments should be invited to agree that the duties on all spirituous liquors imported into African territories placed under their mandates should not be less than the duties in the adjoining territories on similar spirits of equal strength.[151]

The council adopted and recommended to the mandatory powers suggestions submitted by the commission with the object of checking the increase of the imports of liquors into certain territories under B mandate. For this purpose the commission proposed an increase and the unification of duties and the prohibition of the sale of liquor by unauthorized persons. Concerning the proposals on fixing the maximum alcoholic content of beverages which may be regarded as wines and not, therefore, as spirituous liquors, the British Government proposed a standard of 20% and the commission adopted this proposal.[152] At the council's request the mandatory powers signified their acceptance of this definition.[153]

At its twenty-first session, the Mandates Commission noted the information given by Great Britain as to the delimitation in mandated territories of the prohibition zones provided for by Article I of the Convention signed at St. Germain-en-Laye on September 10, 1919. It expressed the hope that Great Britain and the other powers would continue their efforts to control the traffic in these zones and to prevent the natives from making clandestine distilleries. The British replies reveal that, in Togoland and the Cameroons, genuine prohibition zones have been marked out, and in Tanganyika, no delimitations of this kind have been made, but the whole territory is subject to a regime which answers to the provisions of Article 4 of the St. Germain Convention.[154]

The commission also studied the Secretariat's Memorandum based on information supplied by the mandatory powers, regarding the liquor traffic in B- and C-mandated territories. It asked that the Secretariat should keep this information up-to-date, and recommended that, when drawing up the annual statement on liquor traffic, the mandatory powers, in order to add to the technical value of the information, should take account of various suggestions as to the method embodied in the report annexed to the minutes of the session.[155]

On January 25, 1932, the council drew the attention of the mandatory powers entrusted with B and C mandates to the above-mentioned recommendations and requested those powers to be good enough to give effect to them.[156]

The problem of liquor traffic in the African mandated areas is a very difficult problem for both Great Britain and the Mandates Commission, and Great Britain has acted on the commission recommendations, but when all schemes of statesmen in Europe are perfected, when all the barbed wire entanglements and fences have been erected by local governments, there still remains the wily Negro in the brush with his ingenious pot. Those who want to keep the African from drinking something other than disease-infected waters have a tremendous task ahead of them.[157]

From another angle the liquor traffic was very important. In the Council of the League of Nations, M. Hanotaux of France thought the Mandates Commission in this case had a tendency to go beyond the powers with which it was entrusted. Its duty was to advise the council on questions relating to the execution of the mandates. The Permanent Mandates Commission could not on its own initiative make proposals concerning the general administration of the mandate as a whole. But Lord Robert Cecil, the British member, came to the commission's rescue when he said he would not like to contemplate anything that might serve to restrict the liberty of the Mandates Commission and to diminish the value of its work. Nevertheless, Cecil was strongly opposed to the suggestion that the Mandates Commission communicate directly with the governments. The question of whether the Mandates Commission is limited to consideration of the activities of the mandatory on matters mentioned in the mandates or can advise on the entire administration of the areas is still difficult to answer.[158]

VIII. Boundary Negotiations

Tanganyika—Ruanda—Urundi. Each mandate charter stipulates that the consent of the Council of the League of Nations is required for any modification of the terms of the mandate. Therefore, the council's consent is necessary for any boundary changes occurring in the mandates, as the mandate charters contain boundary definitions. The most striking instance of the part which the mandates system can play in securing the revision of a boundary was the first case dealt with by the Mandates Commission—the boundary between Tanganyika under British mandate and the native kingdom of Ruanda under Belgian mandate.

The Council of the League of Nations defined the terms of the British and Belgian mandates in the former colony of German East Africa, July 20, 1922.[159] On August 9, 1922, the Permanent Mandates Commission authorized its chairman to draw the attention of the Council of the League to the unfortunate consequences of the actual boundary line drawn between the parts of former German East Africa allocated under mandate to Great Britain and Belgium.[160] The commission did not make categorical statements to the effect that this practice was in violation of mandate principles. Instead, it merely asked the question as to the expediency of this practice. Only by using patient and conservative methods could the commission expect to enjoy a position of confidence with Great Britain and other colonial governments.[161] The line was originally drawn in such a way as to cut through certain tribes in Ruanda in order to leave room in Tanganyika west of Lake Victoria for the British to send a railway from the north to the south of Africa in territory entirely under their control. It was found later that such a railway could be built without the partition of the kingdom of Ruanda. There was a strong protest from the population of the kingdom.[162] The population was deprived of essential pasturage and other resources. The commission did not recommend a change in the frontier, as it felt that it would be beyond its competence. However, it pointed out in strong terms that the frontier as then drawn was interfering with native welfare.

The council at its meeting on September 4, 1922, instructed the president of the council to transmit for the information of the Belgian and British Governments, the observations of the commission with reference to the situation on the frontier of Ruanda.[163] A letter was addressed to both governments. Almost a year later, August 3, 1923, the British Government sent a letter to the Secretary-General of the League stating:

> In deference to this wish, and desiring only to assure the interests of the native populations, the British and Belgian Governments have examined the possibility of fixing a more suitable frontier and have agreed to request the Council of the League of Nations to amend the British and Belgian mandates for this portion of Africa so as to extend to the Kagera River the boundaries of the territory in respect of which a mandate is held by His Majesty the King of Belgium.
> The new limits of the Belgian mandate would be as follows:
> The mid-stream of the Kagera River from the Uganda boundary to the point where the Kagera River meets the western boundary of Bugufi, thence this boundary to its junction with the eastern and southern boundary of the Urundi to Lake Tanganyika.[164]

This letter was submitted to the council, August 31, 1923, and it approved in consequence the proposed modification of Article I of the Belgian Mandate for East Africa and of Article I of the British Mandate for East Africa.[165]

Although the Tanganyika-Ruanda-Urundi boundary undertakes to respect tribal boundaries, the population density of the area complicates the situation for the native people.[166] Therefore, jointly, Belgium and Great Britain in 1935 asked the council to give its approval to the terms of a treaty signed by them on November 22, 1934, concerning the delimitation of the frontier between Ruanda-Urundi and Tanganyika territory.[167]

The frontier had originally been given in Article I of the respective mandates, of which the texts were modified by a council decision of August 31, 1923. The line was further defined in a protocol signed at Kigoma on August 5, 1924, and confirmed in an exchange of notes between the two governments on May 17, 1926.

The Treaty of November 22, 1934, submitted to the council for approval, makes certain changes in detail considered desirable in view of local geographical conditions. Article 5 of the treaty lays down that the treaty will be ratified by each of the contracting parties after the Council of the League has given its assent thereto.[168]

According to the texts of the mandates, Article 12, any change in their provisions must be approved by the council. The council, in response to the joint request of Belgium and Great Britain, expressed willingness to examine, with a view to approval, the Treaty of November 22, 1934. The Mandates Commission found, after examining the documentation and orally interrogating the accredited representatives of Great Britain and Belgium, that the line fixed by the Treaty of November 22, 1934, called for no special observation on its parts.[169] The council approved the treaty September 6, 1935.[170]

British and French Cameroons. A similar problem arose during the third Mandates Commission session in 1923 in connection with the boundaries between the British and French mandated areas in West Africa. In the British Cameroons' report it was claimed that the greatest injustice had been inflicted on tribes due to the fact that the boundary line did not follow tribal frontiers but cut many tribes in two, leaving one part in British and the other part in French territory. There were cases where grazing land had been taken away.[171]

The commission recommended that the council should request the French Government to collect information and to make known its views on the subject.[172] M. Hanotaux, the French member of the council, said that the frontier between the British and French Cameroons had been established by a Franco-British agreement, which had been communicated to the League of Nations at the time when the mandates were assigned. The British Government had asked for certain rectification of this frontier, and it seemed to him that the commission should simply have declared that this question was not within its competence and have begged the government of Great Britain to communicate directly with the government of France in order that they might examine together the question of the frontier.[173] The British Government believed the Mandates Commission might reasonably propose that the French Government should be asked to make known its opinion on the views of the British Government. It was necessary to know whether the two governments were of the same opinion. The commission was not suggesting a revision of the frontier.[174]

Lord Robert Cecil, the British member on the council, said that the Mandates Commission was responsible for the good administration of the territory under mandate. It might, therefore, perfectly well examine facts which were likely to revert upon the welfare of the natives and draw the attention of the interested powers to these facts. The commission's recommendation was adopted.[175] Negotiations were begun on the Cameroons' boundary and, on the French suggestion, in the thirtieth council meeting the boundary of Togoland was included.[176]

Mr. Palmer, Lieutenant-Governor of the northern province of Nigeria, reported in 1927 at the twelfth session of the Mandates Commission that there were no outstanding questions of any importance concerning the frontier between the British and French Cameroons. In 1919, there had been certain points which the British Administration had desired to raise. In consequence, however, of automatic readjustments which had taken place from 1917-1927 and the effects of the passage of time, the British Administration decided it would be better to leave these questions alone.[177] Ormsby-Gore, Under-Secretary of State for the Colonies, stated that it was not worth while for the governments to raise these questions and it would be better to leave the British and French officials on the spot to come to any understanding as to where the boundaries ran. The actual demarcation of the boundary was a matter for the future, and the position was perfectly secure so long as each tribe on the boundary knew to which administration it belonged. While there were one or two districts in which the British and French Administrations had not yet made final arrangements, the British Government did not desire to ask the Mandates Commission to make any observations on the points.[178]

The delimitation of the frontier between French and British Cameroons was delayed several times. The declaration of the boundary between the British and French spheres of the mandated territory of the Cameroons was signed by the governor of the colony and protectorate of Nigeria and by the High Commissioner of the French Republic in the area under French mandate. This was confirmed by the respective home governments early in 1931. This declaration was not the product of the boundary commission constituted for the purpose of carrying out the provision of Article I of the mandate, but only the result of a preliminary survey conducted in order to determine more exactly than was done in the Milner-Simon Declaration of 1919 the line ultimately to be followed by the boundary commission, but, none the less, the declaration does, in substance, define the frontier.[179] Sir Donald Cameron, the accredited representative of Great Britain at the twenty-second Mandates Commission session, replied that at the request of the French authorities the delimitation of the frontier be postponed again.[180] The French representative, in 1934, told the Mandates Commission Great Britain desired, for financial reasons, to adjourn the operations and France had heard no more of the matter. Since no frontier incidents had occurred, it would seem to show that the matter was not urgent.[181]

The next year the Mandates Commission desired to know whether the delimitation was still in contemplation or whether it had been overlooked.[182] If the commission thought it advisable to remind the two governments concerned of the matter, it was because a provision of the mandate was involved. At the twenty-eighth session of the Mandates Commission in 1935, G. H. Findlay, the accredited representative, said the reason for the postponement was solely financial. The fifteen miles in the northern area had been demarcated because it so happened that competent staff had been available. Nothing had occurred along the rest of the undemarcated frontier during the previous year to make it appear that demarcation was a matter of urgency. However, he brought this matter to the notice of the mandatory powers.

Rappard said fifteen years had elapsed since the delimitation had been decided upon; and he could not see how financial stringency could justify postponement of a question which was an international obligation, the fulfillment of which was incumbent upon the mandatory power and not on the territory.[183] Great Britain announced it was prepared to start on November 1, 1937, with the demarcation of the eastern frontier.[184] In November, 1938 at the thirty-fifth Mandates Commission session, O. W. Firth, the British accredited representative, reported the work of the boundary commission could not be finished in less than five years.[185]

British and French Togoland. Defining the boundary between British and French Togoland did not consume as much time as that of the British and French Cameroons. The Mandates Commission during its fourteenth session noted with satisfaction that the tribal frontiers had been taken into account, and hoped it would be possible for Great Britain to attach the report of the mixed Franco-British Boundary Commission to the next annual report.[186]

The boundary commission had practically finished their work in the field by December, 1928, but the production of the final maps took more time, and if the British and French Governments did not object it would be attached to the report for 1929.[187]

The Secretary-General on November 22, 1930, communicated to the members of the Mandates Commission, members of the League of Nations, and the council the text of a joint note dated September 23, 1930, in which the British and French Governments notified him of their approval, by an exchange of notes, of the final report of the mixed commission for the delimitation of Togoland territory under their respective mandates, in conformity with Article I of the mandate conferred upon the said governments of July 20, 1922.[188]

M. Orts of the Mandates Commission expressed the satisfaction which the commission felt in view of the fact that the work of delimitation between British Togoland and French Togoland was now completed.[189]

The present boundaries in West Africa must be recognized as immature and, therefore, subject to stresses potentially dangerous.[190] Boundary rectification has only been achieved between British Togoland and French Togoland. While the Mandates Commission has attempted to get the boundaries determined, it seems that its attempts have been blocked by administrative officers on the spot.

Tanganyika and Kenya. On September 25, 1925, the British Government communicated to the Secretary-General a copy of the English text of the draft agreement between the British and German Governments which had been prepared in 1914 to define the boundary between British and German East Africa. Great Britain explained that the Acting Governor of Kenya Colony had reported that certain minor difficulties had been experienced in connection with the exact representation of the boundary between that colony and Tanganyika Territory, and had requested that he might be furnished with a copy of the instrument defining the boundary. The British Government assumed that the boundary envisaged by the mandate was that defined in the above mentioned agreement and accordingly instructed the Acting Governor to adopt it as the correct boundary between the two territories.

The council took note of the communication from the British Government.[191] The mandates system has not thus far been extended to any new areas; the possibility of such action was foreseen by some members of the Mandates Commission when discussing the rectificacation of the Tanganyika-Kenya boundary. Sir Frederick Lugard of the Mandates Commission called attention to the difficulties experienced on the frontier between Tanganyika and Kenya where the boundary bisected the Masai tribe. The Masai had been in the habit of grazing and settling at certain seasons on both sides of the boundary.[192] If the Tanganyika Masai were placed under Kenya, it would mean the splitting up of the mandated territory into two separate mandates. The commission had not yet had before it a question which was of such importance for the future of the mandates system.[193] Should the Masai in Tanganyika be placed under Kenya administration, the jurisdiction of the Mandates Commission would be extended over Kenya native policy in so far as it affects the Masai people. To escape this control Buell thinks Kenya would oppose unification or consent to a concession of the Kenya Masai reserve to Tanganyika.[194]

Rappard of the commission thought the commission should favor boundary changes in the interest of the native inhabitants. Such a change might be effected in this case: (1) by annexing part of Kenya to Tanganyika; (2) by extending the Kenya administration at the expense of Tanganyika but with the understanding that it would be responsible to the League for the whole Masai area; or (3) by the creation of a new mandate for the Masai area alone which would necessitate complicated international arrangement.[195] He said:

> Whatever the solution which might eventually be adopted, the Commission could, he thought, congratulate itself on the possibility of seeing the principle of the mandate system extended to new territories.[196]

Extension of the mandates system to other territories was foreseen in the British official comment on the Covenant.[197]

The chairman stated that Lugard had raised a question of a practical nature and that the scope of the discussion had been enlarged, and Lugard indicated a preference for either of the first two alternatives suggested by Rappard as against the third, and Ormsby-Gore, the accredited representative from Great Britain, questioned the expediency of transferring to Kenya a portion of Tanganyika, formerly under the King of Buganda, and declared a separate report could not be submitted in regard to these thousand persons.[198]

M. Orts did not think that the committee should express any opinion regarding the problem which had arisen in connection with the Masai tribe. Any resolution on its part would be premature, as the question was still under consideration by the British Government. In reply to Rappard, M. Orts said that the question of the Anglo-Belgian frontier was of a different character, and the question here would be the union of part of a mandated territory with a colony; whereas, in the previous case, it had only been a question of transferring a strip of territory under British mandate to Belgian mandate, there was no question of a change of status.

The chairman thought the commission should confine itself to expressing a favorable attitude toward measures in the interest of the natives on condition that the League's supervision over areas now under mandate was not reduced.[199]

The proximity of the Tanganyika mandate with Kenya invites comparison of the administration of two territories under the control of the same power.[200]

Frontier between Tanganyika and Mozambique. Great Britain submitted to the council jointly with the Portuguese Government on December 22, 1936, a request seeking the approval of the agreement dated May 11, 1936, defining the frontier between Tanganyika and Mozambique.[201] On January 22, 1937, the council declared its willingness to examine this agreement with a view to approval, and invited the Mandates Commission to inform it of its opinion as to the effect of the agreement on the execution of the mandate.[202]

The commission studied the documentary material submitted to it, and heard the explanation of the accredited representative of Great

Britain. It noted, in particular, that the object of the agreement of May 11, 1936, between Great Britain and Portugal with regard to the delimitation of the frontier between Tanganyika and Mozambique was to define the boundary more clearly and thereby to put an end to an undesirable state of uncertainty. The commission informed the council that the material placed before it contained nothing which would justify it in affirming that the agreement was incompatible with the interests of the mandated territory.[203] On September 14, 1937, the council approved the agreement.[204]

Iraq. There have been boundary settlements by Iraq with Turkey, Trans-Jordan, Syria, Iran (Persia), and Nejd. But the most important settlements were made before or after the Mandates Commission had any real jurisdiction. The Iraq-Turkey (Mosul) boundary dispute of 1925 was settled before the Mandates Commission was making complete observations on Iraq. The Iraq-Syria boundary recommendations were confirmed by the council in November, 1932, after Iraq had been admitted to the League of Nations,[205] and on July 4, 1937, the Iraq-Iran (Persia) boundary line was settled.[206] Except in the first and last cases named above the opinion of the Mandates Commission was always sought after various boundary commissions had reported to the League of Nations.

Conclusion. Back of a boundary are not only national interest and ambitions but a philosophy of international relations. A boundary is criticized from two quite different standpoints: (1) the technical location of a boundary, which may be good or bad in detail; and (2) the wisdom of putting together or keeping together the people and the resources that the boundary contains.[207] Of great importance is the mandates system in the remedying of unfortunate boundary situations without the resort to elaborate and special machinery such as an international conference. A frontier badly drawn under a colonial regime will probably remain so unless it happens to be changed as the result of a war or a financial transaction.[208]

Great Britain and Belgium set a fine precedent in their settlement of the boundary between Tanganyika and Ruanda for the benefit of the natives. The frontiers of all the British mandate territories have been the subject of international negotiation. The boundaries between the British and French Togoland were delimited without much trouble, but the boundaries of the British and French Cameroons were never completely demarcated. Although from a practical side little harm has been done by the failure to do so, nevertheless the Mandates Commission continually reminded Great Britain and France of this because a provision of the mandate was involved. The boundary recommendation by the Mandates Commission caused M. Hanotaux, the French member of the council, to question the competence of the commission on this matter; he also made a definite request for a study of the commission's powers. The idea of extending the principle of the mandate system to new territories was enlarged by the Masai tribe's relation to the Tanganyika-Kenya boundary problem.

In most of the remaining British boundary negotiations by Iraq with Turkey, Trans-Jordan, Syria, Iran (Persia), and Nejd the opinion of the Mandates Commission was always sought.

IX. Petitions and the Questionnaire

Petitions. Article 22 of the Covenant is silent on the right of petition, and so are the text of the different mandates. The idea that the inhabitants should possess such a right was first mentioned at the initial session of the Mandates Commission. Rappard, then the Chief of the Mandates Section of the Secretariat of the League, received a number of documents of various descriptions addressed to the Mandates Commission.[209]

Ormsby-Gore, British representative on the Mandates Commission, stated that it might be maintained that if the nationals of a colony had the right of appealing to the Parliament of the mother country, the national of a mandated territory might similarly have the right to appeal to the League of Nations in the name of which the mandate was exercised.[210] On July 22, 1922, the British Government submitted a memorandum to the Council of the League of Nations, suggesting the procedure which might be adopted with respect to petitions addressed to the League of Nations by communities or sections of the population of mandated territories.[211] During the second session of the Mandates Commission (August 11, 1922) Ormsby-Gore drew attention to the memorandum by the British Government. Since the A and B mandates were definitely issued, the Secretariat would probably receive many petitions, complaints, et cetera, as to the methods of carrying out the mandates. The British Government was anxious that a regular channel should be created for such petitions and complaints and wished the commission to advise the council as to the definite procedure to be adopted.[212] The Mandates Commission, fearing political issues might be involved, decided to await an express instruction from the council. The council gave this permission in September, 1922.[213]

The Chairman of the Mandates Commission consulted his colleagues by correspondence and submitted the British proposal slightly modified to the council. After considerable debate which indicated the subject was a delicate one, the council accepted this procedure with minor modifications on January 31, 1923.[214] The rule as to petitions provides that the commission will receive any petitions emanating from persons or bodies in the mandated territory which are submitted to it through the mandatory power, subject only to the provisions: (a) that the petitions are not incompatible with the principles of the Covenant or the mandates themselves; that they are not anonymous; (c) that they do not simply repeat a petition recently communicated to the mandatory power without containing any fresh facts.[215] The inhabitants are not allowed to address their complaints directly to the Mandates Commission. Their complaints must be sent through the mandatory power who is afforded the opportunity to add any comments it may find desirable. In considering the petition, the Mandates Commission has at the same time the views and explanation of the mandatory. Any complaints that are justiciable in the courts of the territory are not to be considered by the commission.[216]

It was the practice of the commission to submit petitions to one of its members who acts as reporter and advises the commission what answer should be returned or what action should be taken. The commission then frames its conclusions, but does not deal directly either with the petitioner or with the mandatory. It presents its observations on the report of the mandatory and on the petitions, together, to the Council of the League, which is the sole body authorized to make representation to the mandatory. A copy of the report is sent to the government of the mandatory, and the minutes of the whole proceedings of the commission are published for general information, and in order to secure the assistance of public opinion in the moral control exercised by the commission.[217] Due to M. van Rees' proposal petitions may emanate from sources other than the inhabitants of the mandated territories.[218] For petitions of this kind it is provided that they shall be sent to the chairman of the Mandates Commission, who will decide which petitions deserve consideration. If the chairman regards a petition as important, he is to send it to the mandatory powers of whose action the petition complains. The mandatory power is expected to answer this petition within a period not exceeding six months.

The rules of procedure do not define the scope of the word petition. The Commissioners and the Secretariat have received a great deal of material of various sorts not only from inhabitants of the mandated areas but from travelers, investigators, writers, lawyers, humanitarians, religious and other associations with varying degrees and types of interest in the mandated areas. The question was, how much of this material was to be regarded as petitions. During the fifth session of the Mandates Commission the question arose whether the commission could accept a petition coming from an Arab who was a Turkish subject inhabiting a country other than the mandated territory.[219] The Chairman, Marquis Theodoli, held that it would be advisable not to give too narrow a meaning to the word "petition" and to consider as valid, so far as the commission was concerned, not only petitions properly so called but any requests or demands, provided that they were addressed to the League of Nations in accordance with the regular procedure.[220] Sir Frederick Lugard agreed with the chairman and M. van Rees that it would be sufficient for the commission itself to agree to apply this interpretation in practice without making any formal amendment of the rules of procedure.[221] M. Rappard at the seventh session of the Mandates Commission made it clear that the commission's general practice must be to include in the term petition every document, telegram, memorandum, et cetera, received from the petitioners.[222] The Council of the League of Nations at its thirty-seventh session approved this interpretation.[223]

Sir Frederick Lugard brought to the attention of the commission the resolution passed by the Executive Committee of the British League of Nations Union on November 19, 1925:

That the Mandates Commission should suggest to the Council the propriety of requiring that any Mandatory Power which finds it necessary at any time to suspend its ordinary laws should immediately notify the League.[224]

This resolution was obviously suggested by the insurrection in Syria. M. Palacios, the *rapporteur,* expressed the opinion that the document was a petition not from the inhabitants of a mandated area and consequently it should be submitted to the mandatories for their comments. M. van Rees thought the document was not a petition because it was not addressed to the League. M. Rappard thought all documents in the supposed interest of the inhabitants might be considered petitions. M. Freire d' Andrade considered it a petition and Dr. Kastl did not. The majority of the commission thought it was not a petition, and as Sir Frederick Lugard was not present, the commission decided to postpone discussion.[225]

The Permanent Mandates Commission has sought to avoid giving itself the character of a court of appeal for complaints and has treated the report of the mandatory power as its principal source of information.[226] In the fourth session Sir Frederick Lugard submitted a memorandum which maintained that the Permanent Mandates Commission was not a court of appeal and should not accept any petition which had already or could be dealt with by the local courts.[227] The petition dated April 8, 1925, from the Executive Committee of the Palestine Arab Congress protested against the Balfour declaration in the Palestine Mandate. In view of the fact that the very principle of the Palestine Mandate was contested, the commission decided not to take it into consideration.[228] The commission has adopted the policy of refusing to consider petitions that oppose the mandate itself or its principles, on the theory that the commission's functions are confined to advice on the observance of mandates.

Although the matter of petition has proved to be a great help to the inhabitants of mandated territories, it is doubtful whether it has fully accomplished the aims set for it. Hardly any complaints come to the commission from the natives in Africa who are mostly unable to read or write. Of the mandates included in this study petitions have been most numerous from Palestine where they proceed from organized groups. The petitions from the various Jewish and Arab groups of Palestine have been very confusing, and when the commission had to examine the petition emanating from the Executive Committee of the Palestine Arab Congress of April 12, 1925, it did not find itself in a position to formulate, in regard to the numerous questions raised, a unanimous and definite opinion. The commission doubted that it would be possible to base any useful recommendation in a matter so complex and so delicate on the sole basis of written documents.[229]

The discussion in the commission turned on the general question of a visit to a mandated territory.[230]

Sir Frederick Lugard, the British representative on the commission, considered the proposal that the commission should either visit Palestine itself or send a subcommittee to conduct an inquiry was quite impracticable. No mandatory power could accept such a procedure without lowering its prestige, for the commission or subcommittee would be in the position of a court of inquiry in which the mandatory power was the defendant.[231]

That such a visit would be a help to the members of the commission was proven by Rappard who, after having visited Palestine in the Spring of 1925, completely changed his views about the situation there. However, he did not think that the commission as a whole should visit the country, for such a proposal would inevitably give rise in Palestine to an explosion of feeling on the part of all those who were dissatisfied with the administration of the mandatory power.[232] Lugard also maintained that if the Arabs complained that only one side of the case had been submitted to the commission, it was quite possible for the commission to hear a representative of the Arabs. This would be, in his view, a far better procedure than for the commission itself to go to Palestine. He saw nothing to prevent a representative of the Arabs from giving evidence before the commission if it so desired.[233] The council settled this by advising it to give an opinion on the data it had.[234]

There remains for discussion the important question whether petitioners or memorialists should in any circumstances be granted audience. During the seventh session of the Mandates Commission some of the members thought an oral hearing might be desirable. To this there was some dissent though all agreed that the members of the commission might hear petitioners individually, provided no official use was made of the information received. The Secretary-General told the petitioners the Mandates Commission did not think it its duty to receive petitioners; but it was understood that the chairman would always be happy to hear what they had to say.[235]

On the question of legal competence, the commission was divided at its eighth session, and Sir Frederick Lugard proposed to submit his views in writing at the ninth session.[236]

At the ninth session the Waad Leumi National Council of the Jews of Palestine asked to be heard by the commission with regard to the different problems arising out of the establishment of the Jewish National Home.[237] Sir Frederick Lugard, in his memorandum, thought it was entirely within the competence of the commission to hear anyone it might desire to hear. He suggested a procedure for hearing deserving petitioners in order to secure for the commission valuable information and to give satisfaction to those who have genuine cause for submitting a petition. Lugard noted that the right of petition through the mandatory did not in fact exceed the right which exists in every British colony to petition the Secretary of State through the governor.[238] The commission agreed that the hearing of petitioners in exceptional cases might be desirable and drafted a suggestion to that effect in its report to the council.[239]

The suggestion called forth vigorous opposition from Sir Austen Chamberlain, the British representative on the council, and he considered it unwise, imprudent, and even dangerous for the council to take any decision until it had before it the observations of the various mandatory governments upon the suggestion.[240] The views of the rest of the members of the council were almost unanimously unfavorable to the suggestion of the commission. The *rapporteur*, M. Unden of Sweden, saw merit in the suggestion; nevertheless, he associated himself with the proposal of the British representative that this question should be referred to the mandatory powers for their observations.[241] The mandatory governments unanimously denounced it, and Great Britain replied that there were the gravest objections to the grant of any form of audience by an advisory commission of the League to petitioners who either are themselves inhabitants of a territory administered by Great Britain under mandate or are petitioning on behalf of inhabitants of such territories. The British had a wide experience on petitions from the colonies and found that written evidence was sufficient; if more were necessary the commission could ask the mandatory for it.[242] The council, in March, 1927, having taken cognizance of the replies of the mandatory powers on the subject of the hearing, in certain cases, of petitioners by the Mandates Commission, expressed the opinion that there would be no advantages in modifying the procedure followed up to the present time by the commission in this matter.[243]

1. *The Bahais Case.* In most cases, the commission has found little merit in the complaints of petitioners.[244] But an outstanding instance of the commission's criticism came from the petition from the Bahai Spiritual Assembly at Bagdad, dated September 11, 1928.[245] The Bahais, a very small religious group of Persian origin, complained that they had been deprived of certain property in Bagdad. The case went through the entire hierarchy of courts ending with a four-to-one decision in the Court of Appeal against the Bahais, the British presiding justice casting the minority vote. The matter was brought to the League on the principle of liberty of conscience and religion as safeguarded in the treaty of 1922, in the organic law, and in Article 22 of the Covenant. The letter of Iraq's prime minister and the memorandum of the British Government accompanying the petition presented divergent views. The letter maintained that the decision was according to law, that it was free from religious prejudice, being rendered by a court of mixed religious opinion, and that there was no further recourse.[246]

The British memorandum states:

That there has been injustice the British Government is compelled to recognize in that property which has been for years in the possession of the Bahais, without its ownership being legally established, has passed into the ownership of persons who have no conceivable claim to it whatever.[247]

Two prior questions remained to be settled:

1. Did any lawful remedy lie open to the petitioners after the decree of the Bagdad Court of Appeal? No, it was proved that this court gave a final judgment and that this judgment could not be quashed or received by any higher court.

2. The rule of the Mandates Commission had been to regard any petition, the author of which appeals to the commission from a decision given by a court of law, as not being in order. This rule was based on the assumption that any duly constituted court functioning in a mandated territory was free from suspicion of partiality, servility, and sectarianism.

As this assumption was shown to be erroneous by the evidence of the mandatory power itself, the general rule referred to did not apply in this particular case and the Mandates Commission accepted the petition.[248] The commission recognized the injustice done this insignificant sect and so reported to the Council of the League which, in turn, demanded that the wrong be righted.[249] The Iraq Government offered money compensation to the Bahais, who refused the offer.[250] A solution of this problem satisfactory to the Bahais was reported to the commission in November, 1932, following the termination of the mandate.[251]

The questionnaire. The Permanent Mandates Commission came into first real conflict with Great Britain concerning the revised questionnaire. A brief questionnaire on B and C mandates was approved by the commission during its first session and by the council at its fourteenth session.[252] The purpose of this questionnaire was to bring about a certain uniformity in the order of treatment in the reports of the mandatories. These questionnaires were soon found to be inadequate as guides to the content of reports.[253] The first questionnaire had thirteen sections, of which the first seven dealt with the special guarantees of the Covenant and the mandates—slavery, labor, arms traffic, trade and manufacture of alcohol and drugs, liberty of conscience, military clauses, and economic equality. The next five sections dealt with general provisions implied by the letter or spirit of these documents—education, public health, land tenure, moral, social, and material welfare, public finance. Only the last section, demographic statistics, covered general information not immediately suggested by the texts. In the discussion of this questionnaire, the commission seemed to be preoccupied with the need for conforming the questions, especially when they dealt with such controversial matters as military recruiting and immigration, to the texts in order to avoid offending the mandatory powers.[254]

The task of revising the questionnaire was entrusted to M. Orts and was the subject of discussion in the commission for two years. The commission adopted the lists of questions in its final form at its ninth session. The list contains a total of 118 questions. The list divided itself into three nearly equal parts. About a third of the questions need be answered only once, granting, of course, that the mandatory power would inform the commission of any subsequent changes in the answer. Such are questions regarding the administrative and judicial organization of the territories, descriptions of native customs, and so forth. A third of the questions should be answered about once in every five or ten years. Such are questions of policy and questions like the effect on the health and morals of the natives of the economic activities of the mandatory power. Finally, about a third of the questions should be answered every year. Such are questions of statistics, health, labor supply, finance, and so forth.[255]

This questionnaire intended to elicit the facts necessary to give an accurate indication of the entire political, administrative, economic, and social situation in the territory.[256] Fearing the mandatories might be offended with the title of the new questionnaires, the Mandates Commission decided to call it "a list of questions which the Permanent Mandates Commission desires should be dealt with in the annual reports of the mandatory powers." [257]

Sir Austen Chamberlain, the British member of the Council of the League of Nations, was the main objector.[258] He said:

This immense questionnaire was infinitely more detailed, infinitely more inquisitorial than that which had hitherto been in force with the sanction of the council and it raised the question of the true relative position of the mandatory governments in a mandated territory and the mandates commission which examined their reports, and the council which took action as guardian under terms of the covenant. It seemed to him that there was tendency on the part of the commission to extend its authority where the government would no longer be vested in the mandatory power but in the mandates commission. He was sure that was not the intention of the covenant. It was clear from that document that these territories were to be put under the tutelage of advanced powers and that they would exercise their authority under the supervision of the League, for which the League would have a commission to assist it. But it was not, according to his reading of that document, intended that the governing authority of those territories should be any other than the government which had received the mandate.[259]

It was apparent that Chamberlain entirely misunderstood both the content and the nature of the list of questions.[260] M. van Rees, Vice-Chairman of the Permanent Mandates Commission, defended the list of questions before the council. He said:

He was convinced that all his colleagues would express themselves to the same effect. The Commission had never dreamt of going beyond its province. It had, of course, desired to collect as much information as possible in order to form an enlightened opinion, but this legitimate desire in no way justified the implications made. Its duties were not only delicate: they were, moreover, extremely arduous. They had been entrusted five years ago to a Commission composed of persons who were absolutely independent and who had worked with the utmost conscientiousness. He thought that he might, therefore, state that the reproach which had been addressed to the Commission was not all deserved.[261]

Chamberlain expressed his appreciation of the commission's services, and the council decided to submit the commission's suggestions to the mandatory powers before taking action.[262]

The British Government, in its note, cited Article 22 and the mandates and said:

In his report to the Council in August, 1920, the Belgian delegate (M. Hymans) who acted as *rapporteur,* suggested that in the case of B mandates, "the mandatory Power will enjoy, in my judgment, a full exercise of sovereignty, in so far as such exercise is consistent with the carrying out of the obligations imposed by paragraphs 5 and 6 (of Article 22 of the Covenant)." In paragraph 6, which deals with C mandates, the scope of these obligations is perhaps narrower than in paragraph 5, thus allowing the mandatory Power more nearly to assimilate the mandated territory to its own.

In dealing with the question of the annual reports, M. Hymans further said: "The annual reports should certainly include a statement as to the whole moral and material situation of the people under the mandate." It is in the light of this purpose and of the terms of the Covenant itself that we should read M. Hymans' further statement that "the Council should examine the question of the whole administration." The object of the report is to satisfy the Council as to the moral and material situation of the inhabitants, but clearly the Council is not called upon, either by itself or through the Commission, to check and examine every detail of administration, nor can it have the means to discharge such a Herculean task. Its duty is to see that the administration of the mandated territories is conducted generally in accordance with the ideas enunciated in Article 22 of the Covenant. If it should have reason to suppose that these ideals were not being realized, it would naturally pursue its inquiries in such detail as might be found necessary to ascertain the facts, and would make such recommendations as it thought proper for remedying any particular abuses that might be revealed. But there is nothing to lead to the conclusion that it was ever intended that the mandatory Government should be called upon to submit annually for confirmation or criticism by the Council or the Commission all the details of its administrative and legislative activities. On the contrary, M. Hymans excluded the idea of such a procedure when he observed, in the same report from which these quotations have been made, that the Council will obviously have to display extreme prudence, so that the exercise of its rights of control should not provoke any justifiable complaints, and thus increase the difficulties of the task undertaken by the Mandatory Powers.

In the light of these considerations, the mandatory Government of the British Empire feels that both the proposals now put forward by the Mandates Commission are based on a misconception of the duties and responsibilities of the Commission and the Council. The theory that petitioners should have a means of making their grievances known is perfectly correct: but the Commission's suggestion that a hearing should be given to the petitioners is, they submit, an incorrect and dangerous application of the theory. The implication, in the new list of questions, that the Commission should claim to check and investigate every activity of the mandatory power is unnecessary for the purpose for which the mandatory system was established, and irreconcilable with the principles laid down by M. Hymans and accepted by the Council for its execution.[263]

The British note based its argument on insufficient premises, as it paid no attention to the fact, however conclusive, that hitherto not one of the mandatory powers had manifested the least objection to furnishing all the details of its administration. Other objections to the list of questions are equally unfounded. The fact that in no question, with the exception of those touching principles expounded by the commission and approved by the council, had the commission shown a preference for one answer rather than another, precluded the idea that it was trying to administer the territories itself.[264]

In the report on its eleventh session, the commission pointed out that it was entirely for the mandatory powers to decide whether they desire to use or not to use the list of questions according to whether they share or do not share the commission's opinion as to its usefulness.[265] The council concurred with the Mandates Commission on this point and forwarded the commission's observations to Great Britain with no special recommendation.[266]

Thus by implication if not by word, the council answered a question which had proved difficult to answer, namely: Is the commission limited to consideration of the activities of the mandatory on matters mentioned in the mandate or can it advise on the entire administration of the areas? [267] The council endorsed the right exercised by the commission of inquiring into and giving advice on all phases of the mandatory administration. A contrary attitude on the part of the council would undoubtedly have meant the death of the mandates system.[268]

Conclusion. Great Britain's past colonial experience, no doubt, caused her to be the first mandatory power to suggest that a regular channel should be created for petitioners from the inhabitants of mandated territories. England's memorandum sustaining the charges of the injustices of the Bahais religious minority's petition in Iraq was a splendid example of putting a minority principle into practice.

The first real clash between the Mandates Commission and Great Britain came over the desire of the commission to grant an audience to a petitioner and the revised questionnaire. In each case, Britain appeared to be afraid the Mandates Commission was attempting to supervise or assume its duties directly. The Mandates Commission prided itself on being very diplomatic and cautious with the mandatory power, and resented greatly Britain's contention that it was trying to infringe upon the mandatory's power. England had been scrupulously faithful to their mandatory obligations and in their severe criticism of the commission they may have been actuated by nothing more than conscious rectitude.[269]

CHAPTER THREE

Nauru, British Togoland, and the British Cameroons

I. Nauru

The little island of Nauru lies twenty-six miles below the equator in the South Pacific Ocean. It is shaped like a three-quarters moon, and is about twelve miles round. Nauru has an area of only 5,396 acres, practically the whole of which, with the exception of small allotments held by the government and missions, is owned by individual natives.[1] There is a native population of 1,239.

The importance of this little island lies in the fact that it contains a phosphate of a high grade. From 1888 to 1914 the islet carried the German flag, and the phosphate was worked by a German company registered in Great Britain. In 1914, it surrendered, with the other German Pacific Islands to the Australian forces. The island was included in the cession of colonies made by Germany in 1919 to the allied and associated powers, whose representatives agreed that a mandate over it should be given to His Majesty, the King of Great Britain.

Agreement over administration and phosphate monopoly. The mandate over Nauru was conferred upon the British Empire. An agreement was made July 2, 1919, between Great Britain, Australia, and New Zealand for joint administration of the government under the direction, during the first five years, of an administrator appointed by Australia.[2] By this agreement, the executive, legislative, and judicial powers in Nauru were vested in an administrator, to be appointed by the governor of Australia for the first five years, and he was given practically unlimited authority over all matters other than the business relating to the phosphate deposits. The title to the phosphate was vested in a board of commissioners, one from each of the three governments, which manages the business and divides the output in a prescribed ratio: Great Britain, 42 per cent; Australia, 42 per cent; and New Zealand, 16 per cent.[3] None of the phosphate can be sold to any other than these countries until the wants of all of them are satisfied.

This agreement was ratified by an act of the British Parliament on August 4, 1920.[4] The Nauru agreement presents a clear case of a mandatory monopolizing the natural resources of its mandated territory.[5] Also it was directly opposed to the principle of complete separation of government and business in administering backward areas.[6] The agreement was bitterly attacked in the British Commons. Asquith said, "It is illegal in its origin, unequal in its operation; it is opposed in all respects to the letter and the spirit of the Covenant of the League of Nations."[7]

The British government pointed out in defense that the exclusive right of working the phosphate had previously belonged to a British corporation, the Pacific Phosphate Company, and that the agreement merely transferred the property and rights of a British corporation to the British government. The government was sustained by a vote of 218 to 57.[8]

The Mandates Commission and the monopoly. To the Mandates Commission, Nauru was peculiar on two counts: the special resources of the territory and the system of executing the mandates. The Mandates Commission raised the question whether the establishment of a state organization enjoying the sole right of development of the natural resources of a mandated territory was fully in keeping with the disinterested spirit which should characterize the mission of the mandatory.[9] Great Britain pointed out that the exploitation of phosphate in Nauru had always been a monopoly, first of a German, then of a British corporation, and that the phosphate commissioners were merely business executives subject to control in labor recruiting and other matters by the administrator.[10] Moreover the C mandates to which category Nauru belongs did not contain a provision about economic equality; and the question has not been pressed, as nationalist sentiment, unfortunately, has been too strong to allow the open door regime in the Class C mandates.[11] However, this raises the question: Are the C mandates veiled annexations? It is true that in some respects Nauru has been treated as if it were annexed territory; but this treatment may be regarded as nothing more than administrative convenience, which is perfectly consistent with the mandate theory.[12]

The Mandates Commission and the transfer of the mandate. The transfer or termination of a mandate as well as the modification of its boundaries is a modification which undoubtedly requires council confirmation. The Mandates Commission was not unnaturally surprised to find that neither the agreement between the constituent members of the British Empire made at Paris in 1919 nor the Tripartite Agreement of 1920 constituting Australia the *de facto* administrator for five years had been communicated officially to the League of Nations.[13] M. Orts, the Belgian member, appears further to have doubted whether it was within the competence of the commission to treat as mandatory a power not designated in the mandate.[14] But this view did not prevail with the commission. They observed:

. . . some uncertainty as to whether the Mandate for the Island of Nauru with the responsibility which it entails is to be considered by the League of Nations as having been in effect transferred to the Australian Government.[15]

During the Third Session of the Mandates Commission it was announced that an agreement had been reached to the effect that Sir Joseph Cook of Australia should be the accredited representative appointed to answer any question in connection with the report. In view, however, of the agreement whereby the functions of a mandatory power might conceivably be raised alternatively either by New Zealand or Great Britain, it had also been decided that the representatives of the British and New Zealand governments should be present at the same time. The constitutional question of how Australia came to be the mandatory power had been settled by an agreement which had been signed on May 30, 1923, which made the position clear with regard to the responsibility for the exercise of the mandate.

Sir Joseph Cook said that in this respect the representatives of three powers might be regarded as a trinity in unity. He represented the British Empire for the single reason that Australia had been selected by the three sections of the mandatory power to govern the island of Nauru.[16] This explanation was apparently accepted, but it raises the interesting question whether the A and B mandates similarly assigned to His Brittanic Majesty and now administered by the government of Great Britain might be delegated temporarily or permanently to the government of one of the dominions without first obtaining the council's consent. This would seem to be implied from the statement of Ormsby-Gore, then on the Mandates Commission. There was no government of the British Empire. In this case, it was, presumably, for the British Empire to choose one of its constituent governments to administer the mandate.[17]

II. British Togoland and British Cameroons

British Togoland. The British sphere of Togoland lies between 6° 7' and 11° 8' N. latitude, and 0° 27' W. and 1° 15' E. longitude, and is comprised of an area of 13,040 square miles.[18] British Togoland has a population of 293,671.[19]

The sphere is divided into two sections: the northern being administered as if it formed part of the northern territories of the Gold Coast, the southern as if it formed part of the Gold Coast colony. The southern section is known as the Ho district and has some 100,000 inhabitants, who are more advanced in civilization than their northern neighbors. The chief towns are Ho and Kpando. In this district, large areas are given over to cocoa, and smaller areas to cotton. There is also an oil palm belt. The northern district contains the towns of Kete-Krachi and Yendi. Trade in the north is chiefly in cattle and foodstuffs. The exports of the British sphere, as a whole, are mainly cocoa, cotton, and palm kernels and palm oil; the chief imports are cotton piece goods, clothing, salt, tobacco, and kerosene. The division of Togoland left the whole railway system in the French sphere and the railway from Palime to Lome, which runs close to the border of the British sphere and is near to the chief cocoa farms, takes a large share of the trade. However, there are good roads in the British sphere. Since it is the least suited of all the mandate areas for white settlement, Togoland may be said to come the nearest to being a completely native territory.[20]

British Cameroons. British Cameroons consist of a strip of territory marching with the eastern boundary of Nigeria the whole distance of seven hundred miles (save for one breach of some forty miles from the Atlantic Ocean to Chad).

The total area of the mandated territory is 34,136 square miles and the African population is estimated at about 780,000. The European population is 304. For the purpose of administration the territory is divided up as follows. From the coast the Cameroons provinces, comprising an area of 16,581 square miles, extend some 230 miles inland; to the north and east are the Kentu area, 1,236 square miles, now administered as part of the Benue province of Nigeria, and districts attached to the Adamawo province, 1,117 square miles in the area. To the northeast of the Adamawo district in the Dikwa division, 5,149 square miles.[21]

W. E. Hunt, the accredited representative for the British Cameroons at the sixteenth session of the Mandates Commission said: "The truth of the matter is that the British sphere of the mandated territory is not a country in the ordinary sense of the term, but a geographical expression, the result of international agreement." [22]

It is impossible to regard the British Cameroons as an economic entity. Any trade for which statistics could be produced would be infinitesimal when compared with the internal trade, details of which it is impossible to record. Practically no trade enters or leaves the country from the port of Victoria, because there is no communication between the north and south. This had made supervision of the mandatory administration very difficult.

In the Emirate of Dikwa, the most northern part of the Cameroons, is to be found a fairly well organized native state and a comparatively high stage of civilization resulting from long contact with the Arabs. Of its population of 200,000 nearly half are pastoral Arabs; the main portion of the rest are people called Kanuri, of mixed race and Mohammedan religion, and there are also Fulani nomads and Hill Pagans.

European interests are centered in the plantations on the slopes of Mount Cameroon. In the Victoria and Kumba divisions, 403 square miles, out of a total of 5,222 square miles probably an excessive proportion have been alienated for European private enterprise; in 1927, only 48,000 acres were under cultivation. From 1915-1924 the plantations were in care of a government department. They were sold by auction in London in 1924, realizing £224,670;

the purchasers, who for the most part were Germans, entering into possession in March, 1925. Cocoa is the chief crop, and its cultivation has been taken up by the natives: there are also coffee, banana, and rubber estates. Besides cocoa, the chief exports are kola nuts, palm kernels, and palm oil. The imports are largely textiles, provisions, tobacco, motor spirit, and machinery.[23]

Administrative Unions: British Togoland and the Gold Coast; British Cameroons and Nigeria. The mandated documents or the Mandates Commission do not attempt to lay down any particular system of government applicable in these territories. The mandatory in this respect has a free hand, and may introduce such measures of autonomy as it thinks fit. The guiding principle is that the government must have in view the interests of the native inhabitants. The British Empire has developed an elaborate system for exercising jurisdiction outside of its national domain. Authority to exercise such jurisdiction may flow from the royal prerogative, from an act of a British Parliament, or from the common law.[24]

The authority of the British Agent in the mandated area of the British Cameroons and Togoland flows from the Foreign Jurisdiction Act of 1890.[25] This was the result of orders in council in 1923, concerning British Togoland and the British Cameroons. The first order recited Article 119 of the Treaty of Versailles, the agreement of the principal allied and associated powers that France and Great Britain make a joint recommendation, the joint recommendation made by them to the council proposing the mandates. It continued with Great Britain's agreement to accept the mandate and exercise it on behalf of the League of Nations in accordance with the terms of the mandate, the council's confirmation of the mandate, the provision in Article 9 of the latter that "the mandatory shall have full powers of administration and legislation in the area and may administer it as an integral part of his territory and subject to the above provisions," the expediency of uniting the territory for customs, fiscal, and administrative purposes with the neighboring Gold Coast, and the Foreign Jurisdiction Act of 1890.

The order in council then divides the area into a northern and southern sphere integrated respectively with the Gold Coast colony and the Gold Coast protectorate:

. . . provided always that should any such law so applied or any ordinance enacted by the governors be repugnant to any provision of the mandate, such law or ordinance shall, to the extent of such repugnancy but not otherwise be and remain absolutely void and imperative.[26]

This administrative union is advantageous to Togoland, because it allows its people to enjoy the prosperity and civilization of the Gold Coast.[27] The Cameroons order in council enacted a few months earlier has the same preamble substituting Nigeria for the Gold Coast. In the government of the British Cameroons, the northern part is subject to the legislative power of the governor of Nigeria, while in the southern part it is subject to the governor acting through the legislative council of that territory.

The Mandates Commission's recommendation concerning certain provisions of the mandate. At the first session of the Permanent Mandates Commission held in October, 1921, the attention of the council was called to the dispute which might arise out of the mandates for British Togoland and British Cameroons. The particular provision of the mandate was "the Mandatory shall be at liberty to constitute the territory into a Customs union or federation with the adjacent possessions under his sovereignty or control." [28] On the other hand, according to Paragraph 5 of Article 22 of the Covenant, the territories are to be administered under a system which will secure equal opportunities for the trade and commerce of other members of the League.[29]

The commission expressed the opinion that in approving this provision, the council did not intend to authorize an exception to the principle of economic equality. Also it desired to know whether any preferential system obtained in Nigeria, Dahomey, and the Gold Coast, and, if so, whether the British Cameroons and French and British Togoland have been incorporated into a customs union with those neighboring possessions of the two mandatory powers concerned.[30]

In the mandates for British Cameroons and Togoland, there are provisions against slavery and forced labor. The commission felt that certain dangers might arise from the various interpretations of these provisions and notified the council. It did not believe the council intended to sanction the prohibition of the obligation to work, which is the foundation of civilized society.[31] The provisions referred to are: "eventual emancipation of all slaves," and "essential public works and services." The commission considers that in the case of all these mandates it was the intention of the authors of the drafts to ensure the complete emancipation of all slaves at an indefinite date, and to forbid forced labor, except in the case of works and services which would be at the same time both public and essential.[32] These recommendations may seem to have little value, unless one remembers that the cause of the dissenting opinion in the Mavromatis case was due to a difference in the Tanganyika mandate, and the difference was probably accidental.[33]

Financial administration. The second session of the Mandates Commission (August 1-11, 1922) complained that in the report presented for British Togoland it was not clear to the commission whether this territory had a separate budget of its own.[34] The corresponding report for the British Cameroons contained an itemized statement of the revenue and expenditure of the Cameroons Province showing that the Colony of Nigeria contributed in 1921 no less a sum than £78,000 to make up the deficit incurred by the administration of the mandated territory. The commission wished to enquire whether British Togoland was regarded as a distinct territory separate from the Colony of the Gold Coast or whether it was incorporated for fiscal or any other purposes in the neighboring colony.[35]

The Cameroons and Togoland were incorporated by Great Britain for administrative and fiscal purposes with its neighboring colonies of Nigeria and the Gold Coast respectively, and were authorized by the terms of the mandates. However, at its fifth session in 1924, the Mandates Commission stated that if, as a result of incorporating the mandated territories with its neighboring colonies, Great Britain found it impossible to submit a report which would enable the commission clearly to appreciate the nature and character of its mandatory administration, and in particular the work done in order to ensure the well-being of the populations under the mandate, such incorporation would *ipso facto* appear to be incompatible with the spirit of Article 22 of the Covenant.[36] This had reference to the gap in financial matters in regard to the two mandates. It had been impossible for the commission to gain a clear idea of the financial situation.[37] The commission regretted this for two principal reasons. On the one hand, it was unable to inform the council whether the administration of the two mandated territories showed a deficit or surplus, and, on the other, it had not been able to ascertain with sufficient clearness whether the efforts accomplished, with a view to ensuring the well-being of the natives, especially in matters of education and public health, are in full accordance with the principles of trusteeship to which Great Britain is pledged.[38] The commission said it would be satisfied if it were provided, in respect of these two mandated territories, with budgets and accounts based either wholly or partially on estimates, provided that the methods employed in drawing them up were clearly explained. It would be desirable, in cases in which it is impossible to determine exactly the amount of taxes and expenditure in mandated territories, to indicate the approximate proportion of such common taxes and expenditures which is attributable to mandated territories.[39]

The administrative union between these two mandated territories and the neighboring colonies of Great Britain led the commission to make a further observation.

Under the terms of the mandates the mandatory power has the right to administer the countries concerned "as integral portions of its territory." This does not mean that the countries concerned have become integral portions of the neighboring colonies, as the wording of certain passages in the reports of Togoland and Cameroons would appear to suggest.

While the commission desired to bring this matter to the notice of the council, it did not exaggerate its importance. However, as the passages referred to might lead to annexationist aims being attributed quite erroneously to the mandatory powers, it appeared to the commission that their own interest, no less than that of the League of Nations, required that in the future any formula should be avoided which might give rise to doubts on the subject in the minds of ill-informed or ill-intentioned readers.[40] As long as the council supports the work of the commission, "administered as an integral part" will not become equivalent to complete annexation.[41]

At its seventh session (October 19-30, 1925) the Mandates Commission thanked Great Britain for facilitating its task by inserting in the report separate accounts for the mandated territory.[42]

The examination of the reports on Togoland and the Cameroons under British Mandate was made particularly interesting by the information supplied directly to the commission by the British Under-

Secretary of State for the Colonies, the Honorable W. G. Ormsby-Gore, who had just returned from a journey to West Africa.[43] This occurred at the tenth session (November 4-9, 1926). Also during this session the commission noted with satisfaction the fuller details concerning the finances of Togoland, particularly concerning the amounts actually spent in the territory. The commission desired in future reports to find the comparative statements of revenue and expenditure for the last two or three financial years.[44]

The commission took note of the declaration of the representative of the mandatory power at the sixteenth session, 1929, to the effect that grants-in-aid from the revenue of the Gold Coast to cover the estimated deficit of the administration of Togoland were nonrepayable donations, and would never be charged to the mandated territory.[45] The position, so far as concerns the Cameroons, seemed no less dear to the commission, and the commission requested that the mandatory power should make a similar declaration with regard to grants-in-aid to that mandated territory.[46]

In his comments on this matter, the accredited representative gave the commission to understand that the position of Cameroons was similar to that of Togoland, and that, if necessary, a declaration to that effect would be inserted in the next report. In view of the commission's opinion, he thought it important that a formal declaration on this point should be obtained.[47]

It was impossible, the commission said at its Nineteenth Session (November 4-19, 1930), to give a definite opinion on the actual budgetary situation of the Togoland and Cameroons. Realizing the budgets were established most carefully and as accurately as the administrative situation allowed, they could not regard them as of more than relative value—a view shared by Great Britain.[48]

The Mandates Commission noted with satisfaction the deficits shown in the estimates that had been given were made a charge on the neighboring colonies and Great Britain refrained from demanding repayment from the mandated territories.[49]

The administrative union was legal and in a narrow sense it might be considered as a step to legalize annexation, but the Mandates Commission was more concerned whether Great Britain's administration of the territories showed a deficit or surplus. Also they desired to know if the principle of trusteeship was being carried out. The accredited representative of the British Cameroons really explained Great Britain's difficulty in this matter when he said:

Its [The British Cameroons] size, situation, and bipartite shape at present preclude it from being financially autonomous if the standard of administration and of development is to be maintained at a level which the Commission would consider compatible with the due performance of the obligations of trusteeship.[50]

Title of reports. During the Third Session the Mandates Commission noted the report for British Togoland was addressed to the Secretary of State for the Colonies in London,[51] and the report for the British Cameroons was addressed to the Duke of Devonshire.[52] The commission considered that, under the terms of the Covenant, the annual reports should be issued by Great Britain and should be addressed to the Council of the League of Nations. It hoped that future reports would be submitted in such form to make it clear that Great Britain takes full responsibility for them.[53]

The title of the report from British Togoland in 1925 was *Report by His Brittanic Majesty's Government to the Council of the League of Nations on the Administration of the British Sphere of Togoland for the Year 1925*. The title of the British Cameroons report was the same, substituting British Cameroons for British Togoland. A principle was involved here in that the reports were from the colonial office, and its failure to recognize the League of Nations. The administration of the mandates by the colonial office has been criticized in Parliament on the grounds that it seems to assume that the mandates are *ipso facto* parts of the British Empire. It has been suggested that their affairs should be transferred to the Foreign Office.[54]

Indirect rule. The term "indirect rule" has been applied to various systems of native administration; it is used here to denote the system by which the tutelary power recognizes existing African societies and assists them to adapt themselves to the functions of local government.

Great Britain has adopted the policy of indirect rule in the Cameroons and Togoland, as per quote from the report of the Cameroons for 1921.

In the words of Sir F. Lugard. "To rule through the chiefs, to endeavor to educate them in the duties of rulers, to seek their cooperation and to maintain their prestige." With this object in view, the tribal organizations are studied in order that they may be utilized as frame for government, and the regeneration of the natives may be through their own governing class and their own indigenous institutions.

.   .   .   .

. . . and to reconcile the natives to the adoption of modern conditions and methods in a manner which conflicts as little as possible with their own institutions, and to trust to the spread of education gradually to approach the ideal without resort to immediate compulsion.[55]

The principle of this system of indirect government through native chiefs has been described as "Let the white head think: let the black hand govern." [56] Padmore believes the chief reason for indirect rules is to administer large areas as cheaply as possible.[57]

At the Permanent Mandates Commission's request the policy applied to the Cameroons was further described in the 1925 report.

Notwithstanding the variety of methods necessitated in widely differing localities, the central conception of the problem is everywhere the same. The plan adopted by the mandatory power for guiding the moral and social evolution of native life is to educate the natives to manage their own affairs, and to evolve from their own institutions a mode of government which shall conform to civilized standards. This policy is founded on the belief that every system of government, if it is to be permanent and progressive, must have its roots in the framework of indigenous society.

The mandatory powers welcome with satisfaction the words in which the Permanent Mandates Commission has expressed the problem concerning which information is desired. It is precisely by guiding the moral and social evolution of native life rather than by hasty introduction of alien institutions that the Government of the Cameroons seeks to discharge its obligations to the people entrusted to its care.[58]

It appeared during the fifth session of the Mandates Commission that indirect rule in the Cameroons without adequate control might be dangerous.[59] The Chairman of the Mandates Commission, Marquis Theodoli, said:

. . . the members of the Commission did not desire to criticize the manner in which the British official administered the territories by granting considerable freedom to the natives. He thought, neverthe-less, that the Commission should recall the fact that the mandatory power must not confine itself merely to exercising a control, but must also raise the status of the native to a higher standard of civilization. In this connection the Commission desired to know what had been done to improve the material and moral welfare of the natives and to bring about an improvement in their civilization. This task was the essential object of the mandates system.[60]

The system of indirect rule adopted in Nigeria was applied to the Cameroons. In the north—Dikwa and Adamawa, where well-recog-nized native states already existed—this system presented comparatively few difficulties. In the Cameroons provinces, there were a few organ-ized native states, such as that of Banso, but in many districts there was less to build upon. As a preliminary to the introduction of a system more in accordance with the modern ideas of indirect rule, investigations into tribal organizations and law and a voluntary amal-gamation of groups of independent divisions took place in the British sphere of Togoland.

The Mandates Commission has shown a favorable interest in indi-rect rule, but the Chairman made it plain that indirect rule must improve the native's civilization if it is to be a valuable tool in native administration.

While indirect rule has many advantages, it should not be for-gotten that the impossibility of directly ruling millions of Africans makes a temporary delegation of power to native authority inevitable.[61]

Land tenure. African natives have been subject to great abuses at the hands of unscrupulous settlers. Before the arrival of the European powers, land, as a rule, was held in common by the tribes. The right of tribal ownership was recognized by the occupant who could neither alienate nor mortgage his land.[62] As the European settlers disregarded this primitive custom and became owners, much of the land possessed by natives came to be alienated from them, with the result that they were deprived of their means of sustenance.[63] Article 5 of the Mandates for British Togoland and Cameroons pre-vents native land from being transferred, except between natives, without the previous consent of the public authorities, and no real right over native land in favor of non-natives may be created except with the same consent.[64]

The Mandates Commission discussed land tenure during its fourth session and stated:

> After having fully considered the question of Land Tenure the Commission adopted the following text as the expression of its opinion:
> The Mandatory Powers do not possess, in virtue of Articles 120 and 257 (Paragraph 2) of the Treaty of Versailles, any right over any part of the territory under mandate other than that resulting from their having been entrusted with the administration of the territory.
> If any legislative enactment relating to Land Tenure should lead to conclusions contrary to these principles, it would be desirable that the text should be modified in order not to allow of any doubt.[65]

This resolution was based chiefly on a memorandum by M. van Rees on "The System of State Lands in B and C Mandated Territories," [66] and on a memorandum by the Legal Section of the Secretariat entitled "Legal Questions Connected with the Expressions *'Domaine de l' Etat'* (State Domain) and 'Crown Lands' Used in Certain Reports and in the Texts of Laws Regulating Land Tenure in the Mandated Territories." [67]

M. van Rees maintained that the cession of sovereign administration powers did not necessarily imply the cession of sovereign rights over the territory.[68]

In the memorandum of the Legal Section of the Secretariat, they stated:

> It will be seen from these Articles (120 and 257 of the Treaty of Versailles) that it is only as Mandatories that the Powers in question have obtained the cession of the territory and the transfer of the property in question. It is not as owners that these Powers have acquired the property, but as trustees (second paragraph of Article 22)—trustees who only possess powers of management.[69]

The conception of the mandates system was administration without ownership, according to these memoranda. On June 7, 1926, the council endorsed the principle expressed by the Permanent Mandates Commission at its Fourth Session on the question of state domains.[70]

Since the Mandates Commission has formulated the principle which satisfied the requirements of the mandates system, the question arises as to whether in British Togoland and Cameroons new laws should be enacted annulling the old. In British Togoland, the question does not arise, as every acre of land is owned by the chiefs or some other individual.[71] The chiefs have attempted to make the transition from communal to individual ownership of property. The government's policy is to watch it carefully lest it break down the old tribal system.[72] In the British Cameroons, the expression "Crown Lands" is employed in the land laws, but, according to the report for 1925, the expression means "lands vested in the mandatory Power in its mandatory capacity." [73]

The government has been obliged to buy back 14,851 acres of alienated land which was required for native communities. The approximate cost was £10,500.[74]

The land tenure policy of Great Britain in West Africa did not call for the enactment of any radical land laws, and where land had been alienated in violation of the mandate principle, the government has recovered it.

Forced labor and slavery. The B and C mandates contain a provision against slavery and forced labor. The mandatory power is allowed to exact forced labor only for essential public works and in return for adequate remuneration. Compulsory labor has been referred to as technical slavery.[75] Compulsory labor is a very difficult problem, and in order to promote the material and moral well-being of the natives, it must often be resorted to by Great Britain. What is, for example, compulsory labor, and what public works and services may be called essential? A literal interpretation of the provisions against compulsory labor would harm rather than benefit the territories in which they are to apply. The economic development of the mandated areas would be greatly handicapped.[76]

The term "forced labor" has been given a liberal interpretation by the Mandates Commission and judges the acts of a mandatory by the question whether the natives are being abused and exploited for the benefit of others. In its first report, the Permanent Mandates Commission recognized the obligation to work as the foundation of all civilized society.[77] However, the members of the commission have manifested considerable difference of opinion in memoranda submitted on the subject. M. van Rees expressed the opinion that, by the terms of the mandates, natives could not be compelled to work at all except on public works and services and that they must be remunerated, though he admitted that this standard could not be lived up to in practice. Grimshaw, the representative of the International Labor Organization at the Mandates Commission, preferred an interpretation which would confine the expression "forced labor" to work for an employer, for the benefit of someone other than the laborer himself. Thus, compulsory local road-making, sanitation, education for which the worker himself benefits, is not forced labor and need not be remunerated. M. d' Andrade based his opinion on the obligation to work, thus sanctioning vagrancy laws which practically forced all natives to find work.[78] At the tenth session, M. van Rees and Grimshaw suggested in a joint report that whatever might be the words the intention of the mandates was that the conditions of labor should be the best existing at the time in any of the colonies. M. Orts feared this standard might be interpreted as a policy of overbidding by the commission. What was intended was a generous application of the terms of the mandates.[79] The definition of "forced labor" has also been considered by the Temporary Commission on Slavery set up by the council in 1924.[80] A Committee on Native Labor was set up by the governing body of the International Labor Office in 1927. Freire d' Andrade, Merlin, van Rees, and Lugard of the Mandates Commission also are members of the committee.[81] Article 5 of the Geneva Slavery Convention of 1926 imposes limitations upon resort to forced labor but does not define the term.[82]

A conference on the question of forced labor was convened by the International Labor Office of the League of Nations in June, 1929. The conference considered a questionnaire which was issued to all the colonial powers designed to bring to an end forced labor in the colonies except on terms and conditions similar to those laid down for restricting such labor in the mandates.

The Convention of 1930 defined forced labor as all work or services which are extracted from any person under menace of penalty, and for which such person has not offered himself voluntarily. It exempted from the definition labor impressed in cases of emergency and labor for minor services in the direct interest of the community, also compulsory military service and service extracted from persons as a consequence of a conviction in court, provided they are not hired to work for private persons or companies. Further provision requires that forced labor for the transport of persons or goods, while tolerated for the time being in the case of government or urgent needs, shall be abolished within the shortest possible period.[83]

Concerning slavery in the Cameroons the Mandates Commission proposed, in its report to the council, that the British and French Governments should examine means of collaboration, and in its report on the work of the ninth session it was able to note the accredited representative's statement that effective cooperation existed between the British and French officials with a view to preventing any cases of slave-dealing on the northern frontier of the territory.[84] In the report of its tenth session, it added that steady progress had been made in that direction.[85]

At its third session, the commission came to the conclusion that the well-being of the natives in some of the mandated territories was being adversely affected by the recruiting of workers in one area for employment in another in which climatic conditions appreciably differ.[86] At its sixth session, the commission noted that the recruiting of natives from Togoland under British mandate for mines of the Gold Coast, which was having a bad effect on their health, was, for the time being, prohibited.[87]

In the British Cameroons, no forced or compulsory labor has been employed recently, and the annual report for 1935 refers to an ample supply of voluntary labor.[88] The report is interesting, for a shortage of workers had always presented a serious problem from the early days, when the colony was confined to the coast, till 1914 when the control was extended to the interior.[89]

As to the problem of native labor, it is impossible to draft a convention comprising all aspects of native labor. It can only be approached in stages and the Committee on Native Labor, on which there are four members of the Permanent Mandates Commission, has decided to concentrate at the outset upon the most urgent problems.[90]

Buell maintains that if the Mandates Commission does not become bolder in the future than it has been in the past, it will run the danger of losing the opportunity of leading the colonial world. And, for an example, he cites the commission's avoidance of many questions arising out of the forced labor provisions of the mandates. As a result, the leadership in this question has been taken by the International Labor Office.[91]

CHAPTER FOUR

Tanganyika

Tanganyika Territory, formerly German East Africa, is the largest of the mandated territories, having an area of 360,000 square miles which includes about 20,000 square miles of water.[1] It has a population of 5,055,000[2] and includes every variety of tropical country. The northern part of the territory, which is mountainous, is suitable for European settlement, and contains large European plantations. The eastern coast of Tanganyika has long been a field of activity for Arab and Indian traders, who are to be found especially in the port town of Dar-es-Salaam. Elsewhere Tanganyika is chiefly a native territory, but the natives differ widely in language, customs and characteristics, making a uniform administration exceedingly difficult. Where the native authority is strong, it is recognized and supported by the government, but where it is weak, the influence of the political officers is more direct, while still aiming at building up the native authority and the participation of the natives in the management of their own affairs. In the coastal regions the native organization has practically disappeared.

The mandate for Tanganyika was confirmed by the Council of the League of Nations on July 20, 1922,[3] and the authority of the British agents in this territory flows from the Foreign Jurisdiction Act of 1890.[4] The report for Tanganyika was one of the seven reports communicated to the Permanent Mandates Commission at its first meeting in October, 1921. Since the report was drawn up for the British Parliament, no comment was made except to express to Great Britain the commission's gratitude for the courtesy it displayed in permitting the commission to study them.

In the questions and suggestions submitted to the council by the commission, attention was called: (1) to the provision in the Tanganyika mandate which permitted a customs, fiscal or administrative union or federation with adjacent possessions under its sovereignty; (2) to the draft mandate's provision forbidding within the territory all forced or compulsory labor for the benefit of any private enterprise; (3) to the expressions in the mandate "eventual emancipation of all slaves" and "essential public works and services." The first provision did not nullify the equality of opportunity clause in Article 22 of Covenant and the commission desired to make this clear. In the case of Tanganyika such a conflict could not arise, as commercial equality was there assured by the provision of the Berlin and Brussels and the St. Germain Treaty.[5]

In the two remaining provisions of the mandates the questions raised by the Mandates Commission are similar to those concerning the British Cameroons and British Togoland and are discussed in Chapter III.[6]

I. Labor

The Permanent Mandates Commission has not attempted to evolve general principles for all problems relating to labor. The Mandates Commission is divided on the fundamentals of native labor policy. Economic development of backward areas involves intense utilization of native labor. But Lord Lugard of the Mandates Commission expressed the opinion that economic development must take a secondary place since it was dependent on the labor supply and the increase of native population.[7] This opinion was the result of a question raised about native labor in Tanganyika; the question was "whether the demands made on the present generation of natives for labor by reason of the rapidity of the material development of the country were not pressing too heavily upon the people." [8] The requisitioning of labor by chiefs or by the administration for local public works has engaged the special attention of the commission. The Tanganyika mandate recognizes that compulsory labor for essential public works and services is justified, but only in return for adequate remuneration. The Tanganyika Native Authority Ordinance of 1926 authorized native authorities to requisition labor, paid at the ruling rates, up to sixty days per annum for essential public services; and it also sanctions compulsory antifamine cultivation.[9]

In 1926, the Mandates Commission reported to the council that the tribute and the compulsory labor formerly exacted by the Tanganyika chiefs were replaced by a poll tax.[10] The Governor's Memorandum of 1927 requires his consent before labor can be called up for work on the roads.[11] Exceptions are allowed for porterage,[12] loading of steamers, or repairs of bridges in emergencies. The British report for 1936 shows that 6,809 porters were requisitioned by the government for 42,317 days, and 957 other workers for 8,754 days during that period.[13]

The private employers must obtain their labor by offering conditions that will attract. This has been the principle of the Tanganyika administration.[14] The Mandates Commission has also been interested in the Labour Department established in 1926 which understood the supervision of contracts and the activities of recruiting agents, and the investigation of complaints by laborers or employers. It has also studied the flow of labor migration.[15] In 1930, the Labour Department was abolished in the interest of economy, and the administrative officers were made responsible for the department's former duties.[16] The government denied it was an economy measure.[17] The Mandates Commission expressed misgiving at this step and invited a special report on labor conditions to be presented for consideration at the next session.[18] The report submitted did not indicate that the standards developed by the Labour Department had been lowered.[19] In 1938, the Mandates Commission welcomed the announcement of the Tanganyika Government that the Labour Department had been reinstituted.[20]

The unsatisfactory nature of the conditions prevailing among the large population of natives on the scattered workings of the Lupa gold fields was admitted by the government in its report to the Mandates Commission.[21] Steps were taken to improve these conditions, but it is true that the government did not, until 1937, provide adequate control over the operations of the prospectors, nor did it make adequate medical provision for the worker.[22] The Mandates Commission hoped this unsatisfactory situation would not again prevail.[23]

The Mandates Commission has shown great interest in Tanganyika's public and private works program, but the commission is divided on the fundamentals of native labor policy. This supports Buell's contention that unless the Mandates Commission becomes bolder in its labor policy, it will lose its supervision.[24]

II. Land Tenure

According to Article 6 of the Tanganyika Mandate, the framing of laws relating to the holding or transfer of land should take into consideration native laws and customs, and respect the rights and safeguard the interests of the native population. No rights were to be created in favor of non-natives without the previous consent of the public authorities.[25]

In Tanganyika, all lands were declared to be public lands and all public lands were to be administered for the benefit of the natives of the territory.[26] And according to the memorandum by the Legal Section of the Secretariat entitled "Legal Questions Connected with the Expressions *Domaine de l'Etat* (State Domain) and 'Crown Lands' Used in Certain Reports and in the Texts of Laws Regulating Land Tenure in the Mandated Territories," the terminology appears to be in conformity with the principles of mandate law.[27] The Mandates Commission feared the provision might be interpreted so as to render native rights invalid in the absence of a title specifically granted, and asked for a law to make this point clear.[28] Great Britain met this criticism by a law in 1928 in which native customary rights were recognized as equally valid with those held under certificates of occupancy.[29] Later the Mandates Commission expressed further apprehension to the possibility that the power given to the governor to revoke a title to occupancy might be used to interfere with rights obtained from customary occupation;[30] this was met by a declaration that the conditions regarding the revocability of rights of occupancy did not apply to native customary rights.[31] The struggle between white settlement and native production has been of great significance for the mandates system. In Tanganyika, Europeans can live in the highlands and in 1925 there were 127,355 laborers working on their plantations out of a total of 1,225,000 able-bodied adults.[32] In 1923, out of a total value of domestic exports of £1,657,601, only £572,215 worth were attributable to coffee and sisal, the chief European crops. The rest, with the exception of part of the cotton crop, were entirely the fruit of native production.[33]

The encouragement of native agriculture has caused a good deal of opposition among the white settlers already there. The first governor, Sir Horace Byatt, stated the future of Tanganyika lay in devel-

oping native cultivation only.[34]   He made the securing of labor difficult for the white man, and did a great deal to help native production,
including the production of coffee by natives.   Protests were raised
and his successor, Sir Donald Cameron, altered the governmental
policy to one of neutrality between native and white production.   He
permitted the alienation of more than 17,000 acres of land to settlers.[35]
This land was not to encroach upon land occupied or needed by
natives, nor were the natives to be moved into reserves to make room
for the white settlers.

Cameron was opposed to alienating large tracts of land to Europeans and settling the natives in reserves.   He favored intermingling
the natives and the European cultivation.[36]   In this way the native
can work for two or three days on his own cultivation and the rest
of the week on the adjacent cultivation of his European neighbors.
Two hundred and fifty thousand acres have been alienated in Tanganyika by the mandatory government.[37]   But Buell thinks that if the
government adopts a policy of land alienation—thus increasing the
demand for labor—and if it vigorously applies the East African labor
doctrine to which it has subscribed, its efforts in building up a native
institutional life will be doomed to failure.[38]

On the land question, the Mandates Commission has taken a firm
stand.   The principle defined by the commission is compulsory for
Great Britain and refusal to do so would have brought accusation of
bad faith respecting their international obligations.   Great Britain's
declaration appeared to conform with the principles of mandate law
on land tenure, but even this did not satisfy the commission as they
recommended legislation to make native land rights clearer.   Great
Britain enacted the legislation recommended by the commission.   In
Tanganyika where white settlement is possible, native interest has
been given the benefit of the doubt.[39]   This fact should illustrate the
importance of the Mandates Commission on the land question.

III. Indirect Rule

Indirect rule may be defined as a system by which the tutelary
power recognizes existing African societies and assists them to adapt
themselves to the functions of local government.[40]

The German administration had been organized through Arab
officials, but in 1922 Governor Sir Horace Byatt announced his inten-

tion to adopt a form of indirect administration and in 1923 a Native Authority Ordinance was issued to confer on administrative officers, native chiefs, and headmen the authority to issue rules for the maintenance of order and the prevention of crime. Systematic use of native authorities came with the enactment by the new governor, Sir Donald Cameron, of the Native Authority Ordinance of 1926. This ordinance recognized all indigenous authorities as part of an administrative system in which they should exercise real responsibility. The Ordinance of 1926 defines the power of native chiefs, it being understood that their authority remains, in principle, what it was under the tribal law.[42]

In giving reasons for indirect rule, Sir Donald Cameron, before the eleventh session of the Permanent Mandates Commission, in 1927 said:

A very large part of Tanganyika is quite unsuitable, for climatic reasons, for alienation to non-natives. In view of that fact, and in view of the comparatively large native population in those parts of the country which might, for climatic reasons, lie alienated, it is my view that Tanganyika will always remain a predominantly country like Uganda.[43]

The Mandates Commission said it was greatly impressed with the progress made in the building up, in accordance with the program of the governor, whose personal explanations in this connection were greatly appreciated, a system of native administration which made use, as far as possible, of the traditional tribal organization, subject to the supervision of Great Britain. It also declared it would continue to follow closely the further development of this important experiment which aimed at conserving the social and political fabric of native life and moulding it into a solid foundation for the political future of these people.[44] Again at the thirteenth session the commission noted with great interest the account which was given as to the results of the policy of indirect rule in Tanganyika and the consolidation of tribal units into homogeneous organizations.[45]

In an address in 1926 to the administrative officers of the territory, Sir Donald Cameron declared it was Great Britain's duty to develop the native on lines which will not westernize him and turn him into a bad imitation of a European. The aim was to make him a good African.[46] Cameron believed that the first essential for making the native a good African was the re-establishment of the traditional authority of the local chief which had been impaired under the German rule.

A further and most essential feature of indirect rule is the introduction of native courts. The Native Courts Ordinance of 1929 had for its object the institution of a self-contained system of native courts under administrative supervision; it removed the courts from the control of the Supreme Court, and made the executive authorities the sole avenue of appeal.[47] The Mandates Commission announced it would watch the results of this new system with interest.[48] One of the supreme tests of good government is the measure of independence enjoyed by the judiciary, and the confidence felt by the subject in the impartiality and soundness of the judicial administration.[49]

The British Government said it would appear that the commission had misunderstood the reasons for which the native courts have been removed from the supervision of the judicial authorities. The reason was not that those authorities were unable to exercise regular and prompt control of the courts, but that they were less acquainted with the everyday details of native life and, therefore, less favorably situated for supervising these courts than the administrative officers to whom these duties were transferred. A further reason for the transfer of the control of the native courts from the judiciary to the executive was the natives' inability to understand the separation of judicial from executive functions.[50] Nevertheless, most colonial administrators agree that one of the main essentials to safeguard in the administration of justice is that judicial matters should be settled by judicial officers independent of the executive.[51]

M. Merlin, a member of the Mandates Commission at the eighteenth session, said he was entirely in favor of the regime of indirect administration and was particularly glad to support it. The native administration had great advantages. The European authorities only intervened in order to guide, control, redress the wrongs, which was really the duty of the responsible chief. Under the system of direct administration, the European official could, even with the best intentions, incur the enmity of the native by falling foul of their customs, by causing disorder when he believed that he was working to obtain better order.

A good government, according to Western ideas, could sometimes develop a deplorable policy from the colonial point of view.[52]

Rioting occurred in 1937 among the Chagga of Moshi, where the antagonism felt by a small section of the people to the local native cooperative societies, through which the large native coffee crop is marketed, caused the trouble. The African police behaved with commendable discipline and restraint, and, in some cases, arrests were made by the native authorities before the administrative officers were in a position to take action.[53] The Mandates Commission regarded it as being to the credit of the operation of the system of indirect rule in the territory that the native authorities took action on their own motion for the restoration of order in the district of Moshi, without it being necessary for the administration to resort to force.[54]

In the comment which was submitted by D. Mackenzie-Kennedy, the accredited representative of Great Britain, he pointed out that in the one area the use of force by the police in a limited degree had been found necessary for the dispersal of rioters.[55]

In Tanganyika, the prevailing policy is now that of indirect rule, and it has been sanctioned by the Mandates Commission. The native is rapidly becoming a living part of the machinery of government, and the success of indirect rule may well prove of paramount importance to all of Great Britain's East African Dependencies.[56]

IV. Economic Equality

The second paragraph of Article 7 of the Tanganyika mandate reads:

Further, the Mandatory shall ensure to all nationals of states members of the League of Nations, on the same footing as to his own nations, freedom of transit and navigation, and complete economic, commercial, and industrial equality; provided that the Mandatory shall be free to organize essential public works and services on such terms and conditions as he thinks just.[57]

This set an important limitation upon the granting of any form of preference in the Tanganyika Territory. Marquis Theodoli, as Chairman of the Mandates Commission, said:

The principle of economic equality had, therefore, a particularly wide scope, since its application might contribute to the solution of the two greatest problems which lay at the basis of all international disputes, namely, the demographic problem and the distribution of raw materials. So far as the mandates were concerned, its importance lay, in his opinion, not only in the idea which it embodied, but also in its application, which, though it was limited to the fourteen mandated territories, represented an effective step towards the realization of a wider aim. That was a further reason why the commission should follow the application of the principle with the utmost attention in order that the obstacles which might be placed in the way of its application might be reduced and eliminated.

If such were not the case, and if the application of that principle were to remain illusory, the task of the commission would be reduced to extremely modest proportions.[58]

In Tanganyika, the principle of economic equality has been involved in the Mandates Commission's observations and comments on the customs union, postal rates, postal services, and the railways.

Tanganyika, Kenya, and Uganda customs union. The two British protectorates, Kenya and Uganda, created a customs union in 1917. On January 1, 1923, Kenya, Uganda, and Tanganyika adopted identical tariffs; local produce of the three territories was placed on the free list.[59] During the sixth session of the Mandates Commission, Lord Lugard inquired whether the principle of economic equality was contravened by the protective tariff on wheat and timber in Kenya. Ormsby-Gore, the accredited representative, replied that there was an identical tariff in force in the three territories and that the protective tariff on wheat and timber was not preferential nor discriminatory.[60] But M. Rappard said that free trade between Tanganyika and Kenya gave to the inhabitants of Kenya, and, therefore, to Great Britain, advantages which the neighboring colony of the Belgian Congo did not enjoy because of a customs barrier.[61]

On August 1, 1927, a customs agreement for the free interchange of both local produce and imported goods entered into effect.[62]

Postal rates. The question of postal rates has been one of the most troublesome problems in regard to economic equality faced by the Mandates Commission.[63] It originated during the ninth session of the commission, while it was discussing the report from Tanganyika. Marquis Theodoli, chairman of the commission, inquired if there was not an international convention by virtue of which the postal rates were different in Tanganyika according to whether letters were sent to British possessions or to foreign countries.[64] Scott, the accredited representative, promised to furnish this information to the commission. At the twelfth session of the commission, Great Britain's reply showed that rates of postage for matter destined for British possessions had been assimilated to the inland rates of the territory.[65] The question became a tangled one, as members of the commission disagreed as to whether letters were articles of commerce and thus forbidden to be assimilated under the terms of the mandates. It became an important problem when it was brought to the attention of the commission that not only in Tanganyika but also in other mandated territories as well there existed one set of rates for foreign countries and a lower rate for matter destined for the mandatory power's own territory, either in Europe or elsewhere. The commission recommended the mandatory powers furnish particulars concerning (1) their system of postal rates, (2) the reasons which led them to adopt different rates, (3) the practical importance of the question from the financial point of view.[66] M. Kastl, a member of the Mandates Commission, reported to the commission that he concluded the establishment, in A- and B-mandated territories, of lower rates for postal traffic to territories of the mandatory power and its colonies than for traffic with other countries is not consistent with the principle of economic equality.[67] The majority of the Mandates Commission did not accept Kastl's conclusion, as they did not submit any recommendation on this matter to the council.[68]

There can be no doubt that a system of differential postal rates tends to turn business toward the mandatory state.[69]

Postal service. In 1933, the Tanganyika postal service was amalgamated with that of Kenya and Uganda, which had been established as a joint service in 1911. M. Keller, German member of the Council of the League of Nations in 1932, commenting on the twenty-second session of the Mandates Commission, said the commission should not fail to examine carefully the Postal Convention between Kenya and Tanganyika in order to ascertain whether the unification did not go further than mere administrative convenience and did not affect sovereign rights. In this connection, the German Government maintained its point of view that, politically, territories under mandate were separate units.[70]

During the twenty-third session, there was a lengthy debate in the Mandates Commission regarding the interpretation of Article 10 of the mandate for Tanganyika and the probable advantages and disadvantages of the unification of the postal services. Article 10 reads:

The Mandatory shall be authorized to constitute the territory into a customs, fiscal, and administrative union or federation with the adjacent territories under its own sovereignty or control; provided always that the measures adopted to that end do not infringe the provisions of this mandate.[71]

The commission claimed, according to that article, that certain forms of union or federation between Tanganyika and the neighboring territories were admissible, subject to restrictions. It was, however, very important to know what these restrictions were, because, in the future, the commission would be called upon to criticize from the point of view of Article 10, many measures that might be taken in Tanganyika for carrying out this program of coordination and cooperation.[72]

The Mandates Commission suggested that Great Britain should be requested to communicate the texts relating to the amalgamation, together with any useful information which might enable the commission to judge from year to year of the effective results of the measures adopted on the efficiency of the postal service and on the finances and autonomy of the territory. It decided to suspend any further judgment on the amalgamation of the services until adequate experience had enabled it to form a more reliable opinion. Finally, it announced its intention of watching the direct and indirect effects of the amalgamation upon the administrative efficiency and cost of the unified service and the autonomy of the mandated territory.[73]

Also during the twenty-third session of the Mandates Commission, it considered the petitions of September 19, 1932, from the Indian Association, and of January 22, 1933, from the Koloniale Reichsarbeitsgemeinschaft, disputing the legitimacy of the unification. The Indian Association claimed the postal union tended to subordinate the interests of the inhabitants of the mandated territory to those of the predominant elements in Kenya and to impede the duty of supervision falling on the League of Nations and the Mandates Commission. The Koloniale Reichsarbeitsgemeinschaft declared unification was incompatible with the letter and spirit of Article 22 of the Covenant. In the resolution of the petitions attached to their letters, it added that the measure under discussion constituted a unilateral modification of the mandates system and, hence, an infringement of Germany's rights.[74]

The commission adopted as its conclusions on the petitions the observations appearing in its report to the council on the administration of Tanganyika for its twenty-third session.[75]

The accredited representative for Tanganyika in 1934 told the Mandates Commission of Great Britain's decision to issue a common postage stamp for Tanganyika, Kenya, and Uganda.[76] This was the logical consequence of the unification of the postal services, and was based solely on consideration of public convenience, a measure which had resulted in a substantial financial saving to the territory. The commission asked for further details in the next annual report. They desired the reasons for the issuance of the common postage stamp and the allocation of postal, telegraphic, and customs expenditures and revenue between the three territories.[77]

M. Palacios of the Mandates Commission doubted whether the issuing of a common stamp was compatible with the status of the mandated territory, as he thought that its issue might be symbolic of a trend of affairs contrary to what the commission had stipulated on several occasions, more particularly during the discussion on closer union.[78] Calder, the accredited representative, replied that Great Britain thought a common stamp was quite compatible with the status of Tanganyika. Since 1911,. Kenya and Uganda had had a common stamp and no one had suggested that their separate identity was compromised thereby.[79]

At the twenty-ninth session of the Mandates Commission in 1936, it noted the reason for which Great Britain considered the issue of a common stamp for Tanganyika, Kenya, and Uganda was in accordance with the fiscal interests of the mandated territory. It repeated the hope expressed in 1935 that the mandatory power would furnish explicit statements of its views as to the compatibility of this issue with the provisions of the mandate.[80]

The Tanganyika report for 1936 reported that for the second successive year cash revenues exceeded recurrent expenditure of the postal and telegraphic services, and that the amalgamation scheme of individual legislative and financial control in each territory, under technical supervision and central authority of the Postmaster General, combined to function satisfactorily.[81] The report concluded by stating:

It is difficult to understand how a common stamp with the legend Tanganyika, Kenya, and Uganda issued by the amalgamated postal services can be taken to be a symbol of political union.[82]

The accredited representative announced, during the thirty-first mandates session, that Great Britain attached no political significance to the issue of a common stamp for Tanganyika.[83]

Railways. In Tanganyika, all railroad lines are owned by the Tanganyika administration. The Central Railway was constructed by the Germans,[84] and in 1929 the Mandates Commission asked for full information as to the conditions of purchase by the Tanganyika administration.[85] The value of the German lines as taken over by Great Britain was estimated at £4,814,000 for which a sum of £33,995 was paid to certain claim-holders.[86]

The extension of the Central Railway to Mwanza brought it into competition with the Kenya and Uganda Railways. The Secretary of State ruled in 1928 that noncompetitive rates should be arranged, leaving trade to take its natural course, a decision implemented by an agreement permitting the Kenya-Uganda Railways to retain their lake traffic at all points except Mwanza; the rates from Mwanza to either Dar-es-Salaam or Mombasa were to be equalized, and the rates from Tanganyika ports across the lake were made much higher via the Tanganyika route than via Kenya by the cost of transport across the lake. The accredited representative called the attention of Great Britain to the prejudice which the Mandates Commission thought might be caused to the interests of Tanganyika by the application of a program of customs and railways tariff identical with those in force in Kenya.[87]

Changes were suggested, but, in 1934, the Secretary of State decided against a change in the previous arrangement until the total traffic to the Tanganyika lake ports reached the figure of the tonnage handled by the Kenya and Uganda Railways prior to the building of the line. At its twenty-seventh session in 1935 the Mandates Commission discussed the question of competition between the railways of Kenya and Tanganyika. Lord Lugard said:

> The Tanganyika Railway Advisory Council had proposed that, whenever the peculiar circumstances of one of the territories necessitated divergence from the rating policy and classification of commodities, it might impose an exceptional rate under special arrangements to avoid a rate war. The proposal had been accepted by the Secretary of State.[88]

The commission expressed the hope that the effects of that decision would prove advantageous to Tanganyika.[89] A special inquiry made in 1936 expressed the view that it would be preferable to revert to the decision of 1928. The settlement finally arrived at in 1937 provided for equality of rates, freedom of choice by the trader, payment to the transport systems for services rendered, and a division of profits between the two railways. It was estimated that the first year of operation of the agreement would result in a payment by the Kenya and Uganda Railways to the Tanganyika Railways of about £5,000.[90]

Conclusion. The Customs Union of Tanganyika, Kenya, and Uganda was legal, but to the commission there was no doubt that free trade between Tanganyika and Kenya gave the inhabitants of Kenya advantages which the neighboring colony of the Belgian Congo did not enjoy because of a customs barrier. While the commissioners failed to submit a recommendation on the matter of postal rates, they did not support their colleague in his statement that the establishment in A- and B-mandated territories of lower rates for postal traffic to territories of the mandatory power and its colonies than for traffic with other countries is not consistent with the principle of economic equality. The commission suspended judgment on the amalgamation of the Tanganyika-Kenya and Uganda Postal Service until adequate experiences had enabled it to form a reliable opinion. And the commission's observation concerning the probable injury to the Tanganyika Railway by the application of a program of customs and railways tariff identical with those in force in Kenya led later to an equality of rates.

V. Closer Union

Proposals for a federation which would include Kenya, Uganda, Tanganyika, Nyasaland, Northern Rhodesia, and Zanzibar were published by Sir Harry Johnston and other writers after the British occupation of Tanganyika.[91] Secretary of State Amery's statement in 1926 that "the ideal of a united East Africa was steadily growing," may be regarded as the only pronouncement by a minister of the Crown in favor of such a development in the near future.[92] In 1924, the British Parliament ordered the appointment of a commission to report on the coordination of policy and administration in the territories. Ormsby-Gore, as Chairman, spent three months traveling through Nyasaland, Kenya, Uganda, and Tanganyika. The commissioners were not instructed to make any proposals for federation.[93] However, they did sound local opinion on the question, and reported that they found little support for the idea. Federation was rejected on the grounds that lack of communications would be a serious obstacle and that federal government would be cumbrous. They recommended, however, a series of interterritorial conferences at regular intervals at which all six dependencies should be represented. Matters of general policy which presented common problems, such as native administration, communications, taxation, land and labor policy should be discussed at a conference of governors.

The first governors' conference was held at Nairobi in 1926 and the second in 1930.[94]

A commission, with Sir E. Hilton Young as chairman, was appointed to inquire into the possibilities of closer union and cooperation, which should have in mind the ultimate federation of all six territories, though it might be found that for the present only a union of Kenya and Tanganyika was practicable.[95] The commission visited East Africa in 1927-1928 and recommended a series of steps towards an ultimate union under a governor-general, who would have powers designed to enable him to exercise at close quarters the functions of supervision and control which are at present the responsibility of the Secretary of State.[96] As a preliminary step, a high commissioner should be appointed for Kenya, Uganda, and Tanganyika, whose functions would be to work out plans for the development of a unified native policy. The report rejected the arguments made by

British officials and settlers in the past that the semitemperate climate of East Africa justifies a native policy which cannot be supported on the west coast.[97]

Considered in its entirety, the Hilton Young report might be regarded as reflecting the highest standard of the present time with reference to the obligations which advanced nations inhabiting temperate climates owe to the backward peoples of the tropics who, through them, are coming into contact with modern occidental civilization.[98]

The British Government sent each member of the Mandates Commission a copy of the Hilton Young Commission's report, and the British accredited representative to the fifteenth session of the Mandates Commission informed the commission that Great Britain had not yet reached any decision on the findings of that report.[99] In view of the importance of the proposals of the report from the point of view of their agreement with the provisions and principles of the mandates, this question was discussed by members of the commission and various opinions were expressed in the course of these discussions.

M. Kastl, the German member of the Permanent Mandates Commission, said:

The report's ultimate aim is to form a centrally administered territory, consisting of the three areas mentioned above, which are destined to become provinces within this territory. Such a measure would, however, deprive Tanganyika of its character as a mandated area. According to the principle of the mandates system, a territory under mandate must remain an inviolable unit, and can, therefore, never be absorbed into another territory of the mandatory power not subject to a mandate. A territory under mandate must be a "separate entity," not only in its relations with the League of Nations, but also in its relations with other countries, and, particularly, in this special case, with the other British colonial possessions. When the report says, on page 220, that eventually a Central Council may be established as, for instance, in India with provinces under Lieutenant-Governors, it becomes plain that the proposals made in the report do not contemplate the maintenance of the territory under mandate as an inviolable unit.

In conclusion, I would point out that it is of the essence of the system of guardianship that it should only provide for temporary guidance. But the incorporation of the territory under mandate as a province in another newly created union could not be regarded as compatible with the idea of temporary protection and guidance, and would, therefore, be in contradiction with the system of guardianship and with the character of the mandates.[100]

The commission did not feel that it should at this stage express a definite opinion with regard to the findings of the Hilton-Young report, but it called the attention of the council to its discussion on the subject.[101]

During its sixteenth session, the Mandates Commission reported that it had received from the British Government a report by Sir Samuel Wilson, Permanent Under-Secretary of State for the Colonies, who had visited East Africa to ascertain on what lines a scheme for closer union would be administratively workable.[102] Wilson had recommended the appointment of a high commissioner exercising legislative and administrative control over certain major services, all other matters, including native policy, being left to local legislatures.[103] His report in one respect diverges from the Hilton-Young report, in proposing to turn over native policy to the local governments.[104]

Cameron, the governor of Tanganyika, objected to the scheme of closer union advocated in the Wilson report as not being suitable or acceptable, inasmuch as, while it purported to be no more than a settlement on the economic side, it, no doubt, had a highly important political side which gave encouragement to the aspiration of the British unofficial community in Kenya that they should eventually attain responsible government.[105] The commission, bearing in mind the promise made by the British representative, thought it desirable to postpone the examination of the report which, under the circumstances, it regarded as premature.[106]

At the eighteenth session, the Mandates Commission evinced great interest in the scheme for closer administrative customs and fiscal union between Tanganyika, Kenya, and Uganda. The accredited representative told the commission that Great Britain proposed to submit this question for examination to a joint committee of the two Houses of Parliament.[107] Great Britain promised to communicate its final decision to the Mandates Commission so that the latter should be in a position to submit its observations to the council before the decision was actually enforced.[108] The council left it to the Mandates Commission to decide to what extent it was expedient and possible to accede to the desires expressed by Great Britain.[109]

The commission felt that to express an opinion before the mandatory power for Tanganyika had communicated the terms of its decision would not release it from the obligation to examine the final conclusion reached by the British Government. Therefore, the commission again deferred the consideration of the question.[110]

The statement of conclusions issued by Lord Passfield, when Secretary of State in 1930, embodied a proposal for the appointment of a high commissioner who would both advise the Secretary of State on native policy and legislate for all three territories on certain matters of common concern to them. In legislating for these matters, he would have the assistance of a council of three officials and twenty-one nominated members, seven of these coming from each of the three territories.[111]

These proposals were submitted to the consideration of a joint select committee of both Houses of Parliament, which sat in 1930-1931, and came to the conclusion that any far-reaching step in the direction of closer union at that time would be inopportune, on account of the increased financial cost in time of economic depression, the reluctance of the native witnesses from Tanganyika to be more closely associated with Kenya, the obstacles presented by inadequate communications, and the absence of any common consciousness in the population of the territories. They recommended, however, that there should be regular conferences of the governors of Kenya, Uganda, and Tanganyika, with periodical extraordinary conferences including the governors of Northern Rhodesia, Nyasaland, Zanzibar, and that a joint secretariat should be created which would serve also for interterritorial conferences on technical subjects.[112]

The Permanent Mandates Commission considered the British Government's decision at its twenty-third session. M. Merlin of the commission did not think Great Britain could be justly criticized on any positive, established, undisputed fact.[113] Three trends of thought had emerged in the Mandates Commission concerning Great Britain's decision. According to M. Ruppel, the German member of the Mandates Commission, any union involving the creation of a common executive organ was, *eo ipso,* a breach of the territory's political status and, therefore, incompatible with the mandate. If that were so, according to M. van Rees, the commission should object to all the administrative unions of mandated territories with neighboring colonies or protectorates hitherto effected, as, for instance, the administrative amalgamation of the Cameroons under British mandate with Nigeria, of Togoland under British mandate with the Gold Coast, and of Ruanda-Urundi with the Belgian Congo. In all these cases, this amalgamation led to an administrative situation in which the administration of the mandated territory was necessarily subordinated to that of the neighboring territory. This inevitable consequence of unions or federations, formally authorized under B mandates, affected the exercise of the full powers of legislation and administration conferred by these mandates on the local authority, but did not in any way affect the political status of the mandated territories, which was unimpaired.[114] This represented the second trend of thought.

The third trend held that, although Article 10 authorized administrative unions, there was a danger that they might lead, in the end by imperceptible stages, to political union, which was incompatible with the principle of the mandate. Hence, the commission should watch the position carefully and constantly.[115]

Although three views existed in the commission, they finally agreed that a political or constitutional union of Tanganyika with the neighboring territories could not be carried out as long as the present mandate is in force.[116] But, concerning the regular and periodical conferences of governors, two viewpoints were maintained as was evidenced by a minority report. The majority of the commission considered that the conferences of the Governors of Tanganyika, Kenya, and Uganda should not assume executive responsibilities which would unduly restrict the necessity of autonomy of the mandated territory.[117] M. van Rees, Lord Lugard, M. Merlin, and M. Orts did not agree to these passages and submitted a minority report saying:

It is of opinion that the Governors' Conference affords a valuable and necessary means of consultation between the Governors in the interest of their respective territories. It takes cognizance of the fact that the Conference is "purely advisory," that full liberty of action is reserved to each Governor and his Legislative and Executive Councils. The minority, therefore, cannot conceive how it could be feared that a conference so constituted could possibly exercise executive powers, or endanger the political individuality of the mandated territory.[118]

VI. *Liberty of Conscience*

Article 8 of the Tanganyika Mandate concerning liberty of conscience reads as follows:

The Mandatory shall ensure in the territory complete freedom of conscience and the free exercise of all forms of worship which are consonant with public order and morality; missionaries who are nationals of states members of the League of Nations shall be free to enter the territory and to travel and reside therein, to acquire and possess property, to erect religious buildings and to open schools throughout the territory, it being understood, however, that the Mandatory shall have the right to exercise such control as may be necessary for the maintenance of public order and good government, and to take all measures required for such control.[119]

Ormsby-Gore, the accredited representative of the British Government for Tanganyika, reported religious rivalry between the various sects had a very bad effect on the natives. There were three groups, belonging: (1) to the Roman Catholic Church, (2) to the Church of England, and (3) to the other Protestant churches.[120]

The governor of Tanganyika had asked the permission of the British Secretary of State for the Colonies to allow him to take measures similar to those adopted some years ago in Kenya, where various missionary bodies had been allotted definite spheres of influence. This delimitation had been effected in Kenya with the mutual assent of the missionaries.

The accredited representative pointed out the difficulty of getting mutual assent in Tanganyika, for, when the heads of the three groups of missionaries were approached, they would invariably quote the mandate.[121]

M. Orts and Sir Frederick Lugard thought that the point of the maintenance of public order could be raised by the governor in the event of necessity.[122] In other words, Article 8 of the mandate made the free exercise of religion subordinate to the maintenance of public order. This was the point of view which eventually prevailed in the commission in its report to the council.[123]

During the next session the commission noted:

. . . the mandatory Power's statement that the Governor of the territory did not consider that any special measures had become necessary to ensure the normal and peaceful development of the activities of missionaries of various creeds in the territories.[124]

Probably, it seemed the Mandates Commission showed a weakness in applying this principle.[125] In the case of land tenure, the principle defined by the commission is compulsory for all the mandatory powers; unless they embody it in all their land legislation they will be accused of bad faith respecting their international obligations. In the case of freedom of conscience, the commission defined no line of action, but informed Great Britain of the principle which would guide it in the consideration of whatever measures Great Britain put into effect.

VII. *Other Observations by the Mandates Commission*

The Permanent Mandates Commission considers all official documents of the mandatory powers relating to the mandate, whether they are submitted to it by the mandatory powers or not.

The *Tanganyika Gazette* of October 18, 1925 contained the declaration made by the Secretary of State for the Colonies at an East African banquet held on June 25, 1925:

He wished to correct the idea that there was something transient in their hold upon Tanganyika. It was as essentially a part of the British framework as any other Protectorate.[126]

This was a definite assertion of the nationalistic view of the mandates.[127]

Marquis Theodoli, Chairman of the Commission during the ninth session, did not ask the accredited representative to express any opinion, but said Great Britain would perhaps wish to give some explanation to the commission.[128] The chairman also drew the attention of the commission to the *Tanganyika Exhibition Handbook* which had been prepared for the British Empire Exhibition. This handbook contained a history of the territory, but it might be noted that neither in this part of the book nor in any other did the word mandate appear, nor was there any evidence of the fact that the territory was administered under the supervision of the League of Nations. It would seem, therefore, that the handbook showed an important omission in this respect.[129]

M. van Rees called Sir Donald Cameron's attention at the eleventh Mandates Commission session to a statement made before the Legislative Council in Tanganyika. Van Rees did not get the impression that the declaration implied any idea of annexation which was irreconcilable with the mandates, as had been inferred. He thought he desired to remove, in the interest of the territory itself, certain fears manifested by capitalists, who were ready to contribute to the economic development of the territories under mandate, because of the presumed uncertainty of the legal title of the mandatory power over the territories in question.[130]

Sir Donald Cameron said the misunderstanding was due to his attempt to use clear and simple language to the natives, and it was impossible to explain, as was first attempted, to the chiefs and natives that Tanganyika was regarded "as part of the framework of the British Empire and administered as such." [131]

M. Rappard also called Governor Cameron's attention to the preamble to the Tanganyika (Legislative Council) Order in Council 1926 which referred specifically, as enabling His Britannic Majesty to make such an order, to the stipulation in the Foreign Jurisdiction Act of 1890, which provided that His Majesty's jurisdiction may be exercised in a foreign country in the same and as ample a manner as if His Majesty had acquired that jurisdiction by the cession or conquest of territory. Reference is also made in the same preamble to the power and jurisdiction which His Majesty had by treaty, grant, usage, sufferance, and other lawful means.[132]

The Mandates Commission suggested that specific mention, in important acts of this kind, of the fact that the territory is governed under mandate on behalf of the League of Nations would make its status and the basis of the jurisdiction of the mandatory power clearer.[133] Great Britain claimed the omission was due to technical reasons arising from the fact that the Order in Council is closely linked with the Tanganyika Order in Council of 1920, upon the wording of which it is based. This Order in Council was published before the mandate for Tanganyika had been formally issued and it was, therefore, impracticable to make any reference therein to the mandate. It assured the commission that steps had been taken to ensure that reference to the mandate should be made in any future Order in Council dealing with the Tanganyika territory.[134]

During the fifth session, Rappard called the commission's attention to the difference in the Tanganyika mandate concerning the Permanent Court of International Justice.[135] All the mandates recognized the Permanent Court of International Justice as the final interpreter of their terms in the following manner:

The mandatory agrees that if any dispute whatever should arise between the mandatory and another member of the League of Nations relating to the interpretation or the application of the provisions of the mandate, such dispute, if it cannot be settled by negotiation, shall be submitted to the Permanent Court of International Justice provided for by Article 14 of the Covenant of the League of Nations.[136]

The Tanganyika mandate contained an additional paragraph:

State members of the League of Nations may likewise bring any claims in behalf of their nationals for infraction of their rights under the mandate before the said court for decision.[137]

This was an important matter as five judges dissented from the court's preliminary decision in the Mavrommatis concession case on claiming the court had no jurisdiction in this case.[138] They directed attention to the absence in the Palestine mandate of the additional paragraph found in the Tanganyika mandate. The case is also very important as it was the first judgment of the International Court on a mandate question.[139]

In the Mavrommatis case, the dispute arose out of the refusal of the Palestine Mandatory Government to recognize certain irrigation, transport, and power concessions made by the former Turkish Government to Mavrommatis, a Greek subject, whose cause was taken up by the Greek Government in 1924. Great Britain objected to the jurisdiction of the court. The court sustained its jurisdiction.[140]

Rappard believed the difference in the mandate was due to accident in the drafting of the Tanganyika mandate.[141] Great Britain declared the clause was not accidental, but they had no objection to its removal. The commission discussed the matter during the sixth session. There were no suggestions to the council, and the texts were not changed.[142]

VIII. Conclusion

Tanganyika may seem to form a part of a community settlement, all within the British Empire in East Africa, which is of very great benefit to her development and well-being.[143] Some scheme of federation in the East is desirable for it is clear that greater coordination in the administration is desirable. The political issue of amalgamation presents a problem of great difficulty. The Permanent Mandates Commission has been unduly susceptible in its criticism of the few measures of coordination so far effected between Tanganyika and the other areas. It has concluded that amalgamation is incompatible with the terms of the mandate. In other words, a mandated territory cannot be brought into a federation of British possessions. This stand emphasized the difference between a colony or protectorate and a mandate, and it, no doubt, helped Germany in thinking she could secure the return of Tanganyika.

It was argued that there are no circumstances that would make it impossible for one reason or other to return the German Colonies to Germany. According to the League Covenant, the object aimed at by the mandatory system is to insure the well-being and progress of the native population.[144] On the other hand, in England, it was said the consent of the United States would be required before Tanganyika could be transferred to another power. The Anglo-American Tanganyika Convention of 1925 was cited, and was held antecedent and superior to any British obligation to the League.[145] However, in England there seemed to exist a feeling that a peaceful solution of German colonial demands could be worked out.[146] Of course, the Mandates Commission would not propose a transfer, but it was the instrument through which a transfer or peaceful solution would come.

In England, opinion was not for returning the mandate, but for an extension of the mandate principle. This proposal was made by the Labor Party in September, 1936.[147] This was an indirect compliment paid to the Mandates Commission by a British political party. Tanganyika is the test case for the B mandates and the student firmly believes that the League of Nations, through the special efforts of Great Britain and the Mandates Commission, could have offered a peaceful solution to the "have not powers."

CHAPTER FIVE

Iraq

I. Great Britain's Relations with Iraq Before the Adoption of the Treaty by the League of Nations

Great Britain became interested in the eastern part of Iraq (known as Mesopotamia in 1918) because of its proximity to British India and to its interests in the Persian Gulf.[1] British occupation occurred as early as November, 1914 in the Province of Bassra. Later in the war, the rest of the country was conquered and put under military administration. Sir Percy Cox, who knew the Arabs and was known by them, was appointed Civil Commissioner in July, 1917.[2] A joint declaration was made after the Armistice by Great Britain and France which emphasized the policy of liberation and the grant of autonomy.[3] The inhabitants of the country were early dissatisfied with the steps taken to give effect to the declaration and in 1919 there was a serious outbreak against the British Administration. The suppressing of this outbreak was a slow and costly process, and there arose in Great Britain a general demand that the government should entirely withdraw from Mesopotamia.

But Usher, an Englishman, writing in *The Contemporary Review* in 1921 said:

If ever Great Britain was committed to anything or anybody, she is surely committed to the tutelage of Mesopotamia for at least a reasonable period until its people are able to defend themselves.[4]

Winston Churchill, the Colonial Secretary, opposed withdrawal as he no doubt realized that England's removal would precipitate anarchy, imply the occupation of the country by forces of unrest, and encourage the spread of disaffection throughout the Eastern world.[5] An Arab National Government headed by a Provisional National Ministry was established. Emir Faisal was chosen King of Iraq with British support. He ascended the throne in August, 1921. Faisal was made King with the understanding that his government should be constitutional, representative, and democratic.[6]

Early in 1921, the British Government created the Middle East Department of the Colonial Office and placed under its purview Mesopotamia, Palestine, and other Arab districts within the British sphere of influence that had previously been under the Foreign Office. On the whole, the change was a good one. Unfortunately, it did give some color to the view widely held in the East that the mandates were merely up-to-date camouflage for annexation, insured, so to speak, at a low rate by the League of Nations.[7] Before the World War in the Near East, an alliance with Russia or Turkey by England was considered a diplomatic necessity; after the war, it was impossible to have an alliance with either of these powers, and Iraq now was to form an important part in this chain of buffer states to give India a sense of security.[8] W. Ormsby-Gore, a member of the British Parliament and later a member of the Mandates Commission, said in 1920:

Finally, it must be emphasized that the problem of Mesopotamia is only a part of the wide Arab problem. Unless the Arab world is envisaged as a whole, the wrong perspective is obtained. We cannot confine our policy within a number of new artificial boundaries.[9]

The Mesopotamian mandate had been on the agenda of the council as early as December, 1920, but the terms were not made public until February, 1921.[10] The contests over the mandates in this part of the world were bitter, and there were long-drawn-out diplomatic negotiations between Great Britain, France, Italy, and the United States. Great Britain ruled in Iraq without a mandate, her relations with the Iraq government being regulated by the treaty of October 10, 1922, and known as the Treaty of Iraq.[11] There was much opposition in Iraq to the word "mandate," as it was taken in the sense of an authoritative requirement, as by a sovereign.[12] Great Britain, realizing Arab nationalism was a force and not a farce, agreed to abrogate the mandate.[13] Therefore, Britain resolved to set out the main terms of the mandatory relation in the form of a treaty instead of an instrument from the League to the mandatory.[14] The treaty was to remain in force for not more than five years from the date of ratification of the Treaty of Peace with Turkey, and might terminate as soon as Iraq became a member of the League of Nations. The British

Government undertook in the treaty to furnish the kingdom of Iraq with the advice and assistance it required, but so as not to impair the national sovereignty. And the King of Iraq undertook on his side, during the term of the treaty, to be guided by the advice of the representatives of the British Government in all important affairs concerning the international and financial interests of the British Government.[15] This treaty was supplemented by the Protocol of April 30, 1923, and four subsidiary agreements.[16] The Protocol stipulated the termination of the treaty on Iraq's entry into the League, which, in any case, was to terminate four years after the ratification of peace with Turkey.

The trouble with Turkey on the northern frontier of the Mosul vilayet continued, and the treaty was ratified by the constituent assembly, with the express proviso that it shall become null and void if the British Government should fail to safeguard the rights of Iraq in the Mosul vilayet in its entirety.[17]

Great Britain proceeded to establish definite legal relations between Iraq and the League of Nations. In May, 1923, the British Government made a declaration to the Council of the League that it proposed to carry out its obligations under Article 22 of the Covenant by means of the Treaty. In June, 1924, the question was before the Council of the League, which had already been informed of the new situation.[18] On September 27, 1924, the council adopted the draft instrument of the British Government establishing the legal relationship of the new state and of Great Britain to the League. Great Britain assumed the responsibility for Iraq's fulfillment of the alliance, the terms of which were not to be modified without the consent of the council. Iraq's admission to the League would terminate the alliance, but if at the end of the period Iraq were not in the League of Nations, the council was to decide on the measures to be taken under Article 22 of the Covenant.[19] The treaty and agreements defined the powers of Great Britain as a trustee in a more elaborate way than in any case of any other mandated territory.[20]

II. *Iraq as a Mandate*

In 1924, Constituent Assembly of Iraq adopted an organic law for Iraq which provided that Iraq was a sovereign state, free and independent. Its sovereign rights were indivisible and inalienable. Its government was that of a hereditary monarchy, and its form, representative.[21] The constitution had no organic growth. It was thrust ready-made on an inarticulate country.[22]

A report from Mesopotamia was presented during the first session of the Mandates Commission in 1921, but the commission considered the state of uncertainty still existing concerning everything that affected the mandates mentioned in Paragraph 4 of Article 22 of the Covenant would make the study of little use.[23] Although the British Government did not, at any rate originally, regard itself as under any legal obligation, before confirmation of its mandate, to submit reports on its administration, it declared itself willing to do so and, in fact, submitted reports,[24] and further, according to the statement of its representative on the council, regarded itself throughout as acting solely on behalf of the League of Nations.[25] This statement and the submission of reports amounted to a recognition of responsibility to the League for the governance of the country, and it could be accurately said that Great Britain was advising and assisting Iraq under the supervision of the League, and in accordance with the principles laid down in Article 22.[26]

At the seventh session in 1925, the Mandates Commission was ready to consider the first report since the mandate had been confirmed, but Great Britain requested that the consideration of the first report be postponed until the Mosul boundary question, which involved a quarter of the territory, was settled.[27]

The Mosul question was connected with the northern boundary of Iraq which remained unsettled by the Treaty of Lausanne (1923), but under the terms of that Treaty the question was submitted to the League of Nations Council which awarded most of Mosul to Iraq on December 16, 1925.[28] The award, however, was contingent upon British continuance of the mandate for twenty-five years unless Iraq earlier became a member of the League. A new treaty complying with this requirement was concluded between Great Britain and Iraq in January, 1926, and on March 11, 1926, the council finally ratified the Mosul award.[29] But, opinion was expressed that the League of Nations would have to be much stronger and the powers of the Permanent Mandates Commission vastly extended before the peoples of the Near East could hope for much help from Geneva in the working out of their national destinies.[30] By an agreement of June 5, 1926, between Great Britain, Iraq, and Turkey, the latter recognized the boundary with slight rectification in return for 10 per cent of Iraq oil royalties and the neutralization of the frontier.[31] In England the question was asked whether Iraq was an asset or liability as there was a possibility of war with Turkey over this boundary.[32]

On December 14, 1927, Great Britain signed a new treaty with Iraq. Among the provisions were new financial and military arrangements between the two powers, and also included was an undertaking by Great Britain to press for the admission of Iraq to the League of Nations in 1932, that is, at the end of the second period of four years from the ratification of the Treaty of Peace, provided the state was progressing satisfactorily.[33] But the catch, according to the Iraqis, was in Article 8, "Provided the present rate of progress in Iraq is maintained and all goes well in the interval, His Britannic Majesty will support the candidature of Iraq for admission to the League of Nations in 1932." The Iraqis claimed that independence meant League entrance and that, with the foreign qualifications, British control could prevent it indefinitely.[34] Further evidence of the trends in Iraq had occurred on March 10, 1927, when the last battalion of English troops was withdrawn, leaving only five air squadrons and one Indian battalion.[35]

Consideration of the first report for Iraq was taken up at the tenth session of the Mandates Commission in the Fall of 1926. The High Commissioner, Sir Henry Dobbs, appeared as the accredited representative, and gained commendation for his policy of Iraq governed for Iraqi and by Iraqi helped by small numbers of British advisers and inspectors, and the commission found nothing to criticize.[36] Iraq was considered at the twelfth session of the commission and information was requested on the protection of minorities suggested by the League's commission on the Mosul dispute and on economic equality with respect to the customs drawback law of 1926 and various oil concessions.[37] The Anglo-Persian oil concession extension to 1996 was approved by the Fourteenth Mandates Commission, but only after the commission had considered the relation of this agreement to Article II of the Anglo-Iraq Treaty, assuring economic equality. Dr. Kastl, the

German member on Mandates Commission, submitted a report, and he concluded the extension did not violate the treaty.[38] But M. Palacios, another member of the commission observed:

The Mandates Commission had invariably argued that the markets of the mandated territories must be open as widely as possible to the national of all States and has often asked questions regarding public tenders. A statement of the kind contained in the conclusion under consideration might be just in the present case, but it must not be regarded as a general principle to be followed on every occasion.[39]

III. The Termination of the Mandate

The British proposal and the 1930 treaty. At the sixteenth session, the Mandates Commission was preparing to open its examination of the Iraq Report for 1928 when it received a communication from the British Government dated November 4, 1929, announcing the abandonment of the treaty and of its intention to recommend the admission of Iraq to the League of Nations in 1932.[40] As the commission had not been asked by the council to give an opinion on the treaty, it did not make any observations on the subject. Nevertheless, a long discussion took place on the basic principles of the treaty and several members of the commission expressed concern at the loosening of the ties between the League and the mandated territory and the consequent weakening of the League's supervisory power.[41]

With this announcement, Great Britain became popular in the country and the political parties began to do things and ask for British cooperation.[42] The 1927 treaty found little favor in Iraq; two ministers resigned soon after its publication.[43] Trouble continued largely because of the expectation of speedily realizing the hope of entrance into the League of Nations with a new treaty regulating relations with Great Britain. On November 13, 1929, the Prime Minister of Iraq, Abdul Mushain Beg Al Sadun, committed suicide, saying he could no longer endure his treatment by the people of Iraq.

The nations expect service but the British do not agree to our demands. I have never had sufficient support. The Iraq people, who are demanding independence are in fact weak and very far from independence, yet they have been unable to appreciate advice given by men of honor like myself. They have thought me a traitor to my country.[44]

Negotiations were begun for a new treaty on April 1, 1930. This treaty had for its purpose the definition of Anglo-Iraqi relations after the termination of the mandate.[45] The treaty was signed June 30, 1928, and it was to be for twenty-five years. Provisions were made for each of the powers to have a representative at the court of the other. In case of war against either of the parties, the other will come to his aid in the capacity of an ally. But the peculiar part of the treaty provided Great Britain with air bases and permission to maintain forces in Iraq territory.[46] In place of the tutor and tutored relation, a special alliance was set up, one in which the former tutor remains on the spot in the capacity of a silent partner in the affairs of Iraq rather than as an active participant.[47] The Council of the League of Nations later asked the Mandates Commission to study this treaty mainly because of these provisions just mentioned.

The Mandates Commission and the Iraq special report. The Permanent Mandates Commission was called on to participate in setting precedents regarding the termination of mandates. Therefore, the reports of Iraq for 1928 and 1929 were subject to greater scrutiny by the commission as they became more inquisitive and more sensitive to their responsibility. In its report to the council on the sixteenth session, it warned the British Government that in the future its accredited representative would be expected to answer questions, particularly relating to,

Iraq's ability effectively to govern itself with its relations with states members of the League of Nations, religious liberty and economic equality, and also with the guarantees of the rights of racial and religious minorities.

It was hoped, too, that Great Britain would endeavor in the future to make clear how much of the result was due to British officials in the Iraq government service and how much to the efforts of the Iraq Government itself and it would be well that the extent to which Iraqi officials were dependent upon British support, the efforts made, the opposition encountered and the results achieved in each sphere, the difficulties which had been settled and those which were still to be overcome should be described as far as possible.[48] It was upon this information that the commission proposed to rest its recommendations to the Council of the League as to Iraq's fitness for release from mandatory guidance.

On January 13, 1930, the Council of the League approved a resolution requesting the Mandates Commission to submit any suggestion that would assist the council in coming to a conclusion on the admission of Iraq to the League of Nations.[49] At the nineteenth session of the Mandates Commission (November 4-19, 1930), the report for Iraq was unsatisfactory. M. Rappard made the following comment:

The Permanent Mandates Commission was, in fact, placed in a very difficult position if it were now to be called upon to declare, on the basis of the present report, that Iraq was ready for independence. The mandatory power itself, by the very fact that it had made provision for British advisers to remain in the country after 1932, showed quite clearly that it did not consider that Iraq was ready for full and unfettered independence.[50]

The accredited representative, Major Young, suggested there should be prepared for the commission's use a comprehensive report covering the entire ten years' administration. This would enable the commission to estimate progress in all respects throughout the period.[51]

M. Orts of the Mandates Commission was very critical of the report; also, to him the British representative seemed a little more than a "diplomatic observer." [52] The commission reported to the council that it had not obtained sufficient information to begin to formulate an opinion on the progress achieved by Iraq as a result of eight years under the mandate regime.[53]

Examination of the Special Report on the Progress of Iraq during the period 1920-1931 began on June 18, 1931 by the Mandates Commission.[54] Sir Francis Humphrys, High Commissioner for Iraq, and three other British representatives appeared before the commission.[55]

Humphrys admitted that Iraq was not free from imperfections and probably Iraq could never challenge comparison with the more highly developed and civilized nations of the world. He also claimed from Article I of the Covenant it seemed that the principal qualification for membership of the League was that a state should be "fully self-governing" and should give effective guarantees of its sincere intention to observe international obligations. Therefore, membership should not be restricted to those states only which had attained a specially high level of cultural and political development.⁵⁶ To make himself clearer, Humphrys added:

Nobody would think of excluding a Moth aeroplane from an international exhibition merely because it is not so powerful or so swift as (say) a three-engined Fokker. Both machines serve a useful function in their own spheres and it would be absurd to suggest that the "Moth" should not be allowed to leave the ground merely because it cannot travel so fast or carry so many passengers as a more powerful aeroplane.

Similarly I submit that it would not be right to attempt to argue that Iraq is not fit to function independently merely because the machinery of government there may not run quite so smoothly or so efficiently as in some more advanced or more highly developed State. As my Government has attempted to show in the special report, the Iraqi State, given the support and inspiration of membership of the League, is now fit to stand alone; it is now capable of self-government, indeed for all practical purposes it is already governing itself; it has shown itself jealous of the sanctity of international engagements. I submit that, in those circumstances, there is no longer justification for the continuance of mandatory control, and that to grant Iraq independence and the opportunity for progress and development offered by admission to the League would be in full accord with the spirit of the Covenant and the high ideals with which the founders of the League were inspired.⁵⁷

Mandates Commission's criteria for an independent Iraq. Statements from the mandatory powers, the Covenant of the League, and mandates with treaties accompanying them, gave little clue to the procedure for the termination of a mandate, and the Mandates Commission, realizing this, dealt extensively and thoroughly with the Iraqi conditions. Certain members of the Mandates Commission sought to evade for that body the responsibility of specifying conditions of emancipation from a mandate. This was a political matter and should be dealt with by the council. M. Rappard made the following statement:

Those who denied the Commission's responsibilities implicitly acknowledged that its work was in vain. The Council of the League had a political responsibility but, if the Commission, after a profound study of the question, stated that the Council could proceed without demur, it assumed in so doing full and complete responsibility for its advice. It should not attempt to shirk this, but should make its opinion to the Council as authoritative as possible. It was tantamount to suicide if it refused to give a decision on the question whether Iraq could be granted self-government without risk to the rest of the world.[58]

The number of petitions which had reached the commission at this time from the Kurds and non-Moslem minorities impressed them with the apprehension felt by the petitioners in view of the prospective termination of the mandate. The future welfare of the minorities troubled the commission most.[59] High Commissioner Humphrys brought needed relief to the commission with a statement concerning tolerance:

Realizing the heavy responsibility which lay on him, he could assure the Commission that, in his thirty years' experience of Mohammedan countries, he had never found such tolerance of other races and religion as in Iraq. He attributed this partly to the fact that Moslems, Jews and Christians had been used to live amicably together in some villages for centuries. The present rulers of Iraq had, until the last twelve years, formed a minority themselves, and had every reason now to feel sympathy for fellow minorities. One of the chief difficulties in regard to the Assyrians was the constant influx of refugees from Turkey, Prussia, and Persia. If these immigrants had really felt that the Moslems in Iraq were intolerant, it was hardly conceivable that they should come into the country as they did.

His Majesty's Government, he declared, fully realized its responsibility in recommending that Iraq would be admitted to the League, which was, in its view, the only legal way of terminating the mandate. Should Iraq prove herself unworthy of the confidence which had been placed in her, the moral responsibility must rest with His Majesty's Government, which would not attempt to transfer it to the Mandates Commission.[60]

M. Orts, in answer to whose question this statement was made, was greatly pleased with the statement as perhaps the most important that had been made during this examination of the situation in Iraq.[61]

In reply to the suggestion that a representative of the League of Nations should be placed in Iraq to supervise the guarantees to be provided for the minorities, the accredited representative gave the commission the following objections: (1) Iraq would doubtless regard it as a derogation of sovereignty and lack of faith in her ability to implement the guarantees; (2) since the Moslems, Jews, and Christians have lived peaceably together for so long, such a measure would be provocative of the things they proposed to avoid; (3) it would tend to enhance present animosity; (4) it would keep alive the idea of separation; (5) minorities would go to such a representative with imagined grievances as well as real ones.[62]

It was also suggested at this session that a special committee of the Permanent Mandates Commission might be sent to study and report on Iraq conditions before making its decision. Reference was made to the fact that Great Britain's accredited representative had been misled as to the conditions in Palestine in 1929.[63] As a whole, the commission seemed greatly pleased to base its conclusion upon evidence furnished by Great Britain. During this study, M. Rappard went so far as to say that:

The story of Anglo-Iraqi relations in the last ten years was an extremely interesting record of the gradual withdrawal by the mandatory power in successive stages (in 1922, 1926, 1927, and again in 1929) in deference to Iraqi aspirations. It was a very remarkable episode in the history of liberty; and, as the citizen of a small State, he welcomed this unusual instance of voluntary concessions by the stronger to the weaker party.[64]

But it was clear that the majority of the members of the commission did not feel that Iraq had yet reached a degree of maturity for statehood. Yet the report to the council accepted the recommendation of Great Britain for the termination of the mandate. The declaration of High Commissioner Humphrys, as to the continuing responsibility of Great Britain, appears to have been the principal factor influencing the decision.[65]

After much discussion, the commission suggested that the following conditions must be fulfilled before a mandated territory can be released from the mandatory regime—conditions which must apply to the whole of the territory and its population:

The first requirement of a settled government and an administration capable of maintaining the regular operation of essential government service.

The second requirement that the territory concerned must be capable of maintaining its territorial integrity and political independence.

The third requirement that the territory must be able to maintain the public peace throughout the whole territory.

The fourth requirement that the territory must have at its disposal adequate financial resources to provide regularly for normal government requirements.

The fifth requirement that it possess laws and a judicial organization which will afford equal and regular justice to all.[66]

This was the first set of conditions and they deal with the measures of the capacity of a people to govern themselves without external assistance. The second group of guarantees are primarily concerned with the ability of such a people to fulfill their international obligations as a member of the Family of Nations. They are:

1. The effective protection of racial, linguistic, and religious minorities.

2. The privileges and immunities of foreigners (in the Near Eastern territories), including consular jurisdiction and protection as formerly practiced in the Ottoman Empire in virtue of the capitulation and usages, unless any other arrangement on the subject has been previously approved by the Council of the League of Nations in concert with the powers concerned.

3. The interests of foreigners in judicial, civil, and criminal cases, in so far as these interests are not guaranteed by the capitulations.

4. Freedom of conscience and public worship and the free exercise of the religious, educational, and medical activities of religious missions of all denominations, subject to such measures as may be indispensable for the maintenance of public order, morality, and effective administration.

5. The financial obligations regularly assumed by the former mandatory power.

6. Rights of every kind legally acquired under the mandate regime.

7. The maintenance in force for their respective duration and subject to the right of the denunciation by the parties concerned of the international conventions, both general and special, to which, during the mandate, the mandatory power acceded on behalf of the mandated territory.

In addition to the foregoing essential clauses, the Permanent Mandates Commission considered that it would be desirable that the new state, if hitherto subject to the economic equality clause, should consent to secure to all States Members of the League of Nations the most-favored-nation treatment as a transitory measure on condition of reciprocity.[67]

This last requirement can scarcely be supported as a criterion of capacity to exercise sovereignty, especially when the whole world seemed to be placing new emphasis on the value of a national economy.[68]

The Mandates Commission was now occupied with applying these criteria to Iraq. The council also requested the commission to study the 1930 Treaty which, in the opinion of some, was not compatible with Iraq's independence. The commission, after examining the 1930 Treaty, concluded the agreement did not infringe upon the independence of Iraq,[69] although the commission said certain provisions were unusual in treaties of this kind.[70]

Before coming to any decision, the commission had to rely on the reports of Great Britain, and the information received from the accredited representatives.[71] Thus, the only information officially available was British, and some of the members argued that the commission should go no further than a declaration that it could see no reason to oppose the statement of the British Government as to the maturity of Iraq and should not declare its own opinion on this point.[72] The British High Commissioner at the twentieth session of the Mandates Commission made the statement that, should Iraq prove unworthy of the confidence which had been placed in her, the moral responsibility would rest with Great Britain.[73] Had it not been for this declaration, the commission would have been unable to contemplate the termination of a regime which appeared some years ago to be necessary in the interests of all sections of the population.[74]

The application of the criteria. The five test points to the case of Iraq were applied by the commission in the light of the information supplied by the British report and extracted in personal examination from the British representative. To Great Britain the ideal standard of administrative efficiency was not a necessary condition of the termination of the mandatory regime or of the admission of Iraq to the

League of Nations.[75] The commission accepted this view in its application of the five points.

The first requirement was a settled government and an administration capable of maintaining the regular operation of essential governmental services. Since the commission had no information to the contrary, it accepted the assumption.

The second requirement was capability of maintaining territorial integrity and political independence. The commission found that Iraq did not have military forces sufficient to maintain its frontiers and independence, but if released from the mandate it would be protected both by its League membership and its alliance with Britain. On these grounds the commission found Iraq met the second condition. It was a serious problem for Great Britain to be responsible for Iraq's immunity from invasion without any control of her relations with potentially invading nations.[76]

The third point—the territory must be able to maintain internal peace and order. The commission accepted the British assurances in the absence of information to the contrary.

The fourth point was adequate finance. The commission expressed no opinion as Iraq's credit had not yet been tested. On the whole, it found nothing in the information supplied by Britain to cause it to doubt Iraq's ability to provide regularly for normal governmental requirements.

The fifth requirement was laws and judicial organization which would afford equal and regular justice to all. The commission agreed, subject to certain readjustments and improvements, that this point was adequately met.[77]

The commission accepted the British assurances with marked hesitation. In Iraq itself the general feeling of the European communities was that Britain was scuttling out of the mandate too soon. The official reply was repeated, that Iraq was at least as advanced as some states already independent, but Iraq was not yet a homogeneous nation.[78] It seems that some of the members of the Mandates Commission were inclined, on the basis of evidence presented, to disapprove immediate emancipation but were led to acquiesce by the firm stand of Great Britain.[79]

With this uncertainty, it is not surprising that the Mandates Commission should insist on this second group of guarantees by the eman-

cipated state, that it could maintain those conditions whose fulfillment had led to the termination of the mandate.

In the first guarantee concerning the rights of minorities, Great
Britain in its special report suggested the Albanian Declaration as a
model.[80] The Mandates Commission desired a stronger measure, but
Great Britain deprecated any proposal to add further safeguards, and
also opposed every suggestion of a special resident representative of
either Great Britain or the League.[81]

The second guarantee was one safeguarding foreign interests in the
Iraqi courts. There was in existence a judicial agreement of March,
1931, between Iraq and Britain, due to expire on Iraq's entering the
League as an independent state member. This agreement put an end
to special treatment to foreigners in the Iraqi Courts and set up what
was called a uniform system of justice for natives and foreigners alike.
It also provided for nine British judges. The Mandates Commission
felt that the foreign judges selected should not be exclusively of British
nationality. Great Britain was not opposed to the guarantees for the
judicial system but suggested that it might be considered for a transitional period of ten years.[82] Great Britain agreed to the inclusion of
other than British judges in the foreign personnel.[83]

The Mandates Commission recommended to the council that:

Iraq should formally undertake before the Council in accordance
with the resolution of September 4, 1931, to ensure and guarantee
freedom of conscience and public worship, and the free exercise of
the religious, educational and medical activities of religious missions
of all denominations, whatever their nationality, subject to such measures as may be indispensable for the maintenance of morality and
public order.[84]

The remaining guarantees were concerned with the rights and obligations arising under the mandatory, and they were to be assumed by
the new government; this principle had been enunciated by the Council of the League of Nations in 1925.[85]

The commission also recommended that Iraq should make a declaration to the council concerning the financial obligations regularly
assumed on its behalf by Great Britain.[86]

The accredited representative for Great Britain strongly opposed
the condition that Iraq should grant most-favored-nation treatment,
subject to reciprocity, to all States Members of the League for a

transitional period.[87] He said that such a requirement would constitute a derogation from sovereignty, that in its particular economic
position Iraq would benefit little from the reciprocity involved, and
that in any case it should not apply to the special favors granted to
the contiguous territories formerly parts of the Turkish Empire.[88]
The Mandates Commission did not consider this one of the essential
criteria of capacity for independence but it was rather regarded as an
ideal to be pursued in the interests of peace.[89]

The council of January 28, 1932 agreed to the admission of Iraq
provided she gave a declaration guaranteeing minority rights, administration of justice, international law and other safeguards.[90] Iraq
signed this declaration May 30, 1932,[91] and the following October 3,
1932, was admitted to the League of Nations.[92]

Conclusion

Within the period between 1922 and the entrance of Iraq into the
League of Nations, October 3, 1932, two major problems faced Iraq.
One was the application of the documents of the political and social
institutions outlined in them, and the second problem was the termination of the mandate which, in spite of its partial dependence on the
successful solution of the first problem, continued to be demanded by
the majority of Iraqis on the basis of right rather than capacity.[93]
But despite this fact, it was said Iraq's oil reserves were not what they
were estimated and this was given as one reason why Britain desired
to surrender Iraq.[94] It may be further stated that foreign control of
the oil fields was safeguarded by a quite separate seventy-five year
contract, which continued in force whatever the political relations
between the two governments were.[95]

The British request for the termination of the mandate for Iraq
put squarely before the League the problem of improving machinery
which Article 22 had failed to supply. The Permanent Mandates
Commission in its important role as adviser to the council had to
assume the major responsibility for the procedure in the termination
of a mandate. At first the commission seemed more eager to evade
than to meet the responsibility.[96] Of course, the ultimate responsibility
rested with the Council of the League, since it is the council which is
specified in the Covenant as the agency of the League in Mandate

matters. However, the council tended to shift the substance of its decision to the Mandates Commission and the commission in turn shifted a large part of the burden back to Great Britain. The statement of the accredited representative, Sir Francis Humphrys, influenced the commission in favor of Iraq independence, for on several occasions it seemed that the whole commission was unconvinced as to the readiness of Iraq for independence.

The real contribution of the commission was the criteria it set up for determining Iraq's capacity for independence. Two distinct types of standards were advanced in determining Iraq's ability to stand alone, the one dealing with what the Mandates Commission called *de facto* conditions. The second standard was certain moral and spiritual qualities which are incapable of objective appraisal and are, therefore, to be tested by the willingness of the people to offer satisfactory guarantees as to their future conduct in matters in which these qualities might prove the determining factors. The former are the measures of past achievement, the latter are the promise of its permanence.

But the Mandates Commission and Great Britain are in substantial agreement as to the essential criteria, a composite list of which includes settled frontiers, a stable government with stable legislature, judicial and administrative systems supported by public opinion, adequate capacity for national defense and the maintenance of public security, an equitable judicial system, adequate financial resources and fiscal machinery, equitable treatment of minorities, and fulfillment of international obligations and responsibilities. Lacking objective evidence of the public spirit behind these *de facto* conditions, both agreed in demanding further guarantees as to the rights of minorities, the rights and interests of foreigners, freedom of conscience, public worship, and missions, the financial obligations and legal rights arising under the mandate regime, the fulfillment of international conventions entered into prior to emancipation. In addition the commission demanded a guarantee of reciprocal most-favored-nation treatment for all members of the League, a demand which Great Britain found inconsistent with full sovereignty.

Both parties recognized the relative nature of the criteria, the Mandates Commission tending to demand a higher level of achievement than did Great Britain. Likewise, Great Britain was less insistent on the guarantees, seeming to find in the record of past achievement more evidence of the intangible factors than did the Mandates Commission. After applying the criteria to Iraq, the Mandates Commission recommended the termination of the mandate to the Council of the League of Nations. In the Fall of 1932, the kingdom of Iraq became a free and Independent State; the event was differently received in different quarters, according to the point of view of the party concerned. For the League of Nations it represented a political triumph; to the Imperialist, a vindication of the British talent for Oriental administration; to the sentimentalist, a rebirth of the ancient land of the patriarch Abraham, Sargon, Nebuchadnezzar and many other famous names to the Arab press and politicians.[97] The *Nation* magazine observed:

> Our enthusiasm for the accomplishment is dimmed, however, by the fact that Iraq is to remain bound to Great Britain under a twenty-five year alliance concluded in June, 1930. It is difficult to see how the League can justify admitting to its membership a state bound by an agreement which makes it a veiled protectorate of Great Britain. Admittedly, a newly established state may legitimately employ foreign expert assistance. But just as the Lytton report suggests that in Manchuria this assistance should be international rather than Japanese in character, so the League should have insisted that any continuing control over Iraq should not remain in the hands of a single power.[98]

It is to England's credit that Iraq, even in its pioneer condition, is accepted in the Near East as a model according to which neighboring and similarly situated states are openly anxious to mould their destinies.[99] But the most important fact was that never before the creation of the League of Nations (Council, the Permanent Mandates, et cetera) did an international body consider deliberately under an established procedure and long in advance the conditions under which a community could be admitted to statehood.[100]

CHAPTER SIX

Palestine

I. The Special Mandate

At San Remo, April 25, 1920, the mandate for Palestine and Trans-Jordan was allotted by the principal allied powers to Great Britain. The draft mandate was submitted by the British Government to the League in December, 1920. Many complications arose. They were due, in part, to the intervention of the United States, which insisted on the provision of adequate guarantees for American interests in Palestine;[1] in part, to the controversies relating to the membership and functions of the proposed International Commission on the Holy Places.[2] A further complication was created by the fact that France was not at all disposed to see the mandate for Palestine approved in advance of her own mandate for Syria.

These difficulties were eventually settled, and the terms of the Palestine mandate were formally approved by the League Council at a meeting in London on July 24, 1922.[3] The mandate became formally operative on September 29, 1923.[4] The territory included in the Palestine mandate comprised some 15,000 square miles, and at the time of the Peace Conference had a population of about one million. Its boundaries enclose the Biblical land of the twelve tribes of Israel from Dan to Beersheba, extending on the south to the old frontier between Turkey and Egypt; on the east to the Syrian desert.

There are many differences between the terms of the Palestine mandate and those of the other mandates. An examination of the mandate reveals that Great Britain has been commissioned by the League to rule in the spirit of the Balfour Declaration of November 2, 1917. The Balfour Declaration reads:

His Majesty's Government views with favor the establishment in Palestine of a National Home for the Jewish People, and will use their

best endeavors to facilitate the achievement of this object, it being
clearly understood that nothing shall be done which may prejudice
the civil and religious rights of existing non-Jewish Communities in
Palestine or the rights and political status enjoyed by Jews in any
other country.[5]

Article 2 of the mandate may be considered the keynote provision,
and it reads:

The Mandatory shall be responsible for placing the country under
such political, administrative, and economic conditions as will secure
the establishment of the Jewish national home, as laid down in the
preamble, and the development of self-governing institutions, and
also for safeguarding the civil and religious rights of all the inhabitants
of Palestine, irrespective of race and religion.[6]

The special recognition given to the Jews, who at that time formed
only 12 per cent of the population, necessitated important changes in
the provisions of the Palestine Mandate. The first article of the mandate gives Great Britain powers of legislation and administration similar to those possessed by B mandatories. Great Britain is charged with
placing the country under such political, administrative, and economic
conditions as will secure the establishment of the Jewish national
home while at the same time safeguarding the civil and religious
rights of the rest of the population of the country.[7] In doing this,
Britain was to ask the advice of a Jewish Agency recognized as a
public body for the purpose of advising and cooperating with the
Administration of Palestine in such economic, social, and other matters as might effect the establishment of the Jewish national home
and the interests of the Jewish population in Palestine.[8] Among other
privileges extended to Jews, as a result of the recognition of the Balfour Declaration by the Council of the League of Nations, are those
provisions that deal with land settlement,[9] Palestinian nationality,[10]
the construction and operation of public works, services, and utilities,
and the development of natural resources,[11] and the recognition of
Hebrew as one of the three official languages of the country.[12]

It has been claimed that the provision favoring the establishment
of a national home for the Jews in Palestine are contrary to the provisions of Article 22 of the Covenant of the League of Nations.[13] But
it has been denied that there is any inconsistency between the settle-

ment of the Jews in Palestine and either the letter or the spirit of
Article 22 merely because the scheme, which may benefit Palestine,
may also benefit one particular people.[14]

The Balfour Declaration and its consequence, the mandate for
Palestine, ushered in a new concept of international law, widening
the scope of the law; in all other cases it was the actual inhabitants of
the countries in question who were dealt with, as being too backward
to govern themselves. Under the Palestine mandate it is the Jewish
people as a whole who are the beneficiaries. The mandate was for an
absent people who are not yet there on the ground, with the existing
populations secondarily guaranteed full liberty and civil rights.[15]
There is no parallel in history to a state undertaking a task of this
kind, not on behalf of its own subjects, but as a trustee for the conscience of the civilized world.[16]

Under any conditions it was a difficult task as the British were to
permit the Jews to build the national home in Palestine and, at the
same time, to protect the rights of the Arabs.[17] In addition to this,
Great Britain exercises a trust on behalf of civilization, which is deeply
concerned in the good government of a country that contains the
Holy Places of three great religions.[18]

But the Palestine mandate was far from being a liability to Great
Britain; there are certain imponderables in evaluating the worth of
the mandated territories. For example, the defense of the Suez Canal
has been simplified by the possession of the mandate.[19]

II. Trans-Jordan

The eastern part of Palestine, lying to the east of the river Jordan,
has been separated from the rest of Palestine and made into the
Emirate of Trans-Jordan. On September 16, 1922, a Memorandum
from the British Government declared by virtue of Article 25 of the
Palestine Mandate that the articles of that mandate relative to the
establishment of a Jewish national home in Palestine would be inap-
plicable to Trans-Jordan. The Council of the League of Nations
agreed to this change at its twenty-first session in 1922.[20] The territory is almost two and one-half times as large as the rest of Palestine.
No census has been taken, but the total population probably lies
between 300,000 and 350,000.[21]

Since there was no Jewish question, Britain agreed to recognize the independence of this Arab state as soon as possible. A treaty was made with Trans-Jordan on February 20, 1928.[22] This treaty provided for a considerable measure of British control, and the reasons were that Trans-Jordan was a highly artificial creation, with no natural frontiers, and that the British wanted to protect the inhabitants from their tyrannical ruler.[23]

The Mandates Commission questioned the procedure of such an agreement without previous assent of the council.[24] According to the opinion of the accredited representatives, the council, by its decision of September 16, 1922, which implemented Article 25 of the Mandate for Palestine, had already approved this step.[25] The Mandates Commission thought that Article 2 of the agreement, which reads,

The powers of legislation and administration entrusted to His Britannic Majesty as Mandatory for Palestine shall be exercised in that part of the area under mandate known as Trans-Jordan by His Highness the Amir.

was inconsistent with Article 1 of the Mandate for Palestine, which provides that the mandatory shall have full power of legislation and administration, save as they be limited by the terms of this mandate.[26]

The Council of the League considered itself responsible for the application of the mandate, and considered the agreement was in conformity with the mandate.[27]

While Trans-Jordan is governed under a separate administration, the High Commissioner for Palestine is also the High Commissioner for Trans-Jordan.

III. *Placating the Arabs, 1923-1928*

The first report of the British Government on the administration of Palestine was examined in the presence of Sir Herbert Samuel, High Commissioner of the British Government in Palestine, during the fifth session of the Mandates Commission in 1924. Sir Herbert Samuel[28] told of the difficulties encountered by the British Government when endeavoring to establish in Palestine advisory and representative institutions.[29] The commission recorded that the mandate created a conflict of interests between which the balance had to be held.[30] He also furnished explanations with regard to the question of the establishment of a Jewish national home as contemplated by the Palestine mandate. The commission expressed the wish that the Jewish immigration should remain in proportion to the capacity of the economic absorption of the country.[31]

At its seventh session in 1925 the commission was impressed with the broad-minded view presented by Great Britain of the relations between the different racial and religious groups. Regret was expressed that certain elements of the population did not appear to recognize that the essential principles embodied in the mandate provided the only substantial basis for the economic and political development of the country.[32]

While expressing no dissatisfaction with Great Britain's report to its eleventh session, the commission desired to find in its next report more details as to the development of the self-governing institutions provided for in Article 2 of the mandate. It also expressed a wish for additional information with regard to the judicial system, conditions of labor, public health, and finance.[33]

The period from 1923-1928 has been called the period of appeasement.[34] The policy of concession under the two successive High Commissioners, Sir Herbert Samuel and Lord Plumer, went forward. In 1926, the British armed forces in Palestine were reduced to one squadron of the Royal Air Force and two companies of armoured cars. But the Mandates Commission called Great Britain's attention to the danger of not maintaining adequate local forces.[35] Opposition to the national home seemed to be dying. The situation changed in 1928; Arab nationalist sentiment rose in the Middle East, and on the Jewish side the national home began to grow.

IV. Wailing Wall and the 1929 Disturbances

The period of placating the Arabs ended with the Wailing Wall incident of September 24, 1928. The Wailing Wall at Jerusalem represents holy ground for Jews and Moslems alike—the Jews pray at one end because it formed part of the western wall of the Temple; the Arabs venerate the other because it is the part of the Haram-al-Sharif where El Burak, the winged horse of the Prophet, was tethered in the night of his traveling. Under Turkish rule the Jews had established a certain limited right of access, and the Palestine

Government maintained the same right. In preparation for the Day of Atonement, the Jews set up a screen on the pavement to separate the men from the women in accordance with orthodox Jewish ritual. The Arabs complained that the Jews were attempting bit by bit to extend the bounds of the limited right, and their complaints caused the police to remove it. The act of the Day of Atonement engendered high feeling everywhere. On August 15 and 16, 1929, Jewish and Arab demonstrations were held at the Wall; and from August 23 to 29, disturbances broke out all over the country, finally resulting in 133 Jews being killed and 339 wounded, and 116 Arabs were killed.[36] Many of the new settlers knew more than a religious issue was involved if they yielded any privileges, and that the Arabs would follow up their advantage. They knew that a political motive was behind the mask; that the Arabs were really opposed to the Jewish colonization and were exploiting Moslem fanaticism for their own purposes.[37]

The League of Nations Council on September 6, 1929, suggested that if Great Britain could collect the necessary information by March, 1930, an extraordinary session of the Mandates Commission might be held during that month to examine the immediate and remote causes of the Palestine incident, the steps taken to restore order and the measures contemplated to prevent the recurrence of such incidents.[38] On September 14, 1929, the British Colonial Office announced that a commission of enquiry with Sir Walter Shaw as chairman would at once proceed to Palestine to investigate the immediate causes of the disturbances and to make recommendations as to the steps necessary to avoid recurrence.[39]

In November, 1929, the Mandates Commission received a memorandum from the British Government containing a proposal that a special commission should be appointed under the terms of Article 14 of the Palestine Mandate to study, define, and determine finally the rights and claims of Jews and Moslems at the Wailing Wall.[40] To the commission this proposal was a derogation from the terms of Article 14. According to the British proposal, the special commission should be appointed by the president of the council, whereas Article 14 of the mandate stipulates that the special commission for the Holy Places shall be appointed by the British Government with the approval of the council. However, the Mandates Commission expressed its willingness to examine any other proposal submitted, which, without being contrary to the mandate, might settle the differences between Jews and Moslems.[41]

The Council of the League on May 15, 1930, approved the appointment of a three-member commission, and in its report confirmed the status quo.[42] This commission's recommendations were implemented by an order in council, in accordance with which order at the Wall has since been maintained. One of the recommendations of the Shaw Commission provided that a commission should be appointed to determine the rights of both parties at the Wailing Wall.[43]

V. *The Permanent Mandates Commission and the Shaw Commission Report*

The Shaw Commission made its report in March, 1930, and, according to the commission, the fundamental cause of the outbreak was the Arab feeling of animosity and hostility toward the Jews arising from the fear that, by Jewish immigration and land purchase under the Jewish national home project, the Arabs might be deprived of their livelihood and eventually pass under Jewish domination.[44] In the opinion of the Commissioners, the Arab attack was neither provoked, premeditated, nor directed against the British administration.[45] It also exonerated the administration from blame in its handling of the dispute before reinforcements arrived from Egypt and Malta.[46]

Five of the most important recommendations of the Shaw Commission were: (1) that the British Government should issue a clear statement of policy defining the meaning it attached to the passage in the mandate concerning the safeguarding of the rights of non-Jewish communities; (2) that methods of regulating immigration be revised to prevent repetition of the excessive immigration of 1925 and 1926. That non-Jewish interests should be given some voice in the discussion on immigration; (3) that a scientific enquiry should be held into land cultivation and settlement possibilities;[47] (4) that the government should reaffirm the statement it made in 1922 to the effect that the Zionist organization's special position did not entitle it to share in the government of the country; (5) that the government should introduce press legislation enabling them to obtain convictions on articles tending to a breach of peace.[48]

At the Mandates Commission's extraordinary session on the Palestine disturbance in June, 1930, the British Government submitted a special statement with regard to policy, reiterating the intention of Great Britain to fulfill the triple pledge inherent in the mandate, but pointing out the difficulties of promoting self-government in current circumstances.[49] As to the Shaw Report, the Mandates Commission rejected the view that the outbreak was unexpected and unpremeditated, and that it was not directed against British authority. M. van Rees said:

No one would deny that the initial cause of the hostility of the influential Arabs lay in the deep disappointment which they felt upon realizing that their national and political aspirations would not be fulfilled. This fact was recognized in the report on several occasions, and the Arabs themselves made no secret of it. The British Government was held responsible for this disappointment. It was said that the British Government had broken its solemn promises to the Arabs, and that the Zionists, using their influence with the British Government succeeded in obtaining the Balfour Declaration which was an insuperable obstacle to the realization of the national ambitions awakened by and during the war.[50]

The British Government replied that the significant fact remained that during the disturbances no attack was made or attempted on the local representatives of British authority.[51]

M. van Rees also felt it difficult to understand why the Shaw Commission had concluded that there had been no premeditation and no organization by the Arabs in preparing for the disturbances, despite a number of the commission's own observations to which he cited[52] that van Rees considered that these facts were not without importance for anyone who wished to arrive at the unvarnished truth.[53]

Great Britain replied that the opinion of the Shaw Commission was arrived at by an exhaustive inquiry and rigorous cross-examination, in which all the considerations mentioned in subsequent passage of the report were taken into account and that the grounds on which the Mandates Commission differs from the conclusion arrived at are scarcely adequate.[54]

The Mandates Commission considered that the incidents of the Wailing Wall from September, 1928 to August, 1929, contributed largely to the state of mind that led to the outbreak.[55]

The British Government's answer was that the position was complicated by the nonappointment of the Holy Places Commission, a fact for which the British Government accepted no responsibility.[56]

Inadequate armed forces to deal with the outbreak was also charged by the Mandates Commission and it called attention to its recommendations at its ninth session of the danger of excessive reduction of the British forces in Palestine.[57] Great Britain admitted the inadequacy, and pointed out that the Mandates Commission gave no indication that it regarded those forces as inadequate when considering the Palestine Report only a month before the outbreak.[58]

The Mandates Commission also contended that insufficient attention had been paid to the social and economic adaptation of the Arab population to the new conditions due to Jewish immigration. It also argued that more might have been done to bring about that economic fusion of interests which is the best possible means of developing a sense of solidarity and blunting the edge of antagonism.[59]

Great Britain replied that its task was not only to promote conditions securing the establishment of the Jewish national home and the development of self-governing institutions, but that it was also bound to safeguard the civil and religious rights of all the inhabitants of Palestine, irrespective of race or religion. The last obligation was the core of the problem, and its bearing upon the problem of how to execute the other two is largely ignored by the Mandates Commission.[60]

The mandatory was also charged by the Mandates Commission with neglecting agricultural and other development in the interest of the Arabs. The mandatory replied this view implied a fundamental misconception of the British Government's general policy with regard to territories for which it is responsible. This policy, which is justified by long experience, is that such territories must be emancipated as soon as possible from dependence upon grants in and from the British Exchequer; if a territory is to be developed on sound economic lines, it must be developed on a self-supporting basis.[61]

This report was published in London and Geneva on August 25, 1930, together with the British Government's reply.[62] Great Britain stated that the commission scarcely appreciated the complexity of the problem as encountered on the spot, and that its previous comment on British policy could not be said to have foreshadowed these serious charges.[63] Prior to this, the greatest amount of cooperation and mutual confidence had been established between Great Britain and the Mandates Commission, and it was said to be due to the fact that both saw eye to eye with regard to the fundamental issues involved in the Palestine mandate.[64]

In concluding its report, the Mandates Commission declared that if those responsible for the agitation

. . . hoped by its means to secure the triumph of their opposition to the League of Nations as a party to the Mandate, they will find no encouragement from the Mandates Commission.[65]

Probably to atone for the severe criticism of the Mandates Commission, Mr. Henderson, speaking on Palestine before the League Council in September, 1930, stated that the British Government fully appreciated it was the duty of the Permanent Mandates Commission to criticise.[66]

VI. *Report of John Hope Simpson*

As a result of one of the recommendations of the Shaw Commission, Sir John Hope Simpson was appointed in May, 1930 to inquire into land settlement, immigration, and development. The granting of immigration certificates was stopped until Simpson had had an opportunity to make an investigation. This measure was strongly resented in Zionist circles, the Jews appealing to the British Government to reopen the gates of Palestine. Simpson's report was published on October 20, 1930. The estimated cultivable land in Palestine was 6,544,000 duncams (1,638,000 acres, a drop of almost 40 per cent of most previous estimates.[67] The report also said there was not enough cultivable land to give every Arab agricultural family a decent livelihood, and that the government was not in possession of large areas of vacant lands which could be made available for Jewish settlement.[68] Accompanying this report was the government's statement of policy known as the Passfield White Paper which affirmed Great Britain's double obligation to the two groups under the mandate, and accepted the figures of the Simpson Report.[69]

Jewish authorities argued that the White Paper of October, 1930, was inconsistent with the terms of the mandate, and marked the reversal of the policy hitherto followed by Great Britain in regard to the Jewish national home.[70] Attempts at conciliation were made, and in a letter from Prime Minister Ramsay MacDonald to Dr. Weizmann, the President of the Zionist organization and of the Jewish Agency, the White Paper was interpreted in such a way as to completely change the whole situation.[71] With the reverse situation, the President of the Palestine Arab Executive denounced the letter as a breach of faith in which the policy of the White Paper had been thrown over. Many believe it was not enough for the Arabs to be imbued with the desire to drive the tutor out of their country—that was merely destructive—they must demonstrate their powers and their will to construct.[72] Any accurate observer could foresee trouble in the future.

VII. *Increasing Tension*

In 1933, following the German pogrom against the Jews, began another cycle of tension and violence in Palestine. Funds were invested in Palestine by Jews who intended to make their homes there. In October, 1933, there were Arab demonstrations against the British Government for the first time.[73] A vigorous campaign against immigration was launched in the Arab press.[74] The year of 1934 was fairly quiet, and Great Britain drastically cut down the number of Jewish labor immigration permits.[75] In October, 1935, at Jaffa, arms and ammunition were found hidden in a shipment of cement imported from Belgium.[76] Immediately the Arab leaders regarded this as proof that the Jews were secretly arming, and they presented a memorandum to the Administration calling for the establishment of democratic government, for the prohibition of land sales, and for stoppage of Jewish immigration until a competent committee could determine the country's absorptive capacity.

The High Commissioner in December, 1935, proposed a new constitution. It provided for a legislative council with a large unofficial majority. The twenty-eight members were to be made up as follows: five officials, two commercial representatives, eight elected and three nominated Moslems, three elected and four nominated Jews, and one elected and two nominated Christians plus an impartial president from outside Palestine who would neither debate nor vote.[77] The question aroused feeling in England. It was discussed in debates in the House of Lords on February 28, and the House of Commons on March 25, 1936.[78] The plan failed to pass Parliament, and most of the opposition was based on the ground that more time was needed to train both communities in local government.

M. Rappard and Lord Lugard led the criticism against it at the twenty-ninth session of the Permanent Mandates Commission. Lord Lugard said:

That there was a fairly unanimous opinion that the system of secret ballot with a restricted franchise and government by debate and majority vote, which had not proved too successful even in some parts of Europe, were quite unsuited to Oriental people. If, however, the decision to create a legislative council should be irrevocable, he would like to put a further question in reference to the proposed constitution. It was intended that there should be a large unofficial majority over the Government vote, but experience had shown that a majority which was unable to enforce a majority decision and did not control the executive staff was a fertile source of friction.[79]

When Parliament defeated the legislative council plan, the Arabs were convinced that Jewish influence could only be overcome by force. Arab resistance crystallized at a time when a new wave of nationalism swept over the Middle East. Syria and the Lebanese Republic signed treaties with France in which they were soon to become independent.[80] The Italia-Ethiopian War weakened British prestige and Egypt received its independence from Britain in exchange for continued friendship. In the British press it was insinuated that the trouble had been directly fostered by foreign powers.[81]

The trouble broke out again on April 16, 1936, after two Arabs were slain in reprisal for two Jews who were murdered the night before. An Arab Higher Committee was quickly formed; it called and enforced a general strike of all Arabs engaged in labor, transport, and shopkeeping. The strike was to remain in force until the government stopped Jewish immigration.[82] The government failed in an attempt to persuade the Arabs to call off the strike, and announcement of the British Cabinet to appoint a Royal Commission to conduct another investigation made matters worse. Clashes were frequent with the police and the British forces.

On September 6, the British Government announced that it would send strong reinforcements to the country to crush resistance,[83] and late in September with the arrival of twenty thousand British troops, the resistance began to crumble, and the strike was called off on October 12. During the struggle at least one thousand Arabs had been killed, and eighty-two Jews were known to have been killed, and property losses were high.[84]

VIII. Partition and the Royal Commission

The Royal Commission, appointed in May, 1936, with Lord Peel as chairman, departed for Palestine on November 5, 1936. The commission spent over two months in Palestine and issued its report on July 7, 1937. The real aim of the Royal Commission, in addition to investigating the real causes of the disturbance, was to see what could be done to make the mandate work smoothly.[85] The Royal Commission made the customary recommendations that a commission of its nature was supposed to make, but they also announced they had little faith in them. They were quite inadequate for the situation. Of the recommendations, the Royal Commission said:

They are the best palliatives we can devise for the disease from which Palestine is suffering, but they are only palliatives. They might reduce the inflammation and bring down the temperature, but they cannot cure the trouble. The disease is so deep-rooted, that, in our firm conviction, the only hope of a cure lies in a surgical operation.[86]

The commission then suggested a plan of partition in which the territory would be split up into three political units. By this plan the new Arab state would include Trans-Jordan and the largest portion of the present Palestine. The Jews would receive about one-fifth of Palestine. Great Britain's imperial interests would be safeguarded by military agreements permitting her to station armed forces in their territory, to use their ports and communication facilities, and to safeguard the oil pipe line to Haifa. Also Great Britain was to assume a permanent mandate over Jerusalem and Bethlehem, Nazareth, and the Sea of Galilee. For the time being, Great Britain would administer Haifa, Acre, and other centers in the Jewish state which had an important Arab population.

This was indeed a surprise, for it not only meant that the mandate was unworkable, but it also recommended a radical transformation of the existing regime. But in another sense it was not a surprise, for in 1933 the policy of the mandate was considered impracticable by K. Williams in an article in the *Fortnightly* magazine. He said:

The policy of the Palestine Mandate is impracticable. It has failed, and so long as it is persisted in, there will be trouble for Great Britain.[87]

The Mandates Commission agreed to hold an extraordinary session to consider the Royal Commission's report and Great Britain's attitude toward it. The extraordinary session began on July 30, 1937, and the commission was given an entirely new task.[88] There was no longer a question of examining the annual reports of Great Britain and advising the council on all matters relating to the observance of the mandate. The Commission's task was to express a preliminary opinion on the intentions of Great Britain which proposed to the council the termination of the mandate it had been carrying out for fifteen years, and which, in support of this proposal, adduces not so much the attainment of maturity by the ward as the difficulties of guardianship.[89] After the Royal Commission's report, the British Government in an official statement announced that, in its opinion, a plan of partition on the general lines recommended by the commission constituted the best and most hopeful solution of the problem.[90] It is clear that partition negatives the original mandate for all Palestine.[91]

The Mandates Commission's first task was to examine, with assistance of the accredited representatives of Great Britain, the whole of the documentary material submitted to it, and to formulate a perfectly clear opinion on the administration of Palestine under the mandatory regime. The commission's second task was to explore carefully and cautiously the other extraordinary solutions, alien to the mandate pointing out such advantages and drawbacks as it might find them to contain.[92]

M. Ormsby-Gore, former member of the Permanent Mandates Commission, was one of the accredited representatives for Great

Britain. At the first hearing he said, "An endeavor must be made to consider how best to formulate some scheme for the better government of Palestine in accordance with the spirit of the League and the Balfour Declaration." [93]

Therefore, the Mandates Commission confined itself to formulating, in general terms, certain conclusions which, in its view, would constitute the preliminary opinion asked for by the council. Great Britain believed that the aspirations of the Arabs and the Jews in Palestine were constantly growing more irreconcilable, and hoped by petitioning the country in accordance with the general views of the Royal Commission, it would be possible to establish a regime more in accordance with justice and less opposed to the conflicting interests at issue.

The members of the commission were asked to express an opinion on whether it considered the mandate unworkable.[94] M. Palacios and Lord Hailey were the only two members of the commission who thought the mandate was unworkable. M. Palacios said:

As a matter of fact the question under discussion was not whether, in view of the present state of affairs in Palestine the existing mandate was capable of execution and whether it was advantageous or disadvantageous to maintain it; the point to be considered was whether the decision of the mandatory Power was fixed and unalterable. If that were really the case, and so far there had been no doubt on the subject, and if the British Parliament and the Government were agreed as to the impossibility of enforcing the mandate by reason of the essential incompatibility of its terms, the Mandates Commission could only acquiesce in the statements made to it on that first point.[95]

Lord Hailey regarded the mandate as unworkable, not merely because of recent experiences, not merely because there had been riots and disturbances, but because the future political development of the country was essentially and intrinsically impossible on the lines which appeared to be implicit in the mandate.[96]

The seven other members reached the conclusion:

The present mandate became almost unworkable once it was publicly declared to be so by a British Royal Commission speaking with the twofold authority conferred on it by its impartiality and its unanimity, and by the Government of the mandatory Power itself.[97]

The Mandates Commission was also asked to express an opinion on the advantages and drawbacks of the various solutions, modifications of the existing mandate, cantonisation, partition, and any other solution that might be contemplated.[98]

It is interesting to note that not a single member of the Mandates Commission expressed approval of the partition plan suggested by the Royal Commission.[99]

M. Ort, Chairman of the Mandates Commission, said:

But the Chairman would regard partition as a dangerous solution if it involved, as was proposed in the Royal Commission's report the creation of two States, which would shortly be recognized as completely independent. It would be dangerous, because it would place those two States face to face without any transition period and at a time immediately following on a period of violence preceded by a long record of friction and disagreement, which had left behind a legacy of hatred and resentment.[100]

He also said:

The worst error of all would be to create a Jewish State that could not live, and the worst mistake would be to constitute it in such form that its creation would mark the end of the effects of the Balfour Declaration which was confirmed by the Mandate.[101]

What did the Mandates Commission have to offer since they opposed the immediate creation of two independent states? They favored a more gradual movement, and the commission offered two plans, (1) provisional cantonisation or (2) two mandates. Three pages are devoted to cantonisation in the Royal Commission's report.[102] M. Rappard is the proponent of provisional cantonisation which contemplates a central mandatory government under a mandate involving far-reaching autonomy for both cantons, with ultimate reunion within the territory as the aim of the mandatory.[103] The two mandates plan was proposed by M. Orts and contemplates a mandatory power over Arab and over Jewish territories until they had demonstrated their ability to stand alone. As is the case with the provisional cantonisation project, the aim is not final separation, and Orts thought it safeguarded the future. He stated:

It opened the door to all eventualities, and in particular, to the eventuality that, as time passed and memories faded into oblivion, a rapproachment might be brought about by the growth of a conviction, which was at present lacking, of the community of material and moral interests of both sections of the populations, which undoubtedly existed.[104]

These proposals also had their difficulties but temporary zoning to permit the conditions of reconciliation to strengthen is less objectionable than setting up two quasi-sovereign states. A resolution was passed by the Mandates Commission which agreed in principle to partition, but opposed the immediate creation of two independent states in Palestine. The commission favored a prolongation of the period of political apprenticeship under the mandate.

The Council of the League of Nations decided that the mandate for Palestine remain in force, and this was unanimously adopted by the council on September 16, 1937.[105] Ten days later Lewis Y. Andrews, the British District Commissioner of Galilee, was murdered; the government took firmer steps, but it was apparent that the Arabs were dissatisfied with the partition plan and Arab nationalism could not be wiped out. In the early part of 1938, England announced the appointment of a technical commission, under the chairmanship of J. A. Woodhead, which was to go to Palestine to study and draw up a new and full scheme for partition. The commissioners were to take into account the Royal Commission plan for partition, but were given full liberty to suggest modifications of that plan, and the commission was also to report under no less than ten counts, upon various economic and financial questions involved in partition, such as the apportionment of the public debt and the treatment of industrial and other concessions.[106] This technical body came to the conclusion that it was impracticable to carry out the partition plan.[107] It was said that the technical body was appointed to inquire into certain details with terms of reference which made it impossible for that commission to report on certain matters otherwise than against the scheme of partition.[108] Before this report Great Britain had informed the Mandates Commission that partition was the solution which it considered best and most hopeful.[109]

IX. *The White Paper of 1939*

In the early part of 1939, Great Britain conducted conferences with representatives of Arabs and Jews in London, and the discussions failed to bring about the desired agreement. Was it possible to solve the Palestine problem? Apparently for the present it was not possible to devise any final solution of any kind of the Palestine problem.[110] In May, 1939, the British Government issued a White Paper containing a statement of policy for Palestine. The government accepted what may be called the principle of stages. The main provisions were:

1. The mandate should be brought to an end and Palestine become an independent state after ten years.

2. For the next five years Jewish immigration should be limited to a maximum annual quota of ten thousand with an additional twenty-five thousand refugees who should be admitted as soon as the government was assured that there was a provision for their maintenance, and after five years any further immigration should be subject to Arab agreement.

3. The High Commissioner should have full power of regulating the transfer of land from Arabs to Jews, either by prohibition or restriction of transaction in any areas.

4. Immediate steps should be taken to introduce self-governing institutions, Arabs and Jews being appointed to executive positions in the administration in proportion to their population, which is roughly two to one. And after five years, a conference of the Arabs and Jews should be held under the auspices of the British Administration to lay down the principles of the constitution.[111]

Malcom MacDonald, Secretary of State for the Colonies, appeared before the Mandates Commission at its thirty-sixth session in July, 1937, and informed them that Great Britain considered, on the strength of the opinion expressed by its legal advisers, that, in view of the changed situation, the policy which it proposed to pursue as set forth in the White Paper was in agreement with the mandate itself based on Article 22 of the Covenant and on the Balfour Declaration.[112] M. Orts, Chairman of the Mandates Commission, stressed the principle that no safeguarding clauses of any treaty or constitutional provision would be adequate to afford protection to a minority of an independent country, in which, as in Palestine, a spirit of intolerance reigned.[113] Rappard of the commission condemned the White

Paper because it was contrary to the essential principle often affirmed at Geneva, that the dual obligations of the mandatory in Palestine, to facilitate the establishment of the Jewish national home and to safe-guard the rights of the Arabs in Palestine, were equally important.[114]

While Great Britain professed to be applying the principles of the mandate, it was clear to all that it was seeking to whittle down its obligations in the mandate about the Jewish national home to the barest minimum without the direct repudiation of its trust. In July, 1937, Great Britain adopted enthusiastically the report of the Royal Commission which declared the mandate unworkable, and the White Paper of May, 1939, purported to be a fresh interpretation of the mandate that was no longer allowed to be unworkable. The Mandates Commission said:

In 1937, the United Kingdom Government, feeling itself unable equitably to administer Palestine under the present mandate, believed that the possibility of so doing was to be found in a territorial parti-tion for which no provision was made therein, while today it considers its new policy to be in accordance with the mandate. Does this not show that that instrument had at that time a different meaning in the eyes of the mandatory Power than that which it has today?[115]

There were divergent views among the members of the Mandates Commission; but a majority of the members, four against three, judged that the policy of the White Paper was not in conformity with the terms of the mandate, and that, in particular, the British Government would infringe its obligations in respect to immigration land settle-ment and the establishment of the Jewish national home, if it carried out the new policy. The majority members were Orts, Rappard, Dannevig, and Van Asbeck. The minority consisted of Lord Hankey, the British member, who was sitting on the commission for the first time, M. Giraud and Count De Penha Garcia.[116] However, all the members agreed in thinking that the considerations put forward in the report of the Royal Commission of 1937 and in the preliminary opinion presented by the Mandates Commission in August of the same year have not lost their relevance; the solutions envisaged in these two documents (excluding the setting-up of two independent states withdrawn at the outset from mandatory control) should be borne in mind at the appropriate moment.[117]

The Mandates Commission's report on the White Paper was really an attempt to encourage the British Government to continue its policy of the double trust to the Arabs and Jews. This report was issued in August, 1939, and the Council of the League in September was to have considered the report, but World War II postponed consideration by the council. Bentwich observed:

The Council has been known to modify the advice of the Commission on political grounds; but on this occasion it can hardly brush aside the comments that go to the root of the Mandate trust.[118]

While Great Britain faces a difficult problem in finding a solution for Palestine, the White Paper of 1939 created much opposition from various sources, and it may regretfully be said that the White Paper of 1939 is not a solution.[119] With the outbreak of the war in 1939, Jews and Arabs have been forced to sink their differences with the English. While the importance of the problem has been submerged, for the present, its difficulties must not be forgotten, and it will be a major postwar problem in the Middle East.

X. *Conclusion*

Palestine has been the testing ground for Great Britain's relations with the Permanent Mandates Commission. We cannot ignore the fact that Britain has failed thus far in the very difficult task of reconciling the Arabs and Jews in Palestine. It is also true that in 1930, 1937, and 1939 the Permanent Mandates Commission criticized the British Government rather severely for vagueness of its policy and for its apparent tendency to weaken when the Arabs applied pressure. The Shaw Report of 1930 rejected the view that the outbreak of 1929 was unexpected and unpremeditated, and that it was not directed against British authority. The commission also charged that insufficient attention had been paid to the social and economic adaptation of the Arab population to the new conditions due to Jewish immigration. Great Britain replied that the commission scarcely appreciated the complexity of the problem as encountered on the spot. The government charged that the commission's previous comment on British policy could not have foreshadowed these serious charges.

In 1937, after thoroughly examining the accredited representatives of Great Britain, the commission announced that no advantage would be gained by the creation of two new independent states as recommended by the Royal Commission of 1937. Then, for more than two years Great Britain floundered and vacillated from one position to another, and with the White Paper of May, 1939, came a fresh interpretation of the mandate. The majority of the members of the Mandates Commission said the policy of the White Paper was not in conformity with the terms of the mandate, and that the British Government would infringe its obligations in respect to immigration, land settlement, and the establishment of the Jewish national home if it carried out the new policy. The commission recommended again consideration of its 1937 plan.

It appears that the British Government cannot lightly disregard the comments of the commission as a whole, and of those members who have judged that it is not carrying out fairly its obligations under the mandate. No formula, and it may be no policy, can bring at once peace in Palestine. Essentially, any solution must consider Palestine as a binational country—open continuously to Jewish immigration on the one hand, and affording protection against dispossession of the Arabs on the other. Such a solution would encourage Jews and Arabs to develop self-government in their own areas, and later throughout the country. Under this plan they would be prepared to cooperate in a federal system when the mandate expires. Thus the mandates commission's report on the White Paper of 1939 was designed to reemphasize the binational aspects of the situation. Only by its recognition of the two opposing factions in the population can the British Government be expected to deal fairly with Jews and Arabs alike.

CHAPTER SEVEN

Conclusion

The Peace Conference of 1919 created the mandates to provide a system of enlightened government for the surrendered possessions of Germany and Turkey. By receiving Palestine and Trans-Jordan, Iraq, Tanganyika, the British Cameroons, British Togoland, and Nauru, Great Britain became the largest mandatory power.

Of the general problems affecting the mandated territories of Great Britain, the first real clash came over the petitions and the revised questionnaire and in each case England was afraid the Mandates Commission was attempting to supervise or assume its duties directly.

Nauru, the little island rich with phosphate in the South Pacific Ocean, created two questions. The first was, whether the establishment of a state organization enjoying the sole right of development of the natural resources of a mandated territory was fully in keeping with the disinterested spirit which should characterize the mission of the mandatory. Great Britain pointed out that the exploitation of phosphate in Nauru had always been a monoply. The C mandates, to which category Nauru belongs, do not contain a provision about economic equality.

The second question concerned the execution of the mandate. As the mandate for Nauru was conferred upon the British Empire and as there was no government of the British Empire, an agreement was made between Australia, Great Britain, and New Zealand over the administration of the island. Australia was to administer it for the first five years. The Mandates Commission desired to know if the mandate for Nauru had been transferred to Australia, as the agreement had not been communicated to the Council of the League of Nations. The transfer or termination of a mandate requires the council's confirmation. Later, the commission was informed that Australia,

New Zealand, and Great Britain might be regarded as a trinity in unity, and Australia had been selected by the sections of the mandatory power to govern the island of Nauru. This explanation was accepted, but it did not answer the question whether the A and B mandates similarly assigned to His Britannic Majesty and now administered by Great Britain might be delegated temporarily or permanently to the government of one of the dominions without first obtaining the council's consent.

British Togoland and the British Cameroons under the provision of the mandate can be administered as integral portions of the Gold Coast and Nigeria, the British colonies in the area, but this does not mean that the mandates concerned have become integral portions of the neighboring colonies. The commission has not accused Great Britain of attempting an annexation as a result of this clause in the mandate, but they are aware of the danger of annexation through this provision. On the whole, Great Britain's administration of the Cameroons and Togoland have not called for much adverse criticism from the Mandates Commission. Nevertheless, the commission was aware that the status of Togoland and the Cameroons as mandated territories carried with it certain unmistakable advantages as compared with the ordinary colonial status; witness its guarantee of native rights, of publicity, and the right to petition for ventilating grievances, and its provisions restricting the alienation of native lands and preventing militarization.

Tanganyika has been a very good example for the Mandates Commission in illustrating the difference between a colony or protectorate and mandate. In the political issue of the amalgamation between Tanganyika, Kenya, and Uganda, the commission concluded that amalgamation was incompatible with the terms of the mandate. In other words, a mandated territory cannot be brought into a federation of British possessions.

Probably of greater importance was the idea of the extension of the mandate system to nonmandated territory in the Tanganyika-Kenya boundary conflict over the Masai tribe. This was a noble idea that was later supported by the British Labour Party in a modified form. The Labour Party's proposal was the extension of the mandate system to all colonies which are not self-governing, for certain of its members were convinced that the continuance of international unrest was in part due to the sense of frustration and repression of the "have not" powers. In Germany's demand for the return of her colonies, Tanganyika played an important part, and there can be but little doubt that the League of Nations, through the special efforts of Great Britain and the Mandates Commission, could have offered a peaceful solution.

The greatest achievement in the relations of Great Britain and the Permanent Mandates Commission was the creation of a free and independent Iraq. The real contribution of the commission was the criteria it set up for determining Iraq's capacity for independence, and it is to England's credit that Iraq, even in its pioneer condition, is accepted in the Near East as a model according to which neighboring and similarly situated states are openly anxious to mould their destinies. But the most important fact of this great achievement was that never before the creation of the League of Nations (council, the Permanent Mandates Commission, et cetera) did an international body consider deliberately under an established procedure and long in advance the conditions under which a community could be admitted to statehood.

The greatest difficulties in the relations between Great Britain and the Mandates Commission have come over Palestine, and this is only natural as Palestine has been the most difficult mandate to administer. In 1930, the Mandates Commission investigating the quarrel over the Wailing Wall found that the British Government had failed, because it had not clarified the regulation concerning the Wall. England's proposal of 1937 to solve the quarrel between the Arabs and Jews for the possession of Palestine by dividing it into three parts, with England retaining the central one which included Jerusalem, was not acceptable to the Mandates Commission. The British White Paper of 1939, stating Palestine should become an independent state after ten years, was also not approved by a majority of the commission.

Thus far Great Britain has failed in its very difficult task of reconciling the Arabs and Jews in Palestine, and before the present war desired to abandon the mandate. Thus the Mandates Commission's report on the White Paper of 1939 was designed to reemphasize the binational aspects of the situation. Only by its recognition of the two opposing factions in the population can the British Government be expected to deal fairly with Jews and Arabs alike. At present (1941) the problem is submerged by the war, but it will be a major postwar problem in the Middle East, and the history of the relation of Great Britain with the League council and the Mandates Commission reveals that the international machinery exists for the solution of the problem.

Notes

PREFACE

1 House of Commons, Parliamentary Debates, *Official Report 31st Parliament* (London: His Majesty's Stationery Office, 1920), Vol. 118, Column 2188.

Chapter One: THE MANDATES SYSTEM

1 Ernest C. Fayle, *The Great Settlement* (New York: Duffield, 1915), pp. 165-175.
2 J. A. Hobson, *Towards International Government* (New York: The Macmillan Company, 1915), p. 142.
3 H. N. Brailsford, *The War of Steel and Gold* (London: G. Bell and Sons, Ltd., 1914), pp. 336-338.
4 "General Smuts' Plan for the League of Nations," *The Nation,* 108:225-237, February 8, 1919.
5 *Ibid.,* p. 226.
6 Pitman B. Potter, "Origin of the System of Mandates under the League of Nations," *American Political Science Review,* 16:572, November, 1922.
7 Ray Stannard Baker, *Woodrow Wilson and World Settlement* (Garden City, New York: Doubleday, Page and Company, 1922), I, 227.
8 H. W. V. Temperly, editor, *A History of the Peace Conference of Paris* (published under the auspices of the British Institute of International Affairs; London: Hodder and Stoughton, 1924), VI, 500-501.
9 C. Allen True, "Background and Nature of the League of Nations," *International Institutions and World Peace, Proceedings of the Fourth Annual Conference, Institute of Public Affairs* (auspices Carnegie Endowment for International Peace, S. D. Meyers Jr., Editor,

published for the Institute by the Arnold Foundation; Dallas: Southern Methodist University, 1937), p. 99.

10 Alfred Zimmern, *The League of Nations and the Rule of Law 1918-1935* (London: Macmillan and Company, Ltd., 1936), p. 194.

11 Temperley, *op. cit.*, I, 190-193.

12 Robert Lansing, *The Peace Negotiations, A Personal Narrative* (New York: Houghton Mifflin Company, 1921), pp. 78-86.

13 Baker, *op. cit.*, I, 10.

14 James T. Shotwell, *At the Paris Peace Conference* (New York: The Macmillan Company, 1937), p. 75.

15 Joseph Bucklin Bishop, *Theodore Roosevelt and His Time* (New York: Charles Scribner's Sons, 1920), Vol. I, Chaps. XXXVI-XXXVII, pp. 467-505.

16 W. R. Batsell, *The United States and the System of Mandates* (International Conciliation, No. 213. New York: Carnegie Endowment for International Peace Division of Intercourse and Education, October, 1925), p. 270.

17 Pitman B. Potter, "Origin of the System of Mandates under the League of Nations: Further Notes," *American Political Science Review*, 20:843, November, 1926.

18 Ellery C. Stowell, *Intervention in International Law* (Washington, D. C.: John Byrne and Company, 1921), p. 311.

19 Thomas Baty, "Protectorates and Mandates," *British Yearbook of International Law* (1921-1922) (London: Hodder and Stoughton, 1921), p. 115.

20 J. C. Smuts, "General Smuts's Plan for the League of Nations," *The Nation*, 108:222-223.

21 Temperley, *op. cit.*, VI, 351.

22 Potter, "The Origin of the System of Mandates Under the League of Nations," *American Political Science Review*, 16:566-567, November, 1922.

23 David Hunter Miller, *The Drafting of the Covenant* (New York: G. P. Putnam's Sons, 1928), II, 87.

24 David Hunter Miller, "The Origin of the Mandates System," *Foreign Affairs*, 6:281, January, 1928.

25 Baker, *op. cit.*, I, 265, 424.

26 Smuts, *op. cit.*, p. 227.

27 Ellis C. Howard, *The Origin, Structure and Working of the League of Nations* (New York: Houghton Mifflin Company, 1928), p. 84.

28 Zimmern, *op. cit.*, p. 237.

29   David Hunter Miller, "The Making of the League of Nations," *What Really Happened at Paris* (Edward Mandell House and Charles Seymour, editors; New York: Charles Scribner's Sons, 1921), Chap. XVII, pp. 398-424.

30   Ray Stannard Baker, "War Spoils at Paris," *The New York Times,* May 28, 1922, 7:1.

31   Parker T. Moon, *Imperialism and World Politics* (New York: The Macmillan Company, 1927), p. 479.

32   Lieutenant Colonel Lawrence Martin, *The Treaties of Peace, 1919-1923* (New York: Carnegie Endowment for International Peace, 1924), I, 19-20.

33   Miller, *The Drafting of the Covenant,* I, 105.

34   Miller, *loc. cit.*

35   William E. Rappard, *The Quest for Peace since the World War* (Cambridge, Massachusetts: Harvard University Press, 1940), p. 477.

36   Temperly, *op. cit.,* VI, 501.

37   Potter, "Origin of the System of Mandates under the League of Nations," *American Political Science Review,* 16:572, November, 1922.

38   Aaron M. Margalith, *The International Mandates* (Baltimore: The Johns Hopkins Press, 1930), p. 30.

39   Norman L. Hill, *International Administration* (New York: McGraw-Hill Book Company, 1931), p. 119;

E. L. Mathews, "International Status of the Mandatory of the League of Nations; High Treason against Mandatory Authority," *Journal of Comparative Legislation and International Law,* November, 1924, 6:250.

40   Sir Frederick Lugard in a report in 1923 said, theoretically, a mandate may be revoked. League of Nations, Permanent Mandates Commission, *Minutes of the Third Session.* Held in Geneva, 1923, p. 286;

In 1924, he stated: "The possibility of revocation may be dismissed. Wherever the power of revocation (in consequence of breach of contract by maladministration) may exist, there can be no doubt that in this almost inconceivable contingency the International Court of Justice would be the agency employed and that it would make full provision for all legitimate claims and rights. League of Nations, Permanent Mandates Commission, *Minutes of the Fifth Session* (Extraordinary). Held in Geneva, 1924, p. 177.

41   Norman Bentwich, *The Mandates System* (New York: Longman's Green and Company, 1930), p. 17.

42 Potter, "Origin of the System of Mandates under the League of Nations," *American Political Science Review,* 16:570, November, 1922.

43 Smuts, *op. cit.,* p. 226.

44 *Ibid.,* p. 227.

45 Manley O. Hudson, *International Legislation, 1919-1921* (Washington, D. C.: Carnegie Endowment for International Peace, 1931), I, 1-17.

46 Miller, *The Drafting of the Covenant,* I, 115-116.

47 Fedder Tindall, "Progress on the Gold Coast," *Contemporary Review,* 136:54, July, 1929.

48 Temperly, *op. cit.,* VI, 503.

49 In the discussion as to the partition of the country between France and Great Britain in West Africa, the only point at issue was the assignment of the Cameroons estuary with its port of Duala. At first, Duala was administered by the British, but it was recognized that if France was to administer the bulk of the country she must possess its principal port of entry, and this was agreed to by the British. "New Frontiers in West Africa," *Current History,* 21:485, Part II, No. 3, March, 1920.

50 Sir Eric Drummond, *Ten Years of World Cooperation* (Geneva: League of Nations, Secretariat of the League of Nations, 1930), p. 330.

51 Edward M. House, "The Versailles Peace in Retrospect," *What Really Happened at Paris,* Chap. XVIII, pp. 440-443.

52 Japan objected to the C draft because it omitted guaranties for the open door, thus permitting the British dominion to discriminate with regard to immigration and commerce. League of Nations, Permanent Mandates Commission, *Minutes of the First Session.* Held in Geneva, 1921, p. 47.

53 France objected to the B draft because recruiting of natives for service outside mandated territory was forbidden. Manley Ottmer Hudson, "The Protection of Minorities and Natives in Transferred Territories," *What Really Happened at Paris,* Chap. IX, p. 227.

54 League of Nations, "Council, Eighth Session, Second Meeting," *Official Journal,* 1:317, September, 1920.

55 At the time this report was delivered, all the mandatories were already selected by the Supreme Council and were already administering the respective territories.

56 There were a number of disputes with regard to boundaries of some of the mandated territories even after they were once defined.

The most important was as to the province of Mosul in Mesopotamia. The boundary between the British and Belgian mandate in East Africa and the boundaries between the British and French mandate in West Africa were changed subsequent to their creation.

57 League of Nations, "Council, Tenth Session, Second Meeting," *Official Journal,* 1:31, November-December, 1920.

58 H. A. Gibbons, "The Defects of the System of Mandates," *Annals of the American Academy of Social and Political Science,* 96:85, July, 1921.

59 A. H. Snow, "The Disposition of the German Colonies," *The Nation,* 109:530, October 18, 1919.

60 A committee headed by Lord Milner was appointed to prepare the mandates. See *supra,* p. 19.

61 League of Nations, "Council, Tenth Session, Second Meeting," *Official Journal,* 1:31, November-December, 1920.

62 League of Nations, "The Mandate Question, Letter from the Secretary-General to the Members of the League concerning the Terms of C Mandates," *Official Journal,* 2:84, January-February, 1921;

Margalith, *op. cit.,* p. 86.

63 *Papers Relating to the Foreign Relations of the United States, 1921* (Washington, D. C.: The Department of State, United States Government Printing Office, 1936), I, 89.

64 Henry Harford Cumming, *Franco-British Rivalry in the Post-War Near East* (New York: Oxford University Press, 1938), p. 112.

65 League of Nations, "Letter to the Secretary of State of the United States of America, adopted by the Council on March 1st, 1921," *Official Journal,* 2:142, April, 1921.

66 League of Nations, "Council, Nineteenth Session, Third Meeting," *Official Journal,* 3:793, August, 1922.

67 League of Nations, "Council, Nineteenth Session, Thirteenth Meeting," *Official Journal,* 3:825, August, 1922.

68 Hudson, *op. cit.,* I, 123.

69 "What the Mandates Mean to the Empire," *Literary Digest,* 72:75, March 11, 1922.

70 Albert Viton, *Great Britain, An Empire in Transition* (New York: The John Day Company, 1940), p. 332.

71 Hudson, *op. cit.,* "Covenant of the League of Nations, Article 22, Paragraph 9."

72 Bentwich, *op. cit.,* p. 110.

73 League of Nations, "Council, Eighth Session, Seventh Meeting," *Official Journal,* 8:41, July-August, 1920.

74   *Ibid.,* p. 43.

75   League of Nations, "Council Minutes of the Tenth Session: Annex 119a. Report by M. Hymans, Belgian Representative, on the Question of Mandates," *Official Journal,* 10:23, 191, October, 1920.

76   League of Nations, "Council Minutes of the Eleventh Session, Sixth Meeting," *Official Journal,* 11:5-6, November-December, 1920.

77   League of Nations, "Council Minutes of the Eleventh Session, Sixth Meeting," *Official Journal,* 11:13, November-December, 1920.

78   *Ibid.,* p. 14.

79   League of Nations, Secretariat, *Resolutions Adopted by the Assembly during its first session November 15-December 18, 1920.* (Geneva, 1921), p. 32.

80   League of Nations, "Council, Eleventh Session, Seventh Meeting," *Official Journal,* 11:15, November-December, 1920.

81   League of Nations, "Council, Thirteenth Session, First Meeting," *Official Journal,* 2:644, September, 1921.

82   League of Nations, "Constitution of the Permanent Mandates Commission," *Council Minutes of the Eleventh Session. Held at Geneva, November 14 to December 18, 1920.* Annex 133a, November-December, 1920, pp. 90-91.

83   Foreign Policy Association Information Service, *Functions of the Permanent Mandates Commission,* 3:59, April 27, 1927.

84   League of Nations, "Constitution of the Permanent Mandates Commission," *Council Minutes of the Eleventh Session. Held at Geneva, November 14 to December 18, 1920.* Annex 133a, November-December, 1920.

85   Quincy Wright, *Mandates Under the League of Nations* (Chicago: The University of Chicago Press, 1930), pp. 147-148.

86   League of Nations, "Council Minutes of the Fourteenth Session," *Official Journal,* 2:1124, December, 1921.

87   League of Nations, Permanent Mandates Commission, *Minutes of the First Session. Held in Geneva, 1921,* p. 11.

88   See *infra,* p. 147.

89   League of Nations, "Council, Tenth Session, Second Meeting," *Official Journal,* 1:31, November-December, 1920.

90   League of Nations, "Council Minutes of the Eleventh Session, Sixth Meeting," *Official Journal,* 11:13, 90, November-December, 1920.

91   See *infra,* p. 112.

92 League of Nations, Secretariat, Information Section, *The League of Nations and Mandates.* Geneva, 1924, p. 30.

93 League of Nations, "Council, Twenty-third Session, Fourth Meeting," *Official Journal,* 4:208, March, 1923;
League of Nations, Permanent Mandates Commission, *Minutes of the Second Session.* Held at Geneva, 1922, p. 3.

94 League of Nations, Permanent Mandates Commission, *Minutes of the Fourth Session.* Held at Geneva, 1924, p. 34;
League of Nations, Permanent Mandates Commission, *Minutes of the Fifth Session.* Held at Geneva, 1924, p. 6.

95 League of Nations, Permanent Mandates Commission, *Minutes of the Ninth Session.* Held at Geneva, 1926, p. 7.

96 League of Nations, "Administrative Questions, Mandates," *The Monthly Summary,* 7:294, September, 1927.

97 William E. Rappard, *Uniting Europe* (New Haven: Yale University Press, 1930), pp. 256-257.

98 John H. Harris, "The Mandatory System After Five Years' Working," *Contemporary Review,* 127:171 (1), 177, February, 1925.

99 League of Nations, Permanent Mandates Commission, *Minutes of the Fourth Session.* Held at Geneva, 1924, pp. 158-160;
League of Nations, Permanent Mandates Commission, *Minutes of the Fifth Session (Extraordinary).* Held at Geneva, 1924, p. 149;
League of Nations, Permanent Mandates Commission, *Minutes of the Sixth Session.* Held at Geneva, 1925, p. 5.

100 *Ibid.,* p. 7.

101 League of Nations, Permanent Mandates Commission, *Minutes of the Sixteenth Session.* Held at Geneva, 1929, p. 16.

102 League of Nations, "Administrative Questions, Mandates," *The Monthly Summary,* 8:101, March, 1928.

103 League of Nations, "Council, Fiftieth Session, Ninth Meeting," *Official Journal,* 9:962, July, 1928.

104 League of Nations, Permanent Mandates Commission, *Minutes of the Fifteenth Session.* Held at Geneva, 1929, pp. 11-12.

105 League of Nations, "Administrative Questions, Mandates," *The Monthly Summary,* 10:37, February, 1930.

106 League of Nations, "Administrative Questions, Mandates," *The Monthly Summary,* 10:102, May, 1930.

107 League of Nations, Permanent Mandates Commission, *Minutes of the Twenty-seventh Session.* Held at Geneva, 1935, p. 11.

108 League of Nations, Permanent Mandates Commission, *Minutes of the Twenty-eighth Session.* Held at Geneva, 1935, p. 131.

109 League of Nations, Permanent Mandates Commission, *Minutes of the Twenty-ninth Session.* Held at Geneva, 1936, p. 12.

110 League of Nations, Permanent Mandates Commission, *Minutes of the Thirty-fourth Session.* Held at Geneva, 1938, p. 10.

111 League of Nations, "Administrative Questions, The Council," *The Monthly Summary,* 15:6, January, 1935.

112 Lord Hailey, *An African Survey* (New York: Oxford University Press, 1939).

113 League of Nations, "Administrative Questions. Composition of the Permanent Mandates Commission," *The Monthly Summary,* 16:274, September, 1936.

114 League of Nations, "Council, Ninety-seventh Session, Sixth Meeting," *Official Journal,* 18:329, May-June, 1937.

115 League of Nations, "Council, Hundred and Fifth Session, Third Meeting," *Official Journal,* 20:261, May-June, 1939.

116 League of Nations, Permanent Mandates Commission, *Minutes of the Thirty-fourth Session.* Held at Geneva, 1938, p. 10.

117 William Ernest Hocking, "The Working of the Mandates," *Yale Review,* 19:259, Winter, 1930.

118 William E. Rappard, *International Relations as Viewed from Geneva* (published for the Institute of Politics; New Haven: Yale University Press, 1925), p. 39.

119 Norman Bentwich, "Colonies and Mandates," *Contemporary Review,* 149:43, January, 1936.

120 Walter C. Langsam, *In Quest of Empire* (New York: The Foreign Policy Association, 1939), p. 62.

121 A. B. Keith, "Mandates," *Journal of Comparative Legislation and International Law,* 4:80, February, 1922.

122 Marjorie R. Dilley, *British Policy in Kenya Colony* (New York: Thomas Nelson and Sons, 1937), p. 137.

Chapter Two: GENERAL PROBLEMS AFFECTING THE MANDATED TERRITORIES OF GREAT BRITAIN

1 Lausanne Conference on Near Eastern Affairs 1922-1923, *Records of Proceedings and Draft Terms of Peace.* Presented to Parliament by Command of His Majesty. Command 1814 (London: His Majesty's Stationery Office, 1923), pp. 695-698.

2 Norman Bentwich, "Nationality in Mandated Territories Detached from Turkey," *The British Year Book of International Law,*

1926. (Humphrey Milford, editor; London: Oxford University Press), p. 97.

3 League of Nations, Permanent Mandates Commission, *Minutes of the First Session,* 1921, p. 41.

4 League of Nations, "Council, Fourteenth Session," *Official Journal,* 2:1133, December, 1921.

5 League of Nations, "Nationality of the Inhabitants of B and C Mandated Areas," *Official Journal,* 3:593, Annex 340, June 1922.

6 League of Nations, "Council, Eighteenth Session," *Official Journal,* 3:594, Annex 340, June, 1922.

7 League of Nations, "Council, Eighteenth Session, Second Meeting," *Official Journal,* 3:524, June, 1922.

8 League of Nations, Permanent Mandates Commission, *Minutes of the Second Session,* 1922, p. 87.

9 League of Nations, "Administrative Questions: The Nationality of the Inhabitants of Mandated Territories," *The Monthly Summary,* 2:102, May, 1922.

10 George Grafton Wilson and George Fox Tucker, *International Law* (8th edition; New York: Silver Burdett and Company, 1922), p. 131.

11 League of Nations, "Council, Twenty-fourth Session, Fourteenth Meeting," *Official Journal,* 4:604, June, 1923.

12 League of Nations, Permanent Mandates Commission, *Minutes of the Fifth Session,* 1924, p. 186.

13 League of Nations, "Council, Thirty-second Session, Sixth Meeting," *Official Journal,* 6:134, February, 1925.

14 League of Nations, Permanent Mandates Commission, *Minutes of the Fifteenth Session,* 1929, p. 277.

15 League of Nations, "Council, Forty-ninth Session, First Meeting," *Official Journal,* 9:374, April, 1928.

16 Imperial Conference 1926, *Appendices to the Summary of Proceedings.* Presented to Parliament by Command of His Majesty, November, 1926 (London: His Majesty's Stationery Office, 1927), p. 248.

17 League of Nations, "Letter from the British Government to the Secretary-General of the League," *Official Journal,* 9:1364, September, 1928.

18 Royal Institute of International Affairs, *The Colonial Problem* (New York: Oxford University Press, 1937), p. 90.

19 Quincy Wright, *Mandates Under the League of Nations,* p. 528.

20 Quincy Wright, "Some Recent Cases on the Status of Mandated Areas," *American Journal of International Law,* 20:771, October, 1926.

21 Norman Bentwich, "The Mandate for Palestine," *British Year Book of International Law, 1929* (Humphrey Milford, editor; London: Oxford University Press, 1929), p. 141.

22 Quincy Wright, "Status of the Inhabitants of Mandated Territory," *American Journal of International Law,* 18:315, April, 1924.

23 Quincy Wright, "Sovereignty of the Mandates," *American Journal of International Law,* 17:698, October, 1923.

24 League of Nations, Permanent Mandates Commission, *Minutes of the Third Session,* 3:311-312, 1923.

25 League of Nations, "Council, Twenty-seventh Session, Fourth Meeting," *Official Journal,* 5:336, February, 1924.

26 League of Nations, Permanent Mandates Commission, *Minutes of the Fourth Session,* 1924, p. 140.

27 *Ibid.,* p. 141.

28 *Loc. cit.*

29 League of Nations, "Council, Twenty-seventh Session, Fourth Meeting," *Official Journal,* 5:336, February, 1924.

30 League of Nations, Permanent Mandates Commission, *Minutes of the Fifth Session,* 1924, p. 179.

31 *Ibid.,* p. 176.

32 League of Nations, Permanent Mandates Commission, *Minutes of the Fourth Session,* 1924, p. 146.

33 League of Nations, Permanent Mandates Commission, *Minutes of the Fifth Session,* 1924, 5:178.

34 League of Nations, "Council, Thirty-third Session," *Official Journal,* Annex 731a, 6:501, April, 1925.

35 League of Nations, Permanent Mandates Commission, *Minutes of the Sixth Session,* 1925, 6:156.

36 *Ibid.,* p. 52.

37 *Ibid.,* p. 156.

38 *Ibid.,* p. 52.

39 *Ibid.,* p. 172.

40 League of Nations, "Council, Thirty-fifth Session," *Official Journal,* 6:1511, Annex 800, October, 1925.

41 League of Nations, Permanent Mandates Commission, *Minutes of the Eleventh Session,* 1927, p. 66.

42 Elizabeth Van Maanen-Helmer, *The Mandates System in Relation to Africa and the Pacific Islands* (London: P. S. King and Son, Ltd., 1929), p. 158.

43 See *infra,* p. 263.

44 House of Commons, Parliamentary Debates, *Official Report,* Fifth Series, November 22 - December 15, 1926 (London: His Majesty's Stationery Office, 1927), Vol. 200, Column 2369.

45 League of Nations, Permanent Mandates Commission, *Minutes of the Eleventh Session,* 1927, p. 78.

46 House of Commons, *op. cit.,* Vol. 200 Column 2373.

47 M. O. Hudson, *International Legislation,* I, 89.

48 League of Nations, Permanent Mandates Commission, *Minutes of the Eleventh Session,* 1927, p. 78.

49 Colonial Office, *Report by His Britannic Majesty's Government to the Council of the League of Nations on the Administration of Tanganyika Territory for the Year 1926* (London: His Majesty's Stationery Office, 1927), p. 81.

50 League of Nations, Permanent Mandates Commission, *Minues of the Eleventh Session,* 1927, p. 79.

51 League of Nations, Permanent Mandates Commission, *Minutes of the Twelfth Session,* 1927, p. 63.

52 *Ibid.,* p 67.

53 *Loc. cit.*

54 League of Nations, Permanent Mandates Commission, *Minutes of the Thirteenth Session,* 1928, p. 94.

55 *Ibid.,* p. 95.

56 League of Nations, "Council, Fifth-first Session, Third Meeting," *Official Journal,* 9:1451, October, 1928.

57 League of Nations, Permanent Mandates Commission, *Minutes of the Thirteenth Session,* 1928, p. 95.

58 *Ibid.,* p. 197.

59 League of Nations, Permanent Mandates Commission, *Minutes of the Fifteenth Session,* 1929, p. 14.

60 League of Nations, Permanent Mandates Commission, *Minutes of the Sixteenth Session,* 1929, p. 197.

61 League of Nations, "Council, Fifth-eighth Session," *Official Journal,* 11:140, Annex 1185, February, 1930.

62 League of Nations, "Purchase of Material and Supplies by the Public Authorities of the Territories under A and B Mandates," *Official Journal,* 11:843, July, 1930.

63 *Loc. cit.*

64 League of Nations, "Memorandum regarding the practice of the Iraq Government in placing of Government Contracts." *Official Journal,* 11:1826, December, 1930.

65 *Ibid.,* p. 1827.

66 League of Nations, Permanent Mandates Commission, *Minutes of the Sixteenth Session,* 1929, p. 148.

67 *Ibid.,* p. 149.

68 *Ibid.,* p. 151.

69 League of Nations, Permanent Mandates Commission, *Minutes of the Twenty-second Session,* 1932, p. 125.

70 *Ibid.,* p. 359.

71 *Ibid.,* p. 125.

72 *Ibid.,* p. 359.

73 *Ibid.,* p. 127.

74 *Ibid.,* p. 227.

75 *Ibid.,* p. 227.

76 *Ibid.,* p. 229.

77 *Ibid.,* p. 362.

78 League of Nations, "Council, Seventieth Session, First Meeting," *Official Journal,* 14:189, February, 1933.

79 Oscar Newfang, *World Federation* (Pierre Gault, translator; New York: Barnes and Noble, Inc., 1939), p. 60.

80 Benjamin Gerig, *The Open Door and the Mandates System* (London: George Allen and Unwin, Ltd., 1930), p. 177.

81 League of Nations, "Council, Fifth-first Session, Third Meeting," *Official Journal,* 9:1449, October, 1928.

82 League of Nations, Permanent Mandates Commission, *Minutes of the Fourteenth Session,* 1928, p. 236.

83 League of Nations, Permanent Mandates Commission, *Minutes of the Fifteenth Session,* 1929, p. 275.

84 *Ibid.,* p. 289.

85 League of Nations, "Letter from the British Government," *Official Journal,* 11:390, May, 1930.

86 League of Nations, Permanent Mandates Commission, *Minutes of the Eighteenth Session,* 1930, p. 200.

87 *Ibid.,* p. 177.

88 League of Nations, "Council, Thirty-fifth Session," *Official Journal,* 6:1514, Annex 800a, December, 1925;

League of Nations, "Council, Fifty-first Session, Third Meeting," *Official Journal,* 9:1451, October, 1928;

League of Nations, "Assembly, Sixth Session, Resolutions and Recommendations adopted by the Assembly," *Official Journal,* Special Supplement No. 32, October, 1925, p. 29.

89 League of Nations, Permanent Mandates Commission, *Minutes of the Nineteenth Session,* 1930, p. 12.

90 League of Nations, Permanent Mandates Commission, *Minutes of the Third Session,* 1923, p. 90.

91 *Ibid.,* p. 194.

92 *Ibid.,* p. 171.

93 *Ibid.,* p. 194.

94 *Ibid.,* p. 310.

95 League of Nations, "Council, Twenty-seventh Session," *Official Journal,* 5:391, Annex 289, February, 1924.

96 League of Nations, "Letter from the British Government to the Secretary-General of the League," *Official Journal,* 5:851, June, 1924.

97 League of Nations, "Letter from the British Government to the Secretary-General," *Official Journal,* 7:374, March, 1926.

98 League of Nations, "Council, Thirty-fifth Session," *Official Journal,* 6:1514, Annex 800a, October, 1925.

99 League of Nations, "Council, Thirty-fifth Session, Twelfth Meeting," *Official Journal,* 6:1363, October, 1925.

100 United States Senate, Seventy-fifth Congress, Third Session, *Treaties, Conventions, International Acts, Protocols, and Agreements between United States of America and Other Powers, 1923-1937* (Document No. 134; Washington, D. C.: United States Government Printing Office, 1938), IV, 4235, 4244.

101 Quincy Wright, "Treaties Conferring Rights in Mandated Territories," *American Journal of International Law,* 18:787, October, 1924.

102 League of Nations, Permanent Mandates Commission, *Minutes of the Twelfth Session,* 1927, p. 128.

103 *Ibid.,* p. 30.

104 League of Nations, "Council, Forty-ninth Session, Fourth Meeting," *Official Journal,* 9:400, April, 1928.

105 League of Nations, "Letter from the British Government to the Secretary-General of the League," *Official Journal,* 10:800, May, 1929.

106 League of Nations, "Council, Fifth-first Session, Third Meeting," *Official Journal,* 9:1449, October, 1928.

107 League of Nations, Permanent Mandates Commission, *Minutes of the Fourteenth Session,* 1928, p. 142.

108 Colonial Office, *Report by His Majesty's Government in the United Kingdom of Great Britain and Northern Ireland to the Coun-*

cil of the League of Nations on the Administration of Tanganyika
Territory for the Year 1928 (London: His Majesty's Stationery Office,
1929), pp. 6-7.

109 League of Nations, Permanent Mandates Commission, *Minutes of the Fifteenth Session,* 1929, p. 115.

110 *Ibid.,* p. 210.

111 League of Nations, Permanent Mandates Commission, *Minutes of the Twentieth Session,* 1931, p. 230.

112 League of Nations, Permanent Mandates Commission, *Minutes of the Twenty-second Session,* 1932, p. 313.

113 League of Nations, Permanent Mandates Commission, *Minutes of the Twentieth Session,* 1931, p. 211.

114 League of Nations, Permanent Mandates Commission, *Minutes of the Twenty-third Session,* 1933, p. 189.

115 Manley Ottmer Hudson, *International Legislation,* I, 80.

116 George L. Beer, *African Questions at the Peace Conference* (New York: The Macmillan Company, 1923), p. 272.

117 J. C. Smuts, *War Time Speeches* (New York: George H. Doran Company, 1917), p. 82;

Hudson says: "Natives in the African territories and the Pacific Islands should under no circumstances be armed" for other than police purposes and the defense of the territory, Manley O. Hudson, "League of Nations and the Protection of the Inhabitants of Transferred Territories," *Annals of American Academy of Political and Social Science,* 96:81, July, 1921.

Smuts later wrote: "The black manhood of Africa was involved in the war, either as combatants or as porters and carriers. They shared in and endured all the hardships of the African campaigns, and the rude awakening has opened an entirely new chapter in the history of Africa," J. C. Smuts, *Africa and Some World Problems* (Oxford: The Clarendon Press, 1930), p. 26.

118 David Hunter Miller, *The Drafting of the Covenant,* I, 115.

119 David Lloyd George, *Memoirs of the Peace Conference* (New Haven: Yale University Press, 1939), I, 362.

120 League of Nations, Permanent Mandates Commission, *Minutes of the Third Session,* 1923, p. 1157.

121 Great Britain's report on the Cameroons in 1923 stated: "No military bases have been established or maintained in the mandated territory, but it speaks of an occasion where a political officer in the Dikwa Emirate, while visiting a tribe, was given an escort of one officer and thirty rank and file of the Nigerian Regiment." Colonial

Office, *Report by His Britannic Majesty's Government on the British Mandated Sphere of the Cameroons for the Year 1923* (London: His Majesty's Stationery Office, 1924), p. 7.

122 League of Nations, Permanent Mandates Commission, *Minutes of the Third Session,* 1923, p. 151.

123 *Ibid.,* p. 157.

124 *Ibid.,* pp. 196-197.

125 League of Nations, "Council, Twenty-seventh Session, Fourth Meeting," *Official Journal,* 5:338, February, 1924.

126 *Ibid.,* p. 338.

127 League of Nations, Permanent Mandates Commission, *Minutes of the Fourth Session,* 1924, Annex 7.

128 *Ibid.,* p. 179.

129 *Ibid.,* p. 142.

130 *Loc. cit.*

131 *Ibid.,* p. 183.

132 Article I is as follows: "The High Contracting Parties undertake to apply the following measures for the restriction of the liquor traffic in the territories which are or may be subject to their control throughout the whole of the continent of Africa, with the exception of Algeria, Tunis, Morocco, Libya, and the Union of South Africa.

"The provisions applicable to the continent of Africa shall also apply to the islands lying within one hundred nautical miles of the coast." Raymond L. Buell, *The Native Problem in Africa* (New York: The Macmillan Company, 1928), II, 950.

133 Wright, *Mandates Under the League of Nations,* p. 465.

134 League of Nations, "Council, Nineteenth Session, Third Meeting," *Official Journal,* 3:793, August, 1922.

135 League of Nations, Permanent Mandates Commission, *Minutes of the Third Session,* 1923, p. 257.

136 *Ibid.,* p. 309.

137 League of Nations, Permanent Mandates Commission, *Minutes of the Fourth Session,* 1924, p. 11.

138 League of Nations, "Council, Twenty-seventh Session, Fourth Meeting," *Official Journal,* 5:334, February, 1924.

139 *Ibid.,* p. 334.

140 League of Nations, Permanent Mandates Commission, *Minutes of the Fourth Session,* 1924, p. 156.

141 House of Commons, Parliamentary Debates, *Official Report,* Fifth Series, May 5 - May 23, 1924 (London: His Majesty's Stationery Office, 1924), Vol. 173, Column 465.

142 League of Nations, "Letter from the British Government to the Secretary-General of the League," *Official Journal,* 6:332, March, 1925.

143 League of Nations, Permanent Mandates Commission, *Minutes of the Tenth Session,* 1926, p. 182.

144 League of Nations, "Definition of Terms concerning the Liquor Traffic: Opinions of the Mandatory Powers," *Official Journal,* 9:1956, December, 1928.

145 League of Nations, "Letter from the British Government to the Secretatry-General of the League," *Official Journal,* 8:711, June, 1927.

146 League of Nations, "Council, Fifty-fourth Session, First Meeting," *Official Journal,* 10:508, April, 1929.

147 League of Nations, Permanent Mandates Commission, *Minutes of the Thirteenth Session,* 1928, p. 224.

148 League of Nations, Permanent Mandates Commission, *Minutes of the Fourteenth Session,* 1928, p. 269.

149 League of Nations, "Council, Thirtieth Session," *Official Journal,* 5:1404, Annex 662a, October, 1924.

150 League of Nations, "Council, Fifty-fourth Session," *Official Journal,* 10:571, Annex 1100, April, 1929.

151 League of Nations, "Administrative Questions: General Questions," *The Monthly Summary,* 9:58-59, February, 1929.

152 League of Nations, "Council, Forty-fourth Session, First Meeting," *Official Journal,* 10:506, April, 1929.

153 League of Nations, *Report on the Work of the League Since the Last Session of the Assembly.* Distributed to the Council, the Members of the League, and the Delegates at the Assembly, Geneva, June 1, 1929. Official No. A-6, 1929, p. 56.

154 League of Nations, Permanent Mandates Commission, *Minutes of the Twenty-first Session,* 1931, p. 193.

155 *Ibid.,* p. 192.

156 League of Nations, "Council, Sixty-sixth Session, First Meeting," *Official Journal,* 13:450, March, 1932.

157 John H. Harris, "Britain's Negro Problem," *Atlantic Monthly,* 131:553, April, 1923.

158 See *supra,* p. 32.

159 League of Nations, "Council, Nineteenth Session," *Official Journal,* 3:861, Annex 374c, August, 1922.

160 League of Nations, Permanent Mandates Commission, *Minutes of the Second Session,* 1922, p. 72.

161   Raymond L. Buell, "The Mandates System After Ten Years," *Current History*, 31:549, December, 1929.

162   League of Nations, Permanent Mandates Commission, *Minutes of the Second Session*, 1922, p. 72.

163   League of Nations, "Council, Twenty-first Session, Fifth Meeting," *Official Journal*, 3:1178, November, 1922.

164   League of Nations, "Council, Twenty-sixth Session," *Official Journal*, 4:1410, Annex 551a, November, 1923.

165   *Ibid.*, p. 1273.

166   Walter Fitzgerald, *Africa* (New York: E. P. Dutton and Company, 1933), pp. 247-248.

167   League of Nations, "Council, Eighty-sixth Session, First Meeting," *Official Journal*, 16:595, June, 1935.

168   *Ibid.*, p. 660, Annex 1542.

169   League of Nations, Permanent Mandates Commission, *Minutes of the Twenty-seventh Session*, 1935, p. 225.

170   League of Nations, "Council, Eighty-eighth Session, Third Meeting," *Official Journal*, 16:1148, November, 1935.

171   League of Nations, Permanent Mandates Commission, *Minutes of the Third Session*, 1923, p. 307; *West Africa Reports on the British Sphere of the Cameroons for 1922.* Presented to Parliament by Command of His Majesty, May, 1922. Command 1647 (London: His Majesty's Stationery Office, 1922), p. 11.

172   League of Nations, "Council, Twenty-seventh Session, Fourth Meeting," *Official Journal*, 5:335, February, 1924.

173   *Ibid.*, p. 335.

174   *Loc. cit.*

175   *Ibid.*, p. 336.

176   League of Nations, "Council, Thirtieth Session," *Official Journal*, 5:1399, Annex 662, October, 1924.

177   League of Nations, Permanent Mandates Commission, *Minutes of the Twelfth Session*, 1927, p. 72.

178   *Ibid.*, p. 72.

179   Colonial Office, *Report by His Majesty's Government in the United Kingdom of Great Britain and Northern Ireland to the Council of the League of Nations on the Administration of the Cameroons Under British Mandate for the Year 1930* (London: His Majesty's Stationery Office, 1931), p. 7.

180   League of Nations, Permanent Mandates Commission, *Minutes of the Twenty-second Session*, 1932, p. 164.

181   League of Nations, Permanent Mandates Commission, *Minutes of the Twenty-sixth Session*, 1934, p. 67.

182   League of Nations, Permanent Mandates Commission, *Minutes of the Twenty-eighth Session*, 1935, p. 94.

183   *Ibid.*, p. 166.

184   League of Nations, Permanent Mandates Commission, *Minutes of the Thirty-first Session*, 1937, p. 191.

185   League of Nations, Permanent Mandates Commission, *Minutes of the Thirty-fifth Session*, 1938, p. 135.

186   League of Nations, "Council, Forty-fourth Session," *Official Journal*, 10:575, Annex 1100, April, 1929.

187   *Ibid.*, p. 582.

188   League of Nations, "Frontier between Togoland under British Mandate and Togoland under French Mandate," *Official Journal*, 12:10, January, 1931.

189   League of Nations, Permanent Mandates Commission, *Minutes of the Nineteenth Session*, 1930, p. 41.

190   Derwent Whittlesey, "Reshaping the Map of West Africa," *Geographic Aspects of International Relations* (Charles Colby, editor; Chicago: The University of Chicago Press, 1938), p. 143.

191   League of Nations, "Council, Thirty-seventh Session, Sixth Meeting," *Official Journal*, 6:136, February, 1926.

192   League of Nations, Permanent Mandates Commission, *Minutes of the Sixth Session*, 1925, p. 121.

193   *Loc. cit.*

194   R. L. Buell, *The Native Problem in Africa*, I, 497.

195   League of Nations, Permanent Mandates Commission, *Minutes of the Sixth Session*, 1925, p. 123.

196   *Loc. cit.*

197   Frederick Pollock, *League of Nations* (London: Stevens and Sons, 1920), p. 217;
In 1927, it was also suggested that the European powers accept some sort of special mandate from the League of Nations for the administration of all their tropical possessions of the central area of Africa. Harold G. C. Swayne, "Central Area of Africa and the Mandate Principle," *The Contemporary Review*, 132:468, 1927.

198   League of Nations, Permanent Mandates Commission, *Minutes of the Sixth Session*, 1925, p. 124.

199   *Ibid.*, pp. 123-124.

200   Marjorie R. Dilley, *British Policy in Kenya Colony*, p. 4.

201   League of Nations, "Council, Ninetieth Session," *Official Journal*, 17:167, Annex 1581, February, 1936.

202 League of Nations, "Council, Ninety-ninth Session," *Official Journal*, 18:1083, Annex 1668, December, 1937.

203 League of Nations, Permanent Mandates Commission, *Minutes of the Thirty-first Session*, 1937, p. 189.

204 League of Nations, "Council, Ninety-eighth Session, Second Meeting," *Official Journal*, 18:898, December, 1937.

205 League of Nations, "Council, Sixty-ninth Session, Ninth Meeting," *Official Journal*, 13:1955-1956, December, 1932.

206 S. Whittemore Boggs, *International Boundaries* (New York: Columbia University Press, 1940), p. 140.

207 *Ibid.*, p. vi.

208 E. Van Maanen-Helmer, *The Mandates System in Relation to Africa and the Pacific Islands*, p. 230.

209 League of Nations, Permanent Mandates Commission, *Minutes of the First Session*, 1921, p. 28.

210 *Loc. cit.*

211 League of Nations, "Council, Twenty-first Session," *Official Journal*, 3:1245, Annex 409, November, 1922.

212 League of Nations, Permanent Mandates Commission, *Minutes of the Second Session*, 1922, p. 15.

213 League of Nations, "Council, Twenty-first Session," *Official Journal*, 3:1245, Annex 409, November, 1922.

214 League of Nations, "Council, Twenty-third Session," *Official Journal*, 4:298, Annex 457, March, 1923.

215 *Ibid.*, p. 298.

216 League of Nations, Permanent Mandates Commission, *Minutes of the Fourth Session*, 1924, pp. 178-179.

217 League of Nations, Permanent Mandates Commission, *Minutes of the Fifteenth Session*, 1929, p. 15.

218 League of Nations, "Council, Twenty-third Session," *Official Journal*, 4:299-300, Annex 457, March, 1923.

219 League of Nations, Permanent Mandates Commission, *Minutes of the Fifth Session*, 1924, p. 115.

220 *Ibid.*, p. 116.

221 *Loc. cit.*

222 League of Nations, Permanent Mandates Commission, *Minutes of the Seventh Session*, 1925, p. 130.

223 League of Nations, "Council, Thirty-seventh Session, Sixth Meeting," *Official Journal*, 7:136, February, 1926.

224 League of Nations, Permanent Mandates Commission, *Minutes of the Twelfth Session*, 1927, p. 152.

225 *Ibid.*, pp. 153-154.

226   League of Nations, Permanent Mandates Commission, *Minutes of the Eighth Session,* 1926 (Extraordinary, held at Rome), p. 201.

227   League of Nations, Permanent Mandates Commission, *Minutes of the Fourth Session,* 1924, p. 179.

228   League of Nations, Permanent Mandates Commission, *Minutes of the Seventh Session,* 1925, pp. 219-220.

229   League of Nations, "Council, Thirty-seventh Session," *Official Journal,* 7:270, Annex 826, February, 1926.

230   League of Nations, Permanent Mandates Commission, *Minutes of the Seventh Session,* 1925, p. 181.

231   *Ibid.,* p. 124.

232   *Ibid.,* p. 127.

233   *Ibid.,* p. 128.

234   League of Nations, "Council, Thirty-seventh Session," *Official Journal,* 7:270, Annex 826, February, 1926.

235   League of Nations, Permanent Mandates Commission, *Minutes of the Seventh Session,* 1925, p. 35.

236   League of Nations, Permanent Mandates Commission, *Minutes of the Eighth Session,* 1926 (Held at Rome), p. 159.

237   League of Nations, Permanent Mandates Commission, *Minutes of the Ninth Session,* 1926, p. 47.

238   *Ibid.,* p. 192.

239   *Ibid.,* p. 216.

240   League of Nations, "Council, Forty-first Session, Third Meeting," *Official Journal,* 7:1233, October, 1926.

241   *Ibid.,* p. 1236.

242   League of Nations, "Letter from the British Government to the Secretary-General of the League," *Official Journal,* 7:1651, December, 1926.

During the International Labor Conference of 1929, Great Britain opposed the suggestion that the Committee on Native labor should hear petitions from natives and others in regard to the observance of forced labor. Interference with the internal policy of the government was given as the reason. The German representative said there would be little objection to this committee if it had power similar to the Mandates Commission. Raymond L. Buell, "Forced Labor: Its International Regulation," *Foreign Policy Association,* Information Service, 5:42, January 8, 1930.

243   League of Nations, Permanent Mandates Commission, *Minutes of the Eleventh Session,* 1927, pp. 10-11.

244   Quincy Wright, *Mandates Under the League of Nations,* p. 178.

245   League of Nations, Permanent Mandates Commission, *Minutes of the Fourteenth Session,* 1928, p. 221.

246   *Ibid.,* p. 262.

247   *Ibid.,* p. 263.

248   *Ibid.,* p. 264.

249   League of Nations, "Council, Fifty-fourth Session," *Official Journal,* 10:578, Annex 1100, April, 1929.

250   League of Nations, Permanent Mandates Commission, *Minutes of the Twenty-first Session,* 1931, p. 212.

251   League of Nations, Permanent Mandates Commission, *Minutes of the Twenty-second Session,* 1932, p. 42.

252   League of Nations, Permanent Mandates Commission, *Minutes of the Eleventh Session,* 1927, pp. 10-11.

253   Amendments were suggested at the Second Session; League of Nations, Permanent Mandates Commission, *Minutes of the Second Session,* 1922, p. 64.

254   League of Nations, Permanent Mandates Commission, *Minutes of the First Session,* 1921, pp. 32, 47.

255   League of Nations, Permanent Mandates Commission, *Minutes of the Ninth Session,* 1926, pp. 231-237.

256   *Ibid.,* p. 51.

257   *Ibid.,* pp. 51, 231-237.

258   Van Maanen-Helmer and Margalith think the extreme antagonism to the list of questions was probably due to the fact that the discussion of the list became bound up with the discussion of a request from the commission for the views of the council on the advisability of its hearing petitioners in exceptional cases. Van Maanen-Helmer, *The Mandates System in Relation to Africa and the Pacific Islands,* p. 115;

A. Margalith, *International Mandates,* p. 86.

259   League of Nations, "Council, Forty-first Session, Third Meeting," *Official Journal,* 7:1233, October, 1926.

260   Van Maanen-Helmer, *The Mandates System in Relation to Africa and the Pacific Islands,* p. 114.

261   League of Nations, "Council, Forty-first Session, Third Meeting," *Official Journal,* 7:1236-1237, October, 1926.

262   *Ibid.,* p. 1237.

263   League of Nations, "Letter from the British Government to the Secretary-General of the League," *Official Journal,* 7:1650-1651, December, 1926;

The questionnaire was discussed at the Imperial Conference, 1926; Imperial Conference 1926, *Appendices to the Summary of the Proceedings.* Presented to Parliament by Command of His Majesty, November, 1926, pp. 221-243.

264 Van Maanen-Helmer, *The Mandates System in Relation to Africa and the Pacific Islands,* pp. 119-120.

265 League of Nations, Permanent Mandates Commission, *Minutes of the Eleventh Session,* 1927, p. 200.

266 League of Nations, "Council, Forty-sixth Session, Fourteenth Meeting," *Official Journal,* 8:1119, October, 1927.

267 Wright, *Mandates Under the League of Nations,* pp. 147-149.

268 Van Maanen-Helmer, *The Mandates System in Relation to Africa and the Pacific Islands,* p. 121.

269 L. Stein, "Mandates Commission and the Mandatory Powers," *Contemporary Review,* 131:457, April, 1927.

Chapter Three: NAURU, BRITISH TOGOLAND, AND THE BRITISH CAMEROONS

1 The Parliament of the Commonwealth of Australia 1923 (Second session), *Report on the Administration of Nauru During the Year 1922.* (Prepared by the Administrator for Submission to the League of Nations. Presented by Command. Printed and Published for the Government of the Commonwealth of Australia by Albert J. Mullett, [n. d.]), p. 12.

2 In 1927, Australia announced that it had no intention of transferring the administration of Nauru. League of Nations, Permanent Mandates Commission, *Minutes of the Eleventh Session,* 1927, pp. 18-19.

3 G. H. Blakeslee, "The Mandates of the Pacific," *Foreign Affairs,* 1:113, September, 1922.

4 House of Commons, Parliamentary Debates, *Official Report, Second session of the Thirty-first Parliament* (London: His Majesty's Stationery Office, 1920), Vol. 132, Column 2,461.

5 A. Charteris, "The Mandate over Nauru Island," *British Yearbook of International Law, 1923-1924* (London: Hodder and Stoughton, 1923), p. 147.

6 Delisle Burns, *International Politics* (London: Methuen and Company, Ltd., 1920), p. 62.

7   House of Commons, Parliamentary Debates, *Official Report, Second session of the Thirty-first Parliament* (London: His Majesty's Stationery Office, 1920), Vol. 130, Column 1,323.

8   *Ibid.,* Vol. 130, Columns 1,349-1,350.

9   League of Nations, Permanent Mandates Commission, *Minutes of the Second Session,* 1922, p. 3.

10   *Ibid.,* pp. 56-57.

11   R. L. Buell, "Backward People under the Mandate System," *Current History,* 20:388, June, 1924.

12   Luther H. Evans, "Are C. Mandates Veiled Annexations," *Southwestern Political and Social Science Quarterly,* 7:400, March, 1927.

13   League of Nations, Permanent Mandates Commission, *Minutes of the Second Session,* 1922, p. 46.

14   *Loc. cit.*

15   Charteris, *op. cit.,* p. 146.

16   League of Nations, Permanent Mandates Commission, *Minutes of the Third Session,* 1923, pp. 176-177.

17   League of Nations, Permanent Mandates Commission, *Minutes of the Second Session,* 1922, p. 46.

18   Colonial Office, *Report by His Majesty's Government in the United Kingdom of Great Britain and Northern Ireland to the Council of the League of Nations on the Administration of Togoland under British Mandate for the Year 1933* (London: His Majesty's Stationery Office, 1934), p. 4.

19   "British Togoland," *The Encyclopaedia Britannica,* 14th edition, XXII, 268.

20   E. Van Maanen-Helmer, *The Mandates System in Relation to Africa and the Pacific Islands,* p. 65.

21   Colonial Office, *Report by His Majesty's Government in the United Kingdom of Great Britain and Northern Ireland to the Council of the League of Nations on the Administration of the Cameroons under British Mandate for the Year 1933* (London: His Majesty's Stationery Office, 1934), p. 4.

22   League of Nations, Permanent Mandates Commission, *Minutes of the Sixteenth Session,* 1929, p. 85.

23   "British Cameroons," *The Encyclopaedia Britannica,* 14th edition, IV, 663.

24   Quincy Wright, *Mandates under the League of Nations,* p. 405.

25   Colonial Office, *Report by His Britannic Majesty's Government on the British Sphere of the Mandated Territory of Togoland*

for the Year 1923 (London: His Majesty's Stationery Office, 1924), p. 51.

26   From the 20th of February, 1924, the Cameroons districts became an integral part of the northern provinces of Nigeria under the Cameroons Order of His Majesty in Council dated June 26, 1923. Colonial Office, *Report by his Britannic Majesty's Government on the British Mandated Sphere of the Cameroons for the Year 1923* (London: His Majesty's Stationery Office, 1924), p. 5.

27   Freda White, *Mandates* (London: Jonathan Cape, Ltd., 1926), p. 100.

28   League of Nations, "Council, Nineteenth Session," *Official Journal,* 3:869-871, Annex 374f, August, 1922.

29   League of Nations, "The Covenant of the League of Nations," *Official Journal,* 1:9-10, February, 1920.

30   League of Nations, "Council, Twenty-first Session," *Official Journal,* 3:1269, Annex 412a, November, 1922.

31   League of Nations, "Questions and Suggestions submitted to the Council of the League of Nations by the Permanent Mandates Commission," *Official Journal,* 2:1127, December, 1921.

32   *Ibid.,* p. 1127.

33   See *infra,* p. 227.

34   League of Nations, Permanent Mandates Commission, *Minutes of the Second Session,* 1922, p. 58.

35   League of Nations, "Council, Twenty-first Session," *Official Journal,* 3:1270, Annex 412a, November, 1922.

36   League of Nations, "Council, Thirty-second Session," *Official Journal,* 6:213, Annex 711a, February, 1925.

37   League of Nations, Permanent Mandates Commission, *Minutes of the Fifth Session,* 1924, p. 41.

38   League of Nations, "Council, Thirty-second Session," *Official Journal,* 6:214, Annex 711a, February, 1925.

39   League of Nations, Permanent Mandates Commission, *Minutes of the Fifth Session,* 1924, p. 41.

40   *Ibid.,* p. 190.

41   Van Maanen-Helmer, *op. cit.,* p. 210.

42   League of Nations, Permanent Mandates Commission, *Minutes of the Seventh Session,* 1925, p. 51.

43   League of Nations, Permanent Mandates Commission, *Minutes of the Tenth Session,* 1926, p. 106.

44   *Ibid.,* p. 187.

45   League of Nations, Permanent Mandates Commission, *Minutes of the Sixteenth Session*, 1929, p. 101.

46   *Ibid.*, p. 205.

47   League of Nations, "Letter from the Accredited Representative," *Official Journal*, 11:148, February, 1930.

48   League of Nations, Permanent Mandates Commission, *Minutes of the Nineteenth Session*, 1930, p. 24.

49   *Ibid.*, p. 209.

50   League of Nations, Permanent Mandates Commission, *Minutes of the Sixteenth Session*, 1929, p. 83.

51   League of Nations, Permanent Mandates Commission, *Minutes of the Third Session*, 1922, p. 148.

52   *Ibid.*, p. 154.

53   *Ibid.*, p. 316.

54   House of Commons, Parliamentary Debates, *Official Report, Fifth series, Second Session of the Thirty-fourth Parliament*, Vol. 191, Column 2241.

55   *West Africa Reports on the British Sphere of the Cameroons for 1922*, pp. 52-53.

56   Norman Bentwich, *The Mandates System*, p. 94.

57   George Padmore, *How Britain Rules Africa* (London Wishart Books. Ltd., 1936), p. 67.

58   Colonial Office, *Report by His Britannic Majesty's Government to the Council of the League of Nations on the Administration of the British Cameroons for the Year 1925* (London: His Majesty's Stationery Office, 1926), pp. 3-4.

59   League of Nations, Permanent Mandates Commission, *Minutes of the Fifth Session*, 1924, p. 18.

60   *Ibid.*, p. 19.

61   W. R. Crocker, *Nigeria* (London: George Allen and Unwin, Ltd., 1936), p. 221.

62   Paul S. Reinsch, *Colonial Administration* (New York: The Macmillan Company, 1905), pp. 314-356.

63   F. D. Lugard, *The Dual Mandate in British Tropical Africa* (Third edition; London: William Blackwood and Sons, Ltd., 1926), Chaps. 14-16.

64   Manley O. Hudson, *International Legislation,* I, 69.

65   League of Nations, "Council, Thirtieth Session," *Official Journal*, 5:1404-1405, Annex 662a, October, 1924.

66   League of Nations, Permanent Mandates Commission, *Minutes of the Third Session*, 1922, p. 216.

67   League of Nations, Permanent Mandates Commission, *Minutes of the Fourth Session,* 1924, p. 163.

68   League of Nations, Permanent Mandates Commission, *Minutes of the Third Session,* 1923, p. 220.

69   League of Nations, Permanent Mandates Commission, *Minutes of the Fourth Session,* 1924, p. 164.

70   League of Nations, "Council, Fortieth Session, Second Meeting," *Official Journal,* 7:867, July, 1926.

71   League of Nations, Permanent Mandates Commission, *Minutes of the Fifth Session,* 1924, p. 40.

72   League of Nations, Permanent Mandates Commission, *Minutes of the Third Session,* 1923, p. 153.

73   Colonial Office, *Report by His Britannic Majesty's Government to the Council of the League of Nations on the Administration of the British Cameroons for the Year 1925,* pp. 81-82.

74   Colonial Office, *Report by His Majesty's Government in the United Kingdom of Great Britain and Northern Ireland to the Council of the League of Nations on the Administration of the Cameroons under British Mandate for the Year 1933,* p. 80.

75   Mary Evelyn Townsend, *The Rise and Fall of Germany's Colonial Empire, 1884-1918* (New York: The Macmillan Company, 1930), p. 285.

76   See *supra,* p. 162.

77   League of Nations, Permanent Mandates Commission, *Minutes of the First Session,* 1921, pp. 37, 43.

78   League of Nations, Permanent Mandates Commission, *Minutes of the Sixth Session,* 1925, pp. 18-20;

League of Nations, Permanent Mandates Commission, *Minutes of the Seventh Session,* 1925, p. 154;

League of Nations, Permanent Mandates Commission, *Minutes of the Tenth Session,* 1926, pp. 164-168.

79   *Ibid.,* p. 119.

80   League of Nations, "Council, Twenty-eighth Session, Seventh Meeting," *Official Journal,* 5:534, April, 1924;

League of Nations, "Council, Twenty-ninth Session, Second Meeting," *Official Journal,* 5:909, July, 1924.

81   International Labour Conference, First Discussion, Twelfth Session, Geneva, 1929, "Forced Labour," *Report and Draft Questionnaire* (Geneva: International Labour Office, 1929), p. 3.

82   A. L. Warnshuis, Joseph P. Chamberlain, and Quincy Wright, *The Slavery Convention of Geneva, September 25, 1926,* (Interna-

tional Conciliation No. 236. New York: Carnegie Endowment for International Peace, Division of Intercourse and Education, 1928), pp. 16-17.

83 Lord Hailey, *An African Survey,* p. 628.

84 League of Nations, Permanent Mandates Commission, *Minutes of the Ninth Session,* 1926, p. 217.

85 League of Nations, Permanent Mandates Commission, *Minutes of the Tenth Session,* 1926, p. 187.

86 League of Nations, Permanent Mandates Commission, *Minutes of the Third Session,* 1922, p. 310.

87 League of Nations, Permanent Mandates Commission, *Minutes of the Sixth Session,* 1925, p. 175.

88 Colonial Office, *Report by His Majesty's Government in the United Kingdom and Northern Ireland to the Council of the League of Nations by the Administration of the Cameroons under British Mandate for the Year 1935* (London: His Majesty's Stationery Office, 1935), pp. 66-77.

89 Harry R. Rudin, *The Germans in the Cameroons, 1884-1914* (New Haven: Yale Universtiy Press, 1938), p. 316.

90 League of Nations, Permanent Mandates Commission, *Minutes of the Twelfth Session,* 1927, p. 189.

91 R. L. Buell, "The Mandates System After Ten Years," *Current History,* 31:550, December, 1929.

Chapter Four: TANGANYIKA

1 Colonial Office, *Report by His Majesty's Government in the United Kingdom of Great Britain and Northern Ireland to the Council of the League of Nations on the Administration of Tanganyika Territory for the Year 1933* (London: His Majesty's Stationery Office, 1934), p. 4.

2 "Tanganyika," *The Encyclopaedia Britannica,* 14th edition, V, 21.

3 Manley O. Hudson, *International Legislation,* I, 85.

4 Colonial Office, *Report of His Britannic Majesty's Government on the Mandated Territory of Tanganyika for the Year 1923* (London: His Majesty's Stationery Office, 1924), p. 57.

5 League of Nations, "Council, Twenty-first Session," *Official Journal,* 3:1269, Annex 412a, November, 1922.

6 See *supra,* p. 162.

7   League of Nations, Permanent Mandates Commission, *Minutes of the Sixth Session*, 1925, pp. 124-125.

8   *Ibid.*, p. 1269.

9   Colonial Office, *Report by His Britannic Majesty's Government to the Council of the League of Nations on the Administration of Tanganyika Territory for the Year 1926* (London: His Majesty's Stationery Office, 1927), p. 21.

10   League of Nations, "Council Minutes, Forty-first Session," *Official Journal*, 7:1310, Annex 899, October, 1926.

11   League of Nations, "Council Minutes, Forty-sixth Session," *Official Journal*, 8:1260, Annex 985, October, 1927.

12   Porterage constitutes the most conspicuous form of demand for forced labor, and it will be reduced with the development of motor communication. M. H. Hailey, *An African Survey*, p. 629.

13   Colonial Office, *Report by His Majesty's Government in the United Kingdom of Great Britain and Northern Ireland to the Council of the League of Nations on the Administration of Tanganyika Territory for the Year 1936* (London: His Majesty's Stationery Office, 1937), p. 97.

14   L. P. Mair, *Native Policies in Africa* (London: George Routledge and Sons, 1936), p. 144.

15   Colonial Office, *Report of His Britannic Majesty's Government to the Council of the League of Nations on the Administration of Tanganyika Territory for the Year 1926*, pp. 18-19.

16   Mair, *op. cit.*, p. 149.

17   Colonial Office, *Report of His Majesty's Government in the United Kingdom of Great Britain and Northern Ireland to the Council of the League of Nations on the Administration of Tanganyika Territory for the Year 1931* (London: His Majesty's Stationery Office, 1932), p. 54.

18   League of Nations, Permanent Mandates Commission, *Minutes of the Twenty-second Session*, 1932, p. 367.

19   Colonial Office, *Report of His Majesty's Government in the United Kingdom of Great Britain and Northern Ireland to the Council of the League of Nations on the Administration of Tanganyika Territory for the Year 1932* (London: His Majesty's Stationery Office, 1933), p. 139.

20   League of Nations, Permanent Mandates Commission, *Minutes of the Thirty-fourth Session*, 1938, p. 151.

21   Colonial Office, *Report of His Majesty's Government in the United Kingdom of Great Britain and Northern Ireland to the Council*

of the League of Nations on the Administration of Tanganyika Territory for the Year 1936, p. 81.

League of Nations, Permanent Mandates Commission, *Minutes of the Thirty-first Session*, 1937, pp. 41-46.

22 League of Nations, Council, "One Hundred and Second Session, Third Meeting," *Official Journal*, 19:484, November, 1938.

23 League of Nations, Permanent Mandates Commission, *Minutes of the Thirty-fourth Session*, 1938, p. 229.

24 See *supra*, p. 183.

25 Hudson, *op. cit.*, I, 89.

26 Colonial Office, *Report by His Britannic Majesty's Government on the Mandated Territory of Tanganyika for the Year 1923*, p. 42.

27 See *supra*, pp. 174-175.

28 League of Nations, Permanent Mandates Commission, *Minutes of the Ninth Session*, 1926, p. 151.

29 Colonial Office, *Report by His Britannic Majesty's Government to the Council of the League of Nations on the Administration of the Tanganyika Territory for the Year 1927* (London: His Majesty's Stationery Office, 1928), pp. 69-70.

30 Colonial Office, *Report by His Britannic Majesty's Government to the Council of the League of Nations on the Administration of the Tanganyika Territory for the Year 1928* (London: His Majesty's Stationery Office, 1929), p. 63.

31 League of Nations, Permanent Mandates Commission, *Minutes of the Twenty-second Session*, 1932, p. 157;
Colonial Office, *Report by His Majesty's Government in the United Kingdom of Great Britain and Northern Ireland to the Council of the League of Nations on the Administration of the Tanganyika Territory for the Year 1932*, p. 146.

32 Colonial Office, *Report by Major G. St. J. Orde Browne, Upon Labour in Tanganyika Territory* (London: His Majesty's Stationery Office, 1926), p. 18.

33 Colonial Office, *Report by His Britannic Majesty's Government on the Mandated Territory of Tanganyika for the Year 1923*, pp. 10 and 36.

34 R. L. Buell, *The Native Problem in Africa*, I, 491.

35 *Loc. cit.*

36 League of Nations, Permanent Mandates Commission, *Minutes of the Eleventh Session*, 1927, pp. 64-65.

37 Mair, *op. cit.*, p. 143.

38   Buell, *op. cit.,* I, 510.

39   Mair, *op. cit.,* p. 143.

40   Margery Perham, *Native Administration in Nigeria* (London: Oxford University Press, 1937), p. 346.

41   Colonial Office, *Report by His Britannic Majesty's Government on the Mandated Territory of Tanganyika for the Year 1923,* p. 68.

42   Colonial Office, *Report by His Britannic Majesty's Government to the Council of the League of Nations on the Administration of the Tanganyika Territory for the Year 1926,* p. 95.

43   League of Nations, Permanent Mandates Commission, *Minutes of the Eleventh Session,* 1927, pp. 64-65.

44   *Ibid.,* p. 203.

45   League of Nations, Permanent Mandates Commission, *Minutes of the Thirteenth Session,* 1928, p. 228.

46   Colonial Office, *Report by His Britannic Majesty's Government to the Council of the League of Nations on the Administration of Tanganyika Territory for the Year 1925* (London: His Majesty's Stationery Office, 1926), pp. 6-8.

47   Lord Hailey, *An African Survey,* p. 442.

48   League of Nations, Permanent Mandates Commission, *Minutes of the Eighteenth Session,* 1930, p. 202.

49   John H. Harris, "The Challenge of the Mandates," *The Contemporary Review,* 110:470, April, 1921.

50   League of Nations, "Letter from the Accredited Representative Dated July 11, 1930," *Official Journal,* 11:1373, November, 1930.

51   J. H. Harris, "British Justice and Native Races," *The Contemporary Review,* 126:443, October, 1924.

52   League of Nations, Permanent Mandates Commission, *Minutes of the Eighteenth Session,* 1930, p. 25.

53   Colonial Office, *Report by His Majesty's Government in the United Kingdom of Great Britain and Northern Ireland to the Council of the League of Nations on the Administration of Tanganyika Territory for the Year 1937* (London: His Majesty's Stationery Office, 1938), p. 11.

54   League of Nations, Permanent Mandates Commission, *Minutes of the Thirty-fourth Session,* 1938, p. 229.

55   League of Nations, "Letter from the Accredited Representative, Dated June 30, 1938," *Official Journal,* 19:   , November, 1938.

56   Ifor L. Evans, *The British in Tropical Africa* (Cambridge: University Press, 1927), p. 337.

57 Hudson, *op. cit.,* p. 89.

58 League of Nations, Permanent Mandates Commission, *Minutes of the Twelfth Session,* 1927, p. 168.

59 Colonial Office, *Report by His Britannic Majesty's Government on the Mandated Territory of Tanganyika for the Year 1923,* p. 30.

60 League of Nations, Permanent Mandates Commission, *Minutes of the Sixth Session,* 1925, p. 132.

61 League of Nations, Permanent Mandates Commission, *Minutes of the Fourth Session,* 1924, p. 104.

62 Colonial Office, *Report by His Britannic Majesty's Government to the Council of the League of Nations on the Administration of Tanganyika Territory for the Year 1927,* p. 44.

63 Edward C. Jenkins, "Economic Equality and the Mandates Commission," *Journal of Political Economy,* 37:613, October, 1929.

64 League of Nations, Permanent Mandates Commission, *Minutes of the Ninth Session,* 1926, p. 148.

65 League of Nations, Permanent Mandates Commission, *Minutes of the Twelfth Session,* 1927, p. 67.

66 *Ibid.,* p. 198.

67 League of Nations, Permanent Mandates Commission, *Minutes of the Sixteenth Session,* 1929, p. 194.

68 *Ibid.,* p. 201.

69 Benjamin Gerig, *The Open Door and the Mandates System,* p. 180.

70 League of Nations, "Council, Seventieth Session, First Meeting," *Official Journal,* 14:191, February, 1933.

71 Hudson, *op. cit.,* I, 91.

72 League of Nations, Permanent Mandates Commission, *Minutes of the Twenty-third Session,* 1933, pp. 69-70.

73 *Ibid.,* p. 191.

74 *Ibid.,* p. 180.

75 *Ibid.,* p. 195.

76 League of Nations, Permanent Mandates Commission, *Minutes of the Twenty-fifth Session,* 1934, p. 106.

77 League of Nations, "Council, Eighty-sixth Session," *Official Journal,* 16:666, Annex 1543, June, 1935.

78 League of Nations, Permanent Mandates Commission, *Minutes of the Twenty-fifth Session,* 1934, p. 106.

79 *Loc. cit.*

80   League of Nations, "Council, Ninety-fourth Session," *Official Journal,* 17:1347, Annex 1622, November, 1936.

81   Colonial Office, *Report by His Majesty's Government in the United Kingdom of Great Britain and Northern Ireland to the Council of the League of Nations on the Administration of the Tanganyika Territory for the Year 1936,* p. 153.

82   *Ibid.,* p. 157.

83   League of Nations, Permanent Mandates Commission, *Minutes of the Thirty-first Session,* 1937, p. 17.

84   F. S. Joelson, *The Tanganyika Territory* (New York: D. Appleton and Company, 1921), p. 51.

85   League of Nations, "Council, Fifty-fifth Session," *Official Journal,* 10:1653, Annex 1166, November, 1929.

86   League of Nations, Permanent Mandates Commission, *Minutes of the Fifteenth Session,* 1929, pp. 117, 128.

87   League of Nations, "Council, Fifty-sixth Session, Third Meeting," *Official Journal,* 10:1466, November, 1929.

88   League of Nations, Permanent Mandates Commission, *Minutes of the Twenty-seventh Session,* 1935, p. 136.

89   League of Nations, "Council, Eighty-eighth Session, Third Meeting," *Official Journal,* 16:1146, November, 1935;
League of Nations, Permanent Mandates Commission, *Minutes of the Twenty-seventh Session,* 1935, p. 228.

90   Colonial Office, *Report by His Majesty's Government in the United Kingdom of Great Britain and Northern Ireland to the Council of the League of Nations on the Administration of the Tanganyika Territory for the Year 1937,* p. 193.

91   Buell, *op. cit.,* I, 511.

92   *The London Times,* June 12, 1926, p. 13.

93   House of Commons, Joint Committee on Closer Union in East Africa, *Report Together with the Proceedings of the Committee, October 6, 1931* (London: His Majesty's Stationery Office, 1931), I, 8.

94   *Ibid.,* p. 9.

95   Hailey, *op. cit.,* p. 178.

96   House of Commons, Joint Committee on Closer Union in East Africa, *Report Together with the Proceedings of the Committee, October 6, 1931,* I, 10.

97   R. L. Buell, "Two Lessons in Colonial Rules," *Foreign Affairs,* 7:446, April, 1929.

98   Ralston Hayden, "Plans for the Union of Great Britain's Eastern and Central African Colonies," *Current History,* 29:1024, March, 1929.

99   League of Nations, Permanent Mandates Commission, *Minutes of the Fifteenth Session,* 1929, p. 110.

100   *Ibid.,* p. 105.

101   League of Nations, "Council, Fifty-sixth Session," *Official Journal,* 10:1653, Annex 1166, November, 1929.

102   House of Commons, Joint Committee on Closer Union in East Africa, *Report Together with the Proceedings of the Committee, October 6, 1931,* I, p. 11.

103   League of Nations, Permanent Mandates Commission, *Minutes of the Sixteenth Session,* 1929, p. 176.

104   H. H. Schnee, "Mandates System in Germany's Lost Colonies," *Current History,* 31:78, April, 1930.

105   Colonial Office, *Papers Relating to the Question of Closer Union of Kenya, Uganda, and the Tanganyika Territory* (London: His Majesty's Stationery Office, 1931), p. 115.

106   League of Nations, Permanent Mandates Commission, *Minutes of the Eighteenth Session,* 1929, p. 202.

107   *Ibid.,* p. 21.

108   *Ibid.,* p. 27.

109   League of Nations, "Council, Sixty-second Session," *Official Journal,* 12:454, Annex 1266, February, 1931.

110   League of Nations, Permanent Mandates Commission, *Minutes of the Nineteenth Session,* 1930, p. 150.

111   House of Commons, Joint Committee on Closer Union in East Africa, *Report Together with the Proceedings of the Committee, October 6, 1931,* I, 11.

112   *Ibid.,* I, 156.

113   League of Nations, Permanent Mandates Commission, *Minutes of the Twenty-third Session,* 1933, p. 65.

114   *Ibid.,* p. 65.

115   *Loc. cit.*

116   *Ibid.,* p. 189.

117   *Loc. cit.*

118   *Ibid.,* p. 190.

119   Hudson, *op. cit.,* I, 90.

120   League of Nations, Permanent Mandates Commission, *Minutes of the Third Session,* 1923, p. 141.

121   *Ibid.,* p. 142.

122 *Loc. cit.*

123 *Ibid.,* p. 193.

124 League of Nations, "Council, Thirtieth Session," *Official Journal,* 5:1409, Annex 662a, October, 1924.

125 Elizabeth Van Mannen-Helmer, *The Mandates System in Relation to Africa and the Pacific Islands,* p. 187.

126 League of Nations, Permanent Mandates Commission, *Minutes of the Ninth Session,* 1926, p. 135.

127 K. J. Gallagher, "The Problem of the Former German Colonies," *Current History,* 25:664, February, 1927.

128 League of Nations, Permanent Mandates Commission, *Minutes of the Ninth Session,* 1926, p. 135.

129 *Loc. cit.*

130 League of Nations, Permanent Mandates Commission, *Minutes of the Eleventh Session,* 1927, pp. 66-67.

131 *Ibid.,* p. 65.

132 *Ibid.,* p. 67.

133 League of Nations, "Council, Forty-sixth Session," *Official Journal,* 8:1259, Annex 985, October, 1927.

134 League of Nations, "Letter from the British Government to the Secretary-General of the League," *Official Journal,* 9:329, March, 1928.

135 League of Nations, Permanent Mandates Commission, *Minutes of the Fifth Session,* 1924, p. 9.

136 Hudson, *op. cit.,* I, 8-9.

137 *Ibid.,* I, 92.

138 A. K. Kuhn, "The Mavrommatis Case on Readaption of the Jerusalem Concession," *The American Journal of International Law,* 23:383-387, April, 1928.

139 League of Nations, Permanent Mandates Commission, *Minutes of the Fifth Session,* 1925, p. 9.

140 Permanent Court of International Justice, *The Mavrommatis Palestine Concessions* in Publications, Series A, *Collection of Judgments* (Leyden: A. W. Sijthoff's Publishing Company, 1924), No. 2, p. 29.
In 1925 the Permanent Court of International Justice decided Mavrommatis was not entitled to damages, as it was quite possible for Mavrommatis to carry out his undertakings. Permanent Court of International Justice, *The Mavrommatis Jerusalem Concession* in Publications, Series A, *Collection of Judgments* (Leyden: A. W. Sijthoff's Publishing Company, 1925), No. 5, p. 45.

The third case concerning these concessions came before the court in 1927; Mavrommatis complained of a breach of contract. The court declared it had no jurisdiction, and that Mavrommatis should sue in the courts of Palestine. Permanent Court of International Justice, *Judgment No. 10, Readaptation of the Mavrommatis Jerusalem Concessions* (jurisdiction) in Publications, Series A, *Collection of Judgments* (Leyden: A. W. Sijthoff's Publishing Company, 1931), No. 11, pp. 13-23.

141   League of Nations, Permanent Mandates Commission, *Minutes of the Fifth Session,* 1924, p. 9.

142   League of Nations, Permanent Mandates Commission, *Minutes of the Sixth Session,* 1925, p. 56.

143   John C. Chesham, "Tanganyika and the Mandate," *Fortnightly,* 144:591, November, 1938.

144   G. K. Johnann and H. H. Kraft, *Germany's Colonial Problem* (London: Thorton Butterworth, Ltd., 1937), p. 79.

145   L. S. Amery, *The German Colonial Claim* (New York: Longman's Green and Company, 1940), pp. 106-107.

146   Bryce Wood, *Peaceful Change and the Colonial Problem* (New York: Columbia University Press, 1940), pp. 61-71.

Lucy P. Mair, "Colonial Policy and Peaceful Change," *Peaceful Change* (C. A. W. Manning, editor: New York: The Macmillan Company, 1937), pp. 81-98.

147   Arthur H. Steiner, *Principles and Problems of International Relations* (New York: Harper and Brothers, 1940), p. 160;

Charles Roden Buxton, *The Alternative to War* (London: George Allen and Unwin, Ltd., 1936), pp. 115-132.

Chapter Five: IRAQ

1   Isaiah Bowman, *The New World* (Yonkers-on-Hudson, New York: The World Book Company, 1924), pp. 72ff.

2   Colonial Office, *Review of the Civil Administration of Mesopotamia,* presented to both Houses of Parliament by Command of His Majesty (London: His Majesty's Stationery Office, 1920), p. 74.

3   George C. Buchanan, "Why Do We Remain in Iraq," *Nineteenth Century and After,* 93:765, May, 1923.

4   H. B. Usher, "Mesopotamia's Claim on Britain," *Contemporary Review,* 120:323, September, 1921.

5   Ikbal Ali Shah, "Empire and Mesopotamia," *Contemporary Review,* 119:201, February, 1921.

6   Henry A. Foster, *The Making of Modern Iraq* (Norman: University of Oklahoma Press, 1935), p. 115.

7   Robert Machray, "British Policy in the Middle East," *Fortnightly,* 122:653, November, 1924.

8   E. W. P. Newman, "Middle East Mandates," *Contemporary Review,* 136:707, December, 1929.

9   W. Ormsby-Gore, "Mesopotamia and the Arabs," *Nineteenth Century and After,* 88:238, August, 1920.

10   League of Nations, *The Records of the Second Assembly Plenary Meetings* (September 5 to October 5, 1921). Held at Geneva, 1921, p. 115.

11   League of Nations, Treaty Series, *Publication of Treaties and International Engagements Registered with the Secretariat of the League of Nations,* 1925, pp. 14-18.

12   Gertrude L. Bell, *The Letters of Gertrude Bell* (New York: H. Liveright, n.d.), I, 536.

13   H. E. Wortham, "Europe Versus Asia," *Atlantic Monthly,* 131:556-564, April, 1923.

14   League of Nations, Permanent Mandates Commission, *Minutes of the Seventh Session,* 1925, pp. 94-95.

15   League of Nations, Treaty Series, *Publication of Treaties and International Engagements Registered with the Secretariat of the League of Nations,* 1925, pp. 14-18.

16   *Loc. cit.*

17   House of Commons, Parliamentary Debates, *Official Report, Thirty-third Parliament* (London: His Majesty's Stationery Office, 1924), Vol. 176, Column 869.

18   League of Nations, "Council, Twenty-ninth Session, Sixth Meeting," *Official Journal,* 5:923, July, 1924.

19   League of Nations, "Council, Thirtieth Session, Fourteenth Meeting," *Official Journal,* 5:1346-1347, October, 1924.

20   Quincy Wright, "The Government of Iraq," *The American Political Science Review,* 20:769, November, 1926.

21   Richard Coke, "The Newest Constitution in an Ancient Land," *Current History,* 21:241-246, November, 1924.

22   Samuel Henry Slater, "Iraq," *The Nineteenth Century and After,* 99:494, April, 1926.

23   League of Nations, "Council, Fourteenth Session," *Official Journal,* 2:1125, December, 1921.

24   League of Nations, "Note by the Secretary-General," *Official*

Journal, 4:1217, October, 1923. (Reports for the period October, 1920, and March, 1922).

25   League of Nations, "Council, Twenty-third Session, Second Meeting," *Official Journal,* 4:201, March, 1923.

26   P. E. Corbett, "What is the League of Nations?" *The British Yearbook of International Law, 1924* (Humphrey Milford, editor; London: Oxford University Press, 1924), pp. 130-131.

27   League of Nations, Permanent Mandates Commission, *Minutes of the Seventh Session,* 1925, p. 212.

28   League of Nations, "Council, Thirty-seventh Session, Fifteenth Meeting," *Official Journal,* 7:191-193, February, 1926.

29   League of Nations, "Council, Thirty-ninth Session," *Official Journal,* 7:552, Annex 845c, April, 1926.

30   E. P. MacCallum and E. M. Earle, "Trustee or Exploitation," *Asia,* 26:795, September, 1926.

31   Quincy Wright, "The Mosul Dispute," *The American Journal of International Law,* 20:453, October, 1926.

32   Andrew Ryan, "Model Mandate," *Fortnightly,* 125:588, May, 1926.

33   Foster, *op. cit.,* p. 272.

34   Wilbur W. White, *The Process of Change in the Ottoman Empire* (Chicago: The University of Chicago Press, 1937), p. 204.

35   Foreign Policy Association, "Political and Economic Trends in the Near East, 1927," *Information Service,* 3:434, March, 1928.

36   League of Nations, Permanent Mandates Commission, *Minutes of the Tenth Session,* 1926, pp. 50, 183.

37   League of Nations, Permanent Mandates Commission, *Minutes of the Twelfth Session,* 1927, p. 200.

38   League of Nations, Permanent Mandates Commission, *Minutes of the Fourteenth Session,* 1928, p. 247.

39   *Ibid.,* p. 214.

40   League of Nations, Permanent Mandates Commission, *Minutes of the Sixteenth Session,* 1929, p. 203.

41   League of Nations, "Council, Thirty-fourth Session, First Meeting," *Official Journal,* 10:506, April, 1929.

42   George Glasgow, "Independent Iraq," *Contemporary Review,* 137:252, February, 1930.

43   Foreign Policy Association, "Iraq and the British Treaties," *Information Service,* 6:242, August 20, 1930.

44   Albert Howe Lyber, "The Near and Middle East," *Current History,* 31:813, January, 1930.

45   Luther H. Evans, "The Emancipation of Iraq from the Mandates System," *The American Political Science Review,* 26:1033, December, 1932.

46   Foreign Policy Association, "Iraq and the British Treaties," *Information Service,* 2:244-246, August, 1930.

47   D. W. Wainhouse, "Iraq: A British Preserve," *Nation,* 132: 28, January, 1931.

48   League of Nations, Permanent Mandates Commission, *Minutes of the Sixteenth Session,* 1929, p. 204.

49   League of Nations, "Council, Forty-eighth Session, Second Meeting," *Official Journal,* 11:74-75, February, 1930.

50   League of Nations, Permanent Mandates Commission, *Minutes of the Nineteenth Session,* 1930, p. 83.

51   *Ibid.,* p. 85.

52   *Ibid.,* p. 84.

53   *Ibid.,* p. 207.

54   Colonial Office, *Special Report by His Majesty's Government in the United Kingdom of Great Britain and Northern Ireland to the Council of the League of Nations on the Progress of Iraq During the Period 1920-1931* (London: His Majesty's Stationery Office, 1931). 250 pp.

55   League of Nations, Permanent Mandates Commission, *Minutes of the Twentieth Session,* 1931, p. 117.

56   *Ibid.,* p. 124.

57   *Loc. cit.*

58   *Ibid., p,* 116.

59   *Ibid.,* p. 134.

60   *Ibid.,* p. 134.

61   *Loc. cit.*

62   *Ibid.,* p. 140.

63   League of Nations, Permanent Mandates Commission, *Minutes of the Seventeenth Session,* 1930, p. 44.

64   League of Nations, Permanent Mandates Commission, *Minutes of the Twentieth Session,* 1931, p. 131.

65   *Ibid.,* p. 134.

For High Commissioner Humphry's declaration, see *supra,* p. 253.

66   League of Nations, Permanent Mandates Commission, *Minutes of the Twentieth Session,* 1931, p. 229.

67   *Ibid.,* p. 229.

68   Walter H. Ritsher, *Criteria of Capacity for Independence* (Jerusalem: Syrian Orphanage Press, 1934), p. 130.

69 League of Nations, Permanent Mandates Commission, *Minutes of the Twenty-first Session*, 1931, p. 225.

70 L. H. Evans, "General Principles Governing the Termination of a Mandate," *American Journal of International Law*, 20:735, October, 1932.

71 League of Nations, Permanent Mandates Commission, *Minutes of the Twenty-first Session*, 1931, p. 221.

72 League of Nations, Permanent Mandates Commission, *Minutes of the Twentieth Session*, 1931, p. 116.

73 *Ibid.*, p. 134.

74 League of Nations, Permanent Mandates Commission, *Minutes of the Twenty-first Session*, 1931, p. 222.

75 League of Nations, Permanent Mandates Commission, *Minutes of the Twentieth Session*, p. 124.

76 Ghafir, "Great Britain and Iraq," *Contemporary Review*, 139:742-749, June, 1931.

77 League of Nations, Permanent Mandates Commission, *Minutes of the Twentieth Session*, 1931, p. 229.

78 Ernest Main, *Iraq from Mandate to Independence* (London: George Allen and Unwin, Ltd., 1935), p. 107.

79 Ritsher, *op. cit.*, p. 34.

80 League of Nations, Permanent Mandates Commission, *Minutes of the Twenty-first Session*, 1931, pp. 114-115.

81 *Ibid.*, p. 115.

82 *Ibid.*, pp. 205-207.

83 *Ibid.*, p. 110.

84 *Ibid.*, p. 224.

85 League of Nations, "Council, Thirty-fifth Session, Twelfth Meeting," *Official Journal*, 6:1363.

86 League of Nations, Permanent Mandates Commission, *Minutes of the Twenty-first Session*, 1931, p. 224.

87 *Loc. cit.*

88 *Ibid.*, p. 118.

89 *Ibid.*, pp. 118-119.

90 League of Nations, "Council, Sixty-seventh Session," *Official Journal*, Annex 1373, 13:1342, July, 1932.

91 League of Nations, "Note by Secretary General of the League of Nations," *Official Journal*, 13:1483, August, 1932.

92 League of Nations, Permanent Mandates Commission, *Minutes of the Twenty-second Session*, 1932, p. 37.

93   Philip W. Ireland, *Iraq* (New York: The Macmillan Company, 1938), p. 419.

94   R. Lewisohn, "Britain in Iraq, Why England is Surrendering Her Mandate," *Living Age,* 337:668, February 1, 1930.

95   "Will Iraq Go Free?" *New Republic,* 63:304, July 30, 1930.

96   Rupert Emerson, "Iraq: The End of a Mandate," *Foreign Affairs,* 11:355, January, 1933.

97   Richard Coke, "Independent Iraq," *Contemporary Review,* 143:579, May, 1933.

98   "Admission of Iraq into the League of Nations," *Nation,* 135:340, October, 1932.

99   O. Tweedy, "Iraq and Its Problems," *Fortnightly,* 137:221, February, 1932.

100   Quincy Wright, "The Proposed Termination of the Iraq Mandate," *The American Journal of International Law,* 25:437, July, 1931.

Chapter Six: PALESTINE

1   United States Government, State Department, Division of Near Eastern Affairs, *Mandate for Palestine* (Near Eastern Series No. 1; Washington, D.C.: United States Government Printing Office, 1931), pp. 52-53.

2   League of Nations, "Council, Sixteenth Session, Twelfth Meeting," *Official Journal,* 3:112, February, 1922.

3   League of Nations, "Council, Nineteenth Session, Thirteenth Meeting," *Official Journal,* 3:823, August, 1922.

4   Leonard Stein, *Zionism* (New York: Adelphi Company, 1926), p. 125.

5   Aaron M. Margalith, *The International Mandates,* pp. 139-140.

6   Manley O. Hudson, *International Legislation,* I, 111, Article 2.

7   *Loc. cit.*

8   *Ibid.,* p. 111, Article 4.

9   *Ibid.,* p. 112, Article 5.

10   *Ibid.,* p. 112, Article 7.

11   *Ibid.,* p. 113, Article 10.

12   *Ibid.,* p. 118, Article 22.

13   A. Abdul Hadi, "The Balfour Declaration," *The Annals of the American Academy of Political and Social Science*, November, 1932, 164:16.

14   League of Nations, "Mandates," *Official Journal*, 2:331-340, March-June, 1921.

League of Nations, "The Mandates Question," *Official Journal*, 2:444, July-September, 1921.

15   William B. Ziff, *The Rape of Palestine* (New York: Longmans Green and Company, 1938), p. 96.

16   Norman Bentwich, "Mandated Territories: Palestine and Mesopotamia (Iraq)," *The British Yearbook of International Law, 1921-1922* (London: Henry Frowde, 1921), p. 51.

17   David H. Popper, *The Puzzle of Palestine* (New York: The Foreign Policy Association, 1938), p. 37.

18   Norman Bentwich, "The Mandate for Palestine," *The British Yearbook of International Law, 1929* (Humphrey Milford, editor; London: Oxford University Press, 1929), pp. 137-138.

19   Edward Mead Earle, "Economic Value of the Mandated Territories in Relation to Interallied Debts," *International Conciliation*, 230:216, May, 1927.

20   League of Nations, "Council, Twenty-first Session, Eighth Meeting," *Official Journal*, 3:1189, November, 1922.

21   Harry Luke and Edward K. Roach, editors, *The Handbook of Palestine and Trans-Jordan* (3rd edition; London: Macmillan and Company, 1935), p. 435.

22   Colonial Office, *Report by His Majesty's Government in the United Kingdom of Northern Ireland to the Council of the League of Nations on the Administration of Palestine and Trans-Jordan for the Year 1929* (London: His Majesty's Stationery Office, 1930), p. 139.

23   Erik Achorn, *European Civilization and Politics Since 1815* (New York: Harcourt, Brace and Company, 1934), p. 623.

24   League of Nations, Permanent Mandates Commission, *Minutes of the Thirteenth Session*, 1928, pp. 42-45.

25   *Ibid.*, p. 441.

26   *Ibid.*, p. 226.

27   League of Nations, "Mandates," *The Monthly Summary of the League of Nations*, 8:375, December 15, 1928.

28   Samuel was a Jew and he often hinted that it would have been better to have had a non-Jewish British High Commissioner who, not being suspect on account of his race or religion, would have

been more liberal in interpreting and executing his government's promise;

Gershon Agronsky, "Lights and Shadows in Palestine Today," *Current History*, 21:80, October, 1924;

Leonard Stein, "Zionist View of Palestine," *Nation*, 121:742, December 23, 1925.

29 League of Nations, Permanent Mandates Commission, *Minutes of the Fifth Session*, 1924, p. 55.

30 *Ibid.*, p. 188.

31 *Ibid.*, p. 121.

32 League of Nations, Permanent Mandates Commission, *Minutes of the Seventh Session*, 1925, p. 212.

33 *Ibid.*, p. 213.

34 The Royal Institute of International Affairs, *Great Britain and Palestine, 1915-1936* (London: Oxford University Press, 1937), p. 43.

35 League of Nations, Permanent Mandates Commission, *Minutes of the Ninth Session*, 1926, p. 184.

36 Popper, *op. cit.*, p. 82.

37 W. Schack, "The Arabs Attack on the Jews in Palestine," *Current History*, 31:89, October, 1929.

38 League of Nations, "Council, Fifty-sixth Session, Third Meeting," *Official Journal*, 10:1470, November, 1929.

39 Colonial Office, *Report by His Majesty's Government in the United Kingdom of Great Britain and Northern Ireland to the Council of the League of Nations on the Administration of Palestine and Trans-Jordan for the Year 1929*, p. 4.

40 League of Nations, Permanent Mandates Commission, *Minutes of the Sixteenth Session, 1929*, p. 198.

41 *Ibid.*, p. 202.

42 Arnold J. Toynbee, *Survey of International Affairs 1930* (Humphrey Milford, editor; London: Oxford University Press, 1931), pp. 284-286.

43 *Report of the Commission on the Palestine Disturbance of August, 1929.* Presented by the Secretary of State for the Colonies to Parliament by Command of His Majesty March, 1930 (London: His Majesty's Stationery Office, 1930), p. 166.

44 *Ibid.*, pp. 163-164.

45 *Ibid.*, p. 158.

46 *Ibid.*, p. 163.

47 *Ibid.*, p. 166.

48   *Ibid.,* p. 167.

49   *Palestine Statement with Regard to British Policy,* presented by the Secretary of State for the Colonies to Parliament by Command of His Majesty, May, 1930 (London: His Majesty's Stationery Office, 1930), pp. 9-10.

50   League of Nations, Permanent Mandates Commission, *Minutes of the Seventeenth Session,* 1930, pp. 35-36.

51   *Ibid.,* p. 151.

52   van Rees spoke only of the majority. The minority consisted of a single member, Mr. Snell. His report seemed more logical than that adopted by the majority. He said the causes of the disturbances of August were due to fears and antipathies, which convinced him the Moslem and Arab leaders awakened and fostered them for political needs. *Report of the Commission on the Palestine Disturbances of August, 1929,* p. 172.

53   League of Nations, Permanent Mandates Commission, *Minutes of the Seventeenth Session,* 1930, p. 142.

54   League of Nations, "Mandates," *The Monthly Summary of the League of Nations,* 10:147, August, 1930.

55   League of Nations, Permanent Mandates Commission, *Minutes of the Seventeenth Session,* 1930, p. 139.

56   League of Nations, "Mandates," *The Monthly Summary of the League of Nations,* 10:148, July, 1930.

57   League of Nations, Permanent Mandates Commission, *Minutes of the Seventeenth Session,* 1930, p. 141.

58   *Ibid.,* p. 151.

59   *Ibid.,* p. 142.

60   *Ibid.,* p. 149.

61   *Ibid.,* p. 152.

62   The Royal Institute of International Affairs, *Great Britain and Palestine, 1915-1936,* p. 49.

63   League of Nations, Permanent Mandates Commission, *Minutes of the Seventeenth Session, 1930,* p. 149.

64   J. Stoyanovsky, *The Mandate for Palestine* (London: Longmans, Green and Company, 1928), p. 354.

65   League of Nations, Permanent Mandates Commission, *Minutes of the Seventeenth Session, 1930,* p. 143.

66   League of Nations, "Council, Sixtieth Session, First Meeting," *Official Journal,* 11:1295, November, 1930.

67   John Hope Simpson, *Report on Immigration, Land Settlement and Development in Palestine* (Presented by the Secretary of

State for the Colonies to Parliament by Command of His Majesty, October, 1930; London: His Majesty's Stationery Office, 1930), p. 23.

68 *Ibid.,* pp. 141-142.

69 *Palestine Statement of Policy by His Majesty's Government in the United Kingdom,* presented by the Secretary of State for the Colonies to Parliament by Command of His Majesty, October 1930 (London: His Majesty's Stationery Office, 1930), p. 16.

70 Leonard Stein, "Memorandum" on *The Palestine White Paper of October, 1930* (London: Jewish Agency for Palestine, 1930), pp. 83-85.

71 The Royal Institute of International Affairs, *Great Britain and Palestine,* 1915-1936, p. 57.

72 R. Gordon-Canning, "Arab Mandates," *Contemporary Review,* 136:202, August, 1929.

73 Colonial Office, *Report by His Majesty's Government in the United Kingdom of Great Britain and Northern Ireland to the Council of the League of Nations on the Administration of Palestine and Trans-Jordan for the Year 1933* (London: His Majesty's Stationery Office, 1934), p. 5.

74 *Ibid.,* p. 5.

75 The Royal Institute of International Affairs, *Great Britain and Palestine, 1915-1936,* p. 79.

76 Colonial Office, *Report by His Majesty's Government in the United Kingdom of Great Britain and Northern Ireland to the Council of the League of Nations on the Administration of Palestine and Trans-Jordan for the Year 1935* (London: His Majesty's Stationery Office, 1936), p. 6.

77 *Ibid.,* pp. 8-10.

78 House of Commons, Parliamentary Debates, *Official Report, First Session of the Thirty-first Parliament* (London: His Majesty's Stationery Office, 1937), Vol. 309, Column 2111.

79 League of Nations, Permanent Mandates Commission, *Minutes of the Twenty-ninth Session,* 1936, p. 145.

80 League of Nations, "Council, Ninety-third Session," *Official Journal,* Annex 1622, 17:1345, November, 1936.

81 *The London Times,* May 26, 1936, p. 15.

82 Colonial Office, *Report by His Majesty's Government in the United Kingdom of Great Britain and Northern Ireland to the Council of the League of Nations on the Administration of Palestine and Trans-Jordan for the Year 1936,* p. 11.

83   *New York Times,* September 6, 1936, p. 21.

84   Colonial Office, *Report by His Majesty's Government in the United Kingdom of Great Britain and Northern Ireland to the Council of the League of Nations on the Administration of Palestine and Trans-Jordan for the Year 1936,* p. 20.

85   Popper, *op. cit.,* p. 95.

86   Palestine Royal Commission, *Report, presented by the Secretary of State for the Colonies to Parliament by Command of His Majesty, July, 1937* (London: His Majesty's Stationery Office, 1938), p. 368.

87   K. Williams, "Palestine: A New Policy Wanted," *Fortnightly,* 140:665, December, 1933.

88   League of Nations, Permanent Mandates Commission, *Minutes of the Thirty-second Session,* 1937, p. 19.

89   *Ibid.,* p. 227.

90   J. M. N. Jeffries, *Palestine the Reality* (New York: Longmans, Green and Company, 1939), p. 663.

91   Herbert Sidebotham, *Great Britain and Palestine* (London: Macmillan Company, 1937), p. 275.

92   League of Nations, Permanent Mandates Commission, *Minutes of the Thirty-second Session,* 1937, p. 32.

93   *Ibid.,* p. 13.

94   *Ibid.,* pp. 160-168.

95   *Ibid.,* p. 161.

96   *Ibid.,* p. 168.

97   *Ibid.,* p. 229.

98   *Ibid.,* p. 194.

99   *Ibid.,* p. 203.

100   *Ibid.,* p. 201.

101   *Ibid.,* p. 22.

102   Palestine Royal Commission, *Report, Presented by the Secretary of State for the Colonies to Parliament by Command of His Majesty, July, 1937,* pp. 377-379.

103   League of Nations, Permanent Mandates Commission, *Minutes of the Thirty-second Session,* 1937, p. 203.

104   *Ibid.,* p. 202.

105   Herman L. Weisman, *The Future of Palestine* (New York: Lincoln Printing Company, 1937), p. 124.

106   Jeffries, *op. cit.,* p. 675.

107   Palestine Partition Commission, *Report Presented by the Secretary of State for the Colonies to Parliament by Command of*

His Majesty, October, 1938 (London: His Majesty's Stationery Office, 1938), p. 246.

108 Victor Cazalet, "Palestine Policy," *Fortnightly,* 152:267, September, 1939.

109 League of Nations, Permanent Mandates Commission, *Minutes of the Thirty-fourth Session,* 1938, p. 228.

110 Viscount Samuel, *Palestine: The Present Position. The United States and World Organization During 1938* (International Conciliation No. 352; New York: Carnegie Institute, Carnegie Endowment for International Peace, September, 1939), p. 428.

111 League of Nations, "Mandates," *Official Journal,* 20:363-368, July-August, 1939.

112 League of Nations, Permanent Mandates Commission, *Minutes of the Thirty-sixth Session,* 1939, p. 275.

113 *Ibid.,* p. 139.

114 *Ibid.,* p. 105.

115 *Ibid.,* p. 275.

116 *Ibid.,* pp. 171-186.

117 *Ibid.,* p. 275.

118 Norman Bentwich, "Palestine Policy," *Nineteenth Century and After,* 126:419, October, 1939.

119 Viscount Samuel, "Where the White Paper Fails," *Living Age,* 356:457, July, 1939.

Bibliography

A. BIBLIOGRAPHICAL AIDS

Allison, W. H., Sidney B. Fay, A. H. Shearer, *et al., Guide to Historical Literature.* New York: The Macmillan Company, 1931. 1,222 pp.

Brecycha-Vauthier, A. C. de, *Sources of Information.* New York: Columbia University Press, 1939. 118 pp. A Handbook on the Publications of the League of Nations.

Coulter, Edith M., and Melanie Gerstenfeld, *Historical Bibliographies.* Berkeley: University of California Press, 1935. 206 pp.

Langer, William L., and Hamilton F. Armstrong, *Foreign Affairs Bibliography.* New York: Harper Brothers, 1933. 551 pp.

B. SOURCE MATERIAL

I. Books

Bell, Gertrude L., *The Letters of Gertrude Bell.* 2 vols.; New York: H. Liveright, n. d.

Lloyd George, David, *Memoirs of the Peace Conference.* 2 vols.; New Haven: Yale University Press, 1939.

II. Great Britain

Colonial Office, *Appendices to the Report by His Britannic Majesty's Government on the Administration Under Mandate of Palestine and Trans-Jordan for the Year 1924.* London: His Majesty's Stationery Office, 1925. 29 pp.

————, *Correspondence Regarding the Modification of the Boundary Between British Mandated Territory and Belgian Mandated Territory in East Africa.* London: His Majesty's Stationery Office, 1923. 8 pp.

————, *Government of Palestine Report, July, 1920-December, 1921.* London: His Majesty's Stationery Office, 1922.

Colonial Office, *Palestine: Report by His Britannic Majesty's Government on the Palestine Administration, 1923.* London: His Majesty's Stationery Office, 1925. 70 pp.

————, *Palestine: Report on Palestine Administration, 1923.* London: His Majesty's Stationery Office, 1924. 52 pp.

————, *Papers Relating to the Question of Closer Union of Kenya, Uganda, and the Tanganyika Territory.* London: His Majesty's Stationery Office, 1931. 230 pp.

————, *Report by His Majesty's Government in the United Kingdom of Great Britain and Northern Ireland to the Council of the League of Nations on the Administration of the British Cameroons for the Year 1928.* London: His Majesty's Stationery Office, 1929. 138 pp.

————, *Report by His Majesty's Government in the United Kingdom of Great Britain and Northern Ireland to the Council of the League of Nations on the Administration of the Cameroons under British Mandate for the Years 1929, 1930, 1931, 1932, 1933, 1934, 1935, 1936, 1937.* London: His Majesty's Stationery Office, 1930-1937.

————, *Report by His Majesty's Government in the United Kingdom of Great Britain and Northern Ireland to the Council of the League of Nations on the Administration of Palestine and Trans-Jordan for the Years 1928, 1929, 1930, 1931, 1932, 1933, 1934, 1935, 1936, 1937, 1938.* London: His Majesty's Stationery Office, 1928-1938.

————, *Report by His Majesty's Government in the United Kingdom of Great Britain and Northern Ireland to the Council of the League of Nations on the Administration of Tanganyika Territory for the Years 1928, 1929, 1930, 1931, 1932, 1933, 1934, 1935, 1936, 1937, 1938.* London: His Majesty's Stationery Office, 1928-1938.

————, *Report by His Majesty's Government in the United Kingdom of Great Britain and Northern Ireland to the Council of the League of Nations on the Administration of Togoland under British Mandate for the Years 1928, 1929, 1930, 1931, 1932, 1933, 1934, 1935, 1936, 1937, 1938.* London: His Majesty's Stationery Office, 1928-1938.

————, *Report by His Britannic Majesty's Government on the Administration of Iraq for the Period April, 1923-December, 1924.* London: His Majesty's Stationery Office, 1935. 224 pp.

Colonial Office, *Report by His Britannic Majesty's Government on the Administration Under Mandate of British Togoland for the Year 1924.* London: His Majesty's Stationery Office, 1925. 97 pp.

————, *Report by His Britannic Majesty's Government on the Administration Under Mandate of Tanganyika Territory for the Year 1924.* London: His Majesty's Stationery Office, 1925. 79 pp.

————, *Report by His Britannic Majesty's Government on the British Mandated Sphere of the Cameroons for the Year 1923.* London: His Majesty's Stationery Office, 1924. 90 pp.

————, *Report by His Britannic Majesty's Government on the British Sphere of the Mandated Territory of Togoland for the Year 1923.* London: His Majesty's Stationery Office, 1924. 54 pp.

————, *Report by His Britannic Majesty's Government on the Mandated Territory of Tanganyika for the Year 1923.* London: His Majesty's Stationery Office, 1924. 94 pp.

————, *Report by His Britannic Majesty's Government to the Council of the League of Nations on the Administration of the British Cameroons for the Years, 1925, 1926, 1927.* London: His Majesty's Stationery Office, 1926, 1927, 1928.

————, *Report by His Britannic Majesty's Government to the Council of the League of Nations on the Administration of the British Sphere of Togoland for the Years 1925, 1926.* London: His Majesty's Stationery Office, 1926, 1927.

————, *Report by His Majesty's Government in the United Kingdom of Great Britain and Northern Ireland to the Council of the League of Nations on the Administration of Iraq for the Years 1929, 1930, 1931, 1932.* London: His Majesty's Stationery Office, 1929-1933.

————, *Report by His Britannic Majesty's Government to the League of Nations on the Administration of Iraq for the Years 1925, 1926.* London: His Majesty's Stationery Office, 1927, 1928.

————, *Report by His Majesty's Government to the Council of the Council of the League of Nations on the Administration of Palestine and Trans-Jordan for the Years 1925, 1296, 1927.* London: His Majesty's Stationery Office, 1926, 1927, 1928.

Colonial Office, *Report by His Britannic Majesty's Government to the Council of the League of Nations on the Administration of Tanganyika Territory of the Years 1925, 1926, 1927.* London: His Majesty's Stationery Office, 1926, 1927, 1928.

————, *Report by His Britannic Majesty's Government to the Council of the League of Nations on the Administration of Togoland under British Mandate for the Year 1927.* London: His Majesty's Stationery Office, 1928. 72 pp.

————, *Report by Major G. St. J. Orde Browne, O.B.E., upon Labour in the Tanganyika Territory.* London: His Majesty's Stationery Office, 1926. 105 pp.

————, *Report on Iraq Administration, April, 1922-March, 1923.* London: His Majesty's Stationery Office, 1924.

————, *Report on Tanganyika Territory: Covering period from the Conclusion of the Armistice to the End of 1920.* London: His Majesty's Stationery Office, 1921. 109 pp.

————, *Report on Tanganyika Territory for the Year 1921.* London: His Majesty's Stationery Office, 1922. 34 pp.

————, *Review of the Civil Administration of Mesopotamia.* London: His Majesty's Stationery Office, 1920. 149 pp.

————, *Special Report by His Majesty's Government in the United Kingdom of Great Britain and Northern Ireland to the Council of the League of Nations on the Progress of Iraq during the Period 1920-1931.* London: His Majesty's Stationery Office, 1931. 331 pp.

————, *West Africa: Report on the British Mandated Sphere of Togoland for 1920-1921.* London: His Majesty's Stationery Office, 1922. 52 pp.

————, *West Africa: Reports on the British Sphere of the Cameroons.* London: His Majesty's Stationery Office, 1921.

————, *West Africa: Reports on the British Sphere of the Cameroons, May, 1922.* London: His Majesty's Stationery Office, 1922.

France No. 1, 1930. Final Report of the Commissioners Appointed to Delimitate the Boundary between the British and French Mandated Territories of Togoland. Lome, October, 21, 1929. London: His Majesty's Stationery Office, [n. d.].

House of Commons, Joint Committee on Closer Union in East Africa, *Report together with the Proceedings of the Committee. October 6, 1931.* London: His Majesty's Stationery Office, 1931. 2 vols.

House of Commons, Parliamentary Debates, *Official Report,* Fifth series, Vol. 130, June 7-June 25, 1920. London: His Majesty's Stationery Office, 1920.

————, *Official Report,* Fifth series, Vol. 132, July 19-August 6, 1920. London: His Majesty's Stationery Office, 1920.

————, *Official Report*. Fifth series, Vol. 173, May 5-May 23, 1924. London: His Majesty's Stationery Office, 1924.

————, *Official Report*. Fifth series, Vol. 176, July 14-August 7, 1924. London: His Majesty's Stationery Office, 1924.

————, *Official Report*. Fifth series, Vol. 191, February 2-February 19, 1926. London: His Majesty's Stationery Office, 1926.

————, *Official Report*. Fifth series, Vol. 200, November 22-December 15, 1926. London: His Majesty's Stationery Office, 1927.

————, *Official Report*. Fifth series, Vol. 309, February 24-March 13, 1936. London: His Majesty's Stationery Office, 1936.

Iraq: Report on Iraq Administration. October, 1920-March, 1922. London: His Majesty's Stationery Office.

Imperial Conference, *Summary of Proceedings and Appendices.* London: His Majesty's Stationery Office, 1926. 2 vols.

An Interim Report on the Civil Administration of Palestine During the Period July 1, 1920-June 30, 1921. London: His Majesty's Stationery Office, 1921. 29 pp.

Lausanne Conference on Near Eastern Affairs, 1922-1923, *Records of Proceedings and Draft Terms of Peace.* London: His Majesty's Stationery Office, 1923. 861 pp.

Palestine Partition Commission, *Report presented by the Secretary of State for the Colonies to Parliament by Command of His Majesty, October, 1938.* London: His Majesty's Stationery Office, 1938. 310 pp.

Palestine Royal Commission, *Report, Presented by the Secretary of State for the Colonies to Parliament by Command of His Majesty, July, 1937.* London: His Majesty's Stationery Office, 1938. 404 pp.

Palestine: Statement of Policy by His Majesty's Government in the United Kingdom, Presented by the Secretary of State for the Colonies to Parliament by Command of His Majesty, October, 1930. London: His Majesty's Stationery Office, 1930. 23 pp.

Palestine Statement with Regard to British Policy, Presented by the Secretary of State for the Colonies to Parliament by Command of His Majesty, May, 1930. London: His Majesty's Stationery Office, 1930. 10 pp.

The Parliament of the Commonwealth of Australia 1923 (Second Session), *Report on the Administration of Nauru during the Year 1922.* Prepared by the Administrator for submission to the League of Nations. Presented by Command. Printed and published for the Government of the Commonwealth of Australia by Albert J. Mullett.

Report of the Commission on the Palestine Disturbance of August, 1929. Presented by the Secretary of State for the Colonies to Parliament by Command of His Majesty, March, 1930. London: His Majesty's Stationery Office, 1930. 202 pp.

Report by Sir Sydney Armitage-Smith, K.B.E., C.B., on a Financial Mission to Tanganyika, 26th September, 1932. Presented by the Secretary of State for the Colonies to Parliament by Command of His Majesty, October, 1932. London: His Majesty's Stationery Office, 1932. 137 pp.

Reports of Mandatory Powers, *Report by His Britannic Majesty's Government on the Administration under Mandate of the British Cameroons for the Year 1924.* Report No. II. London: World Peace Foundation, 1925. 51 pp.

Simpson, John Hope, *Report on Immigration, Land Settlement and Development in Palestine.* London: His Majesty's Stationery Office, 1930. 185 pp.

III. INTERNATIONAL LABOUR OFFICE

International Labour Conference, First Discussion, Geneva, 1929, "Forced Labour," *Report and Draft Questionnaire.* Geneva: International Labor Office, 1929. 320 pp.

IV. LEAGUE OF NATIONS

League of Nations, *Assembly Records of Assembly.* First to Nineteenth Session, 1920-1938. Geneva.

————, *Council Minutes, Sessions First to Thirteenth,* Geneva: 1920-1921.

————, *The Monthly Summary.* Geneva: 1920-1938.

————, *Official Journal.* Geneva: 1920-1939.

————, *Official Journal Special Supplement, Resolutions and Recommendations.* First to Tenth Assembly, 1920-1929. Geneva: Bureau of Secretariat.

————, The Permanent Mandates Commission, *Minutes,* 1921-1939.

————, *Report on the Work of the League Since the Last Session of the Assembly.* Official No. A-6; Geneva: June 1, 1929.

————, Treaty Series, *Publication of Treaties and International Engagements Registered with the Secretariat of the League of Nations.* Vol. 35; Geneva: 1925. 446 pp.

V. Permanent Court of International Justice

Permanent Court of International Justice, *The Mavrommatis Jerusalem Concession* in Publications, Series A, *Collection of Judgments,* No. 5. Leyden: A. W. Sizthoff's Publishing Company, 1925. 51 pp.

————, *The Mavrommatis Palestine Concessions* in Publications, Series A, *Collection of Judgments,* No. 2. Leyden: A. W. Sizthoff's Publishing Company, 1924. 93 pp.

Permanent Court of International Justice, *Judgment No. 10, Readaptation of the Mavrommatis Jerusalem Concessions* (Jurisdiction) in Publications, Series A; *Collection of Judgments,* No. 1. Leyden: A. W. Sizthoff's Publishing Company, 1931. 64 pp.

VI. United States

Papers Relating to the Foreign Relations of the United States, 1921. Washington, D. C.: The Department of State, United States Government Printing Office, 1936, I, 986.

United States Government, State Department, Division of Near Eastern Affairs, *Mandate for Palestine.* Near Eastern Series No. 1; Washington, D. C.: United States Government Printing Office, 1931. 115 pp.

United States Senate, Seventy-fifth Congress, Third Session, *Treaties, Conventions, International Acts, Protocols, and Agreements between United States of America and Other Powers, 1923-1937.* Document No. 134; Washington, D. C.: United States Government Printing Office, 1938. Vol. IV, 5,755 pp.

C. SECONDARY MATERIAL

Books

Achorn, Erik, *European Civilization and Politics Since 1815.* New York: Harcourt, Brace and Company, 1934. 879 pp.

Amery, L. S., *The German Colonial Claim.* New York: Longmans Green and Company, 1940. 199 pp.

Baker, Ray Stannard, *Woodrow Wilson and World Settlement.* 3 vols.; Garden City, New York: Doubleday, Page and Company, 1922.

Baty, Thomas, "Protectorates and Mandates," *British Yearbook of International Law, 1921-1922.* London: Hodder and Stoughton, 1921. Pp. 109-121.

Beer, George L., *African Questions at the Peace Conference.* New York: The Macmillan Company, 1923. 628 pp.

Bentwich, Norman, "Mandated Territories: Palestine and Mesopotamia (Iraq)," *The British Yearbook of International Law, 1921-1922.* London: Henry Frowde, 1921. Pp. 48-56.

————, "Nationality in Mandated Territories Detached from Turkey," *The British Yearbook of International Law, 1926.* Humphrey Milford, editor; London: Oxford University Press. Pp. 97-109.

————, "The Mandate for Palestine," *British Yearbook of International Law, 1929.* Humphrey Milford, editor; London: Oxford University Press, 1929. Pp. 137-144.

————, *The Mandates System.* New York: Longmans Green and Company, 1930. 200 pp.

Boggs, S. Whittemore, *International Boundaries.* New York: Columbia University Press, 1940. 272 pp.

Bowman, Isaiah, *The New World.* Yonkers-on-Hudson, New York: The World Book Company, 1924. 112 pp.

Brailsford, H. N., *The War of Steel and Gold.* London: G. Bell and Sons, Ltd., 1918. 340 pp.

"British Cameroons," *The Encyclopaedia Britannica,* 14th edition, Vol. IV.

"British Togoland," *The Encyclopaedia Britannica,* 14th edition, Vol. XXII.

Buell, Raymond L., *The Native Problem in Africa.* New York: The Macmillan Company, 1928. 2 vols.

Burns, Delisle, *International Politics.* London: Methuen and Company, Ltd., 1920. 189 pp.

Bishop, Joseph Bucklin, *Theodore Roosevelt and His Time.* 2 vols. New York: Charles Scribner's Sons, 1920.

Buxton, Charles Roden, *The Alternative to War.* London: George Allen and Unwin, Ltd., 1926. 176 pp.

Charteris, A., "The Mandate over Nauru Island," *British Yearbook of International Law, 1923-1924.* London: Hodder and Stoughton, 1923. Pp. 137-152.

Corbett, P. E., "What is the League of Nations?" *The British Yearbook of International Law, 1924.* Humphrey Milford, editor; London: Oxford University Press, 1924. Pp. 119-148.

Crocker, W. R., *Nigeria.* London: George Allen and Unwin, Ltd., 1936. 277 pp.

Cumming, Henry H., *Franco-British Rivalry in the Post-War Near East.* New York: Oxford University Press, 1938. 298 pp.

Dilley, Majorie R., *British Policy in Kenya Colony*. New York: Thomas Nelson and Sons, 1937. 296 pp.

Evans, Ifor L., *The British in Tropical Africa*. Cambridge: The University Press, 1929. 396 pp.

Fayle, Ernest C., *The Great Settlement*. New York: Duffield, 1915. 309 pp.

Fitzgerald, Walter, *Africa*. New York: E. P. Dutton and Company, 1933. 462 pp.

Foster, Henry A., *The Making of Modern Iraq*. Norman: University of Oklahoma Press, 1935. 319 pp.

Gerig, Benjamin, *The Open Door and the Mandates System*. London: George Allen and Unwin, Ltd., 1930. 236 pp.

Hailey, Lord, *An African Survey*. New York: Oxford University Press, 1939. 1837 pp.

Hill, Norman L., *International Administration*. New York: McGraw-Hill Book Company, 1931. 292 pp.

Hobson, J. A., *Towards International Government*. New York: The Macmillan Company, 1915.

House, Edward M., "The Versailles Peace in Retrospect," *What Really Happened at Paris*. Edward Mandell House and Charles Seymour, editors; New York: Charles Scribners Sons, 1921. Chap. XVIII. 528 pp.

Howard-Ellis, Charles, *The Origin, Structure, and Working of the League of Nations*. New York: Houghton Mifflin Company, 1928. 528 pp.

Hudson, Manley O., *International Legislation, 1919-1927*. Vol. 1. Washington, D. C.: Carnegie Endowment for International Peace, 1931. 786 pp. Vol. 1.

————, "The Protection of Minorities and Natives in Transferred Territories," *What Really Happened at Paris*. Edward Mandell House and Charles Seymour, editors; New York: Charles Scribners Sons, 1921. Chap. IX, 528 pp.

Ireland, Philip W., *Iraq*. New York: The Macmillan Company, 1938. 510 pp.

Jeffries, J. M. N., *Palestine the Reality*. New York: Longmans, Green and Company, 1939. 728 pp.

Joelson, F. S., *The Tanganyika Territory*. New York: D. Appleton and Company, 1921. 256 pp.

Johnann, G. K., and H. H. Kraft, *Germany's Colonial Problem*. London: Thornton Butterworth, Ltd., 1937. 96 pp.

Langsam, Walter C., *In Quest of Empire*. New York: The Foreign Policy Association, 1939. 96 pp.

Lansing, Robert, *The Peace Negotiations. A Personal Narrative.* New York: Houghton Mifflin Company, 1921. 328 pp.

League of Nations, *Ten Years of World Cooperation.* Foreword by Sir Eric Drummond. Secretariat of the League of Nations, 1930. 467 pp.

Lewin, Evans, *The Germans and Africa.* New York: Frederick A. Stokes Company, 1915. 317 pp.

Lugard, F. D., *The Dual Mandate in British Tropical Africa.* Third edition; London: William Blackwood and Sons, Ltd., 1926. 643 pp.

Luke, Harry and Edward K. Roach, editors, *The Handbook of Palestine and Trans-Jordan.* London: Macmillan and Company, 1935. Third edition. 549 pp.

Main, Ernest, *Iraq from Mandate to Independence.* London: George Allen and Unwin, Ltd., 1935. 267 pp.

Mair, Lucy P., "Colonial Policy and Peaceful Change," *Peaceful Change.* C. A. W. Manning, editor; New York: The Macmillan Company, 1937. 193 pp.

————, *Native Policies in Africa.* London: George Routledge and Sons, Ltd., 1936. 303 pp.

Margalith, Aaron M., *The International Mandates.* Baltimore: Johns Hopkins Press, 1930. 242 pp.

Martin, Lawrence, Lieutenant Colonel, *The Treaties of Peace, 1919-1923.* New York: Carnegie Endowment for International Peace, 1924. 2 vols.

Miller, David Hunter, *The Drafting of the Covenant.* New York: G. P. Putnam's Sons, 1928. 2 vols.

————, "The Making of the League of Nations," *What Really Happened at Paris.* Edward Mandell House and Charles Seymour, editors; New York: Charles Scribner's Sons, 1921. Chap. XVII. 528 pp.

Moon, Parker T., *Imperialism and World Politics.* New York: The Macmillan Company, 1927. 583 pp.

Newfang, Oscar, *World Federation.* Pierre Gault, translator; New York: Barnes and Noble, Inc., 1939. 117 pp.

Padmore, George, *How Britain Rules Africa.* London: Wishart Books, Ltd., 1936. 402 pp.

Perham, Margery, *Native Administration in Nigeria.* London: Oxford University Press, 1937. 404 pp.

Pollock, Frederick, *League of Nations.* London: Stevens and Sons, 1920. 251 pp.

Popper, David H., *The Puzzle of Palestine.* New York: The Foreign
Policy Association, 1938. 111 pp.

Rappard, William E., *The Quest for Peace Since the World War.*
Cambridge, Massachusetts: Harvard University Press, 1940. 516
pp.

————, *International Relations as Viewed from Geneva.* Published for the Institute of Politics; New Haven: Yale University
Press, 1925. 228 pp.

————, *Uniting Europe.* New Haven: Yale University Press,
1930. 309 pp.

Reinsch, Paul S., *Colonial Administration.* New York: The Macmillan Company, 1905. 422 pp.

Ritscher, Walter H., *Criteria of Capacity for Independence.* Jerusalem: Syrian Orphanage Press, 1934. 152 pp.

Royal Institute of International Affairs, *The Colonial Problem.* New
York: Oxford University Press, 1937. 448 pp.

————, *Great Britain and Palestine,* 1915-1936. London: Oxford
University Press, 1937. 111 pp.

Rudin, Harry R., *The Germans in the Cameroons, 1774-1914.* New
Haven: Yale University Press, 1938. 456 pp.

Schnee, Heinrich, *German Colonization Past and Future.* New York:
Alfred A. Knopf, 1926. 176 pp.

Shotwell, James T., *At the Paris Peace Conference.* New York: The
Macmillan Company, 1937. 444 pp.

Sidebotham, Herbert, *Great Britain and Palestine.* London: Macmillan Company, 1937. 310 pp.

Smuts, J. C., *Africa and Some World Problems.* Oxford: The Clarendon Press, 1930. 184 pp.

————, *War Time Speeches.* New York: George H. Doran Company, 1917. 116 pp.

Stein, Leonard, "Memorandum" on *The Palestine White Paper of
October, 1930.* London: Jewish Agency for Palestine, 1930. 89
pp.

————, *Zionism.* New York: Adelphi Company, 1926. 218 pp.

Steiner, Arthur H., *Principles and Problems of International Relations.* New York: Harper and Brothers, 1940. 835 pp.

Stowell, Ellery C., *Intervention in International Law.* Washington,
D. C.: John Byrne and Company, 1921. 558 pp.

Stoyanovsky, J., *The Mandate for Palestine.* London: Longmans,
Green and Company, 1928. 399 pp.

"Tanganyika," *The Encyclopaedia Britannica,* 14th edition, Vol.
XXI.

Temperly, H. W. V., editor, *A History of the Peace Conference of Paris*. Published under the auspices of the British Institute of International Affairs; London: Hodder and Stoughton, 1924. Vol. I to VI.

Townsend, Mary Evelyn, *The Rise and Fall of Germany's Colonial Empire, 1884-1918*. New York: The Macmillan Company, 1930. 424 pp.

Toynbee, Arnold J., *Survey of International Affairs, 1930*. Humphrey Milford, editor; London: Oxford University Press, 1931. 605 pp.

True, C. Allen, "Background and Nature of the League of Nations," *International Institutions and World Peace. Proceedings of the Fourth Annual Conference, Institute of Public Affairs*. Auspices Carnegie Endowment for International Peace, S. D. Myres, Jr., editor; published for the Institute by the Arnold Foundation; Dallas: Southern Methodist University, 1937. 290 pp.

Van Maanen-Helmer, Elizabeth, *The Mandates System in Relation to Africa and the Pacific Islands*. London: P. S. King and Son, Ltd., 1929. 331 pp.

Viton, Albert, *Great Britain, An Empire in Transition*. New York: The John Day Company, 1940. 352 pp.

Weisman, Herman L., *The Future of Palestine*. New York: Lincoln Printing Company, 1937. 138 pp.

Whittlesey, Derwent, "Reshaping the Map of West Africa," *Geographic Aspects of International Relations*. Charles Colley, editor; Chicago: The University of Chicago Press, 1938. 295 pp.

White, Freda, *Mandates*. London: Jonathan Cape, Ltd., 1926. 196 pp.

White, Wilbur W., *The Process of Change in the Ottoman Empire*. Chicago: The University of Chicago Press, 1937.

Wilson, George Grafton and George Fox Tucker, *International Law*. 8th edition; New York: Silver Burdett and Company, 1922. 360 pp.

Wood, Bryce, *Peaceful Change and the Colonial Problem*. New York: The Columbia University Press, 1940. 166 pp.

Wright, Quincy, *Mandates Under the League of Nations*. Chicago: The University of Chicago Press, 1930. 726 pp.

Ziff, William B., *The Rape of Palestine*. New York: Longmans Green and Company, 1938. 612 pp.

Zimmern, Alfred, *The League of Nations and the Rule of Law 1918-1935*. London: The Macmillan and Company, Ltd., 1936. 527 pp.

D. PERIODICALS

"Admission of Iraq into the League of Nations," *Nation,* 135:340, October, 1932.

Agronsky, Gershon, "Lights and Shadows in Palestine Today," *Current History,* 21:75-80, October, 1924.

Batsell, W. R., *The United States and the System of Mandates,* International Conciliation, No. 213, New York: Carnegie Endowment for International Peace, Division of Intercourse and Education, October, 1925. Pp. 269-315.

Bentwich, Norman, "Colonies and Mandates," *Contemporary Review,* 149-151, January, 1936.

————, "Palestine Policy," *Nineteenth Century and After,* 126: 416-425, October, 1939.

Blakeslee, G. H., "The Mandates of the Pacific," *Foreign Affairs,* 1:98-115, September, 1922.

Buchanan, George C., "Why Do we Remain in Mesopotamia?" *Nineteenth Century and After,* 93:764-766, May, 1923.

Buell, Raymond L., "Forced Labor: Its International Regulation," *Foreign Policy Association,* Information Service, 5:411-428, January 8, 1930.

————, "The Mandates System After Ten Years," *Current History,* 31:545-550, December, 1929.

————, "Two Lessons in Colonial Rule," *Foreign Affairs,* 7:439-453, April, 1929.

————, "The Struggle in Africa," *Foreign Affairs,* 6:22-50, October, 1927.

————, "Backward People Under the Mandate System," *Current History,* 20:386-395, June, 1924.

Cazalet, Victor, "Palestine Policy," *Fortnightly,* 152:265-272, September, 1939.

Chesham, John C., "Tanganyika and the Mandate," *Fortnightly,* 144:585-592, November, 1938.

Coke, Richard, "The Newest Constitution in an Ancient Land," *Current History,* 21:241-246, November, 1924.

————, "Independent Iraq," *Contemporary Review,* 143:579-585, May, 1933.

Earle, Edward Mead, "Economic Value of the Mandated Territories in Relation to Interallied Debts," *International Conciliation,* 230: 215-226, May, 1927.

Emerson, Rupert, "Iraq: The End of a Mandate," *Foreign Affairs,* 11:355-360, January, 1933.

Evans, Luther H., "The Emancipation of Iraq from the Mandates System," *The American Political Science Review,* 26:1024-1049, December, 1932.

————, "Are C Mandates Veiled Annexations," *Southwestern Political and Social Science Quarterly,* 7:381-400, March, 1927.

————, "General Principles Governing the Termination of a Mandate," *American Journal of International Law,* 26:735-758, October, 1932.

Foreign Policy Association, "Political and Economic Trends in the Near East, 1927," *Information Service,* 3:422-441, March 2, 1928.

Foreign Policy Association, Information Service, *Functions of the Permanent Mandates Commission,* 3:45-60, April 27, 1927.

Gallagher, K. J., "The Problem of the Former German Colonies," *Current History,* 25:663-668, February, 1927.

"General Smuts' Plan for the League of Nations," *The Nation,* 108:225-237, February 8, 1919.

Ghafir, "Great Britain and Iraq," *Contemporary Review,* 139:742-749, June, 1931.

Gibbons, H. A., "The Defects of the System of Mandates," *Annals of the American Academy of Social and Political Science,* 96:84-90, July, 1921.

Glasgow, George, "Independent Iraq," *Contemporary Review,* 137:251-252, February, 1930.

Gordon-Canning, R., "Arab Mandates," *Contemporary Review,* 136:199-204.

Gore, W. Ormsby, "Mesopotamia and the Arabs," *Nineteenth Century and After,* 88:225-238, August, 1920.

Hadi, Abdul A., "The Balfour Declaration," *The Annals of the American Academy of Political and Social Science,* 164:12-21, November, 1932.

Hayden, Ralston, "Plans for the Union of Great Britain's Eastern and Central African Colonies," *Current History,* 29:1022-1024, March, 1929.

Harris, John H., "The Challenge of the Mandates," *The Contemporary Review,* 119:462-470, April, 1921.

————, "Britain's Negro Problem," *Atlantic Monthly,* 131:544-555, April, 1923.

————, "British Justice and Native Races," *The Contemporary Review,* 126:443-448, October, 1924.

————, "The Mandatory System After Five Years' Working," *Contemporary Review,* 127:171-178, February, 1925.

Hocking, William E., "The Working of the Mandates," *Yale Review,* 19:244-268, Winter, 1930.

Hudson, Manley O., "League of Nations and the Protection of Inhabitants of Transferred Territories," *Annals of American Academy of Political and Social Science,* 96:78-83, July, 1921.

Jenkins, Edward C., "Economic Equality and the Mandates Commission," *Journal of Political Economy,* 37:604-616, October, 1929.

Keith, A. B., "Mandates," *Journal of Comparative Legislation and International Law,* 4:71-83, February, 1922.

Kuhn, A. K., "The Mavrommatis Case on Readaptation of the Jerusalem Concession," *The American Journal of International Law,* 22:383-385, April, 1928.

Lewisohn, R., "Britain in Iraq. Why England Is Surrendering Her Mandate," *Living Age,* 337:664-669, February 1, 1930.

Lyber, Albert Howe, "The Near and Middle East," *Current History,* 31:811-813, January, 1930.

MacCallum, Elizabeth P., "Iraq and the British Treaties," *Foreign Policy Association, Information Service,* 6:226-246, August, 20, 1930.

MacCallum, Elizabeth P., and E. M. Earle, "Trustee or Exploitation?" *Asia,* 26:792-798, September, 1926.

Machray, Robert, "British Policy in the Middle East," *Fortnightly,* 122:651-659, November, 1924.

Mathews, E. L., "International Status of the Mandatory of the League of Nations; High Treason Against Mandatory Authority," *Journal of Comparative Legislation and International Law,* 6: 245-250, November, 1924.

Miller, David Hunter, "The Origin of the Mandates System," *Foreign Affairs,* 6:277-289, January, 1928.

"New Frontiers in West Africa," *Current History,* 21:482-484, March, 1920.

Newman, E. W. P., "Middle East Mandates," *Contemporary Review,* 136:705-711, December, 1929.

Potter, Pitman B., "Origin of the System of Mandates Under the League of Nations: Further Notes," *American Political Science Review,* 20:842-846, November, 1926.

————, "Origin of the System of Mandates Under the League of Nations," *American Political Science Review,* 16:563-583, November, 1922.

Ryan, Andrew, "Model Mandate," *Fortnightly,* 125:588-596, May, 1926.

Samuel, Viscount, "Where the White Paper Fails," *Living Age,* 356: 457-459, July, 1939.

————, *Palestine: The Present Position. The United States and World Organization During 1938.* International Conciliation No. 352; New York: Carnegie Institute, Carnegie Endowment for International Peace, September, 1939. Pp. 426-433.

Schack, W., "The Arabs Attack on the Jews in Palestine," *Current History,* 31:86-92, October, 1929.

Schnee, H. H., "Mandates System in Germany's Lost Colonies," *Current History,* 32:76-80, April, 1930.

Shah, Ikbal Ali, "Empire and Mesopotamia," *Contemporary Review,* 119:200-206, February, 1921.

Snow, A. H., "The Disposition of the German Colonies," *The Nation,* 109:527-530, October 18, 1919.

Slater, Samuel Henry, "Iraq," *The Nineteenth Century and After,* 99:479-494, April, 1926.

Stein, Leonard, "Zionist View of Palestine," *Nation,* 121:742-743, December 23, 1925.

————, "Mandates Commission and the Mandatory Powers," *Contemporary Review,* 131:451-457, April, 1927.

Swayne, Harold G. C., "Central Area of Africa and the Mandate Principle," *The Contemporary Review,* 132:461-468, October, 1927.

Tindall, Fedden, "Progress on the Gold Coast," *Contemporary Review,* 136:54-60, July, 1929.

Tweedy, O., "Iraq and Its Problems," *Fortnightly,* 137:220-229, February, 1932.

Usher, H. B., "Mesopotamia's Claim on Britain," *Contemporary Review,* 120:322-328, September, 1921.

Wainhouse, D. W., "Iraq: A British Preserve," *Nation,* 132:27-28, January 7, 1931.

Warnshius, A. L., Joseph P. Chamberlain, and Quincy Wright, *The Slavery Convention of Geneva, September 25, 1926.* International Conciliation No. 236; New York: Carnegie Endowment for International Peace, Division of Intercourse and Education, 1928. 67 pp.

"What the Mandates Mean to the Empire," *Literary Digest,* 72:71-75, March 11, 1922.

Williams, K., "Palestine: A New Policy Wanted," *Fortnightly,* 140: 665-773, December, 1933.

"Will Iraq Go Free?" *New Republic,* 63:303-304, July 30, 1930.

Wortham, H. E., "Europe Versus Asia," *Atlantic Monthly,* 131:556-564, April, 1923.

Wright, Quincy, "The Mosul Dispute," *The American Journal of International Law,* 20:453-464, October, 1926.

Wright, Quincy, "Some Recent Cases on the Status of Mandated Areas," *American Journal of International Law,* 20:768-772, October, 1926.

————, "The Proposed Termination of the Iraq Mandate," *The American Journal of International Law,* 25:436-446, July, 1931.

————, "Treaties Conferring Rights in Mandated Territories," *American Journal of International Law,* 18:786-787, October, 1924.

————, "Status of the Inhabitants of Mandated Territory," *American Journal of International Law,* 18:306-315, April, 1924.

————, "Sovereignty of the Mandates," *American Journal of International Law,* 17:691-703, October, 1923.

————, "The Government of Iraq," *The American Political Science Review,* 20:743-769, November, 1926.

E. NEWSPAPERS

The Manchester Guardian Weekly, October 8, 1933.

London Times, June 12, 1926; May 26, 1936.

The New York Times, May 28, 1922; September 6, 1936.

Index